SOUTH ASIA IN MOTION

SOHINI KAR

FINANCIALIZING POVERTY

Labor and Risk in Indian Microfinance

STANFORD UNIVERSITY PRESS

STANFORD, CALIFORNIA

Stanford University Press
Stanford, California

Printed in the United States of America on acid-free, archival-quality paper

Library of Congress Cataloging-in-Publication Data

Names: Kar, Sohini, author.
Title: Financializing poverty : labor and risk in Indian microfinance / Sohini Kar.
Description: Stanford, California : Stanford University Press, 2018. | Series: South
    Asia in motion | Includes bibliographical references and index.
Identifiers: LCCN 2017050722 (print) | LCCN 2017051764 (ebook) |
    ISBN 9781503605893 (e-book) | ISBN 9781503604841 (cloth : alk. paper) |
    ISBN 9781503605886 (pbk : alk. paper) | ISBN 9781503605893 (ebook)
Subjects: LCSH: Microfinance—India—Kolkata. | Microfinance—Social aspects—
    India—Kolkata. | Poverty—India—Kolkata. | Poor women—India—Kolkata.
Classification: LCC HG178.33.I4 (ebook) | LCC HG178.33.I4 K37 2018 (print) |
    DDC 332—dc23
LC record available at https://lccn.loc.gov/2017050722

Cover design: Cadence Design Studio
Cover photo: Tiffen center, Vellore, Tamil Nadu, India. ©McKay Savage
Typeset by Motto Publishing Services in 10/15 Adobe Caslon Pro

For my parents, Syamal and Rita Kar

CONTENTS

List of Abbreviations   ix

Acknowledgments   xi

Introduction: Enfolding the Poor   1

1   Entrepreneurship and Work at the
    "Bottom of the Pyramid"   31

2   From Social Banking to Financial Inclusion   57

3   The Reluctant Moneylender   81

4   The Domestication of Microfinance   107

5   Financial Risk and the Moral Economy of Credit   139

6   Insured Death, Precarious Life   167

    Epilogue   199

    Notes   205

    References   221

    Index   245

BC	business correspondent
BJP	Bharatiya Janata Party
BNCCI	Bengal National Chamber of Commerce and Industry
BOP	bottom of the pyramid
BSE	Bombay Stock Exchange
CGAP	Consultative Group to Assist the Poor
COO	chief operating officer
CSR	corporate social responsibility
EDI	Enterprise Development Institute
GAD	gender and development
GDP	gross domestic product
ILO	International Labor Organization
IMF	International Monetary Fund
IPO	initial public offering
JNNURM	Jawaharlal Nehru National Urban Renewal Mission
KYC	know your customer
LO	loan officer
MFI	Microfinance Institution
MFIN	Microfinance Institutions Network
MGNREGA	Mahatma Gandhi National Rural Employment Guarantee Act
MIV	microfinance investment vehicle

NABARD	National Bank for Agriculture and Development
NGO	nongovernmental organization
NPA	nonperforming asset
OD	overdue
PAN	permanent account number
PMJDY	Pradhan Mantri Jan Dhan Yojana
RBI	Reserve Bank of India
SERP	Society for the Elimination of Poverty
SEWA	Self-Employed Women's Association
SHG	self-help group
WID	women in development

ACKNOWLEDGMENTS

I am extraordinarily grateful to the women and men who are not named but whose voices fill the pages of this book. They have graciously shared their time, knowledge, and kindness with me, and I hope that this book does justice to their concerns.

Numerous peers and colleagues have been central to this book, as intellectual interlocutors, mentors, and friends. I have benefited from the guidance of three remarkable scholars: Lina Fruzzetti, Catherine Lutz, and Kay Warren. Their unfailing encouragement as this project took off and continued feedback as it developed have been invaluable.

At Brown, I am also grateful to Patrick Heller for comments on the project, and to Jessaca Leinaweaver and Paja Faudree for advice on writing. I am grateful to the following people for all their support and camaraderie: James Doyle, Susan Ellison, Colin Porter, Stacey Vanderhurst, Laura Vares, Caitlin Walker, Katie Rhine, Christine Reiser, Andrea Mazzarino, Harris Solomon, Jennifer Ashley, Inna Leykin, Kathleen Millar, Yagmur Nuhrat, Sukriti Issar, and Andrea Flores. Llerna Searle was also a great interlocutor on financialization in my time in Providence. Finally, Kathy Grimaldi deserves recognition for her kindness to everyone who stopped by the corner of Hope and Power.

At Harvard, Ajantha Subramanian was a terrific mentor. I am also grateful to Kerry Chance, Namita Dharia, Amrita Ibrahim, Jeff Kahn, Ramyar Rossoukh, and Naor Ben-Yehoyada, who provided a delightful community in Cambridge. Carly Schuster, in particular, continues to be a brilliant collaborator on all things microfinance. At LSE, I am deeply grateful to my colleagues in International Development. In particular, Catherine Boone very generously organized a book workshop that proved invaluable. Thank you to Deborah James, Kate Meagher, David Lewis, Philipa Mladovsky, Jonathan Parry, Mahvish

Shami, and Austin Zeiderman for their insightful comments on the manuscript.

In India, I would like to thank Jayanta Sinha and Kalyan Mitra for helping arrange contacts in the field. I am grateful to Anup and Rita Thakur for housing me in New Delhi. Thank you to Dilip and Bani Mitra, Debkumar and Manju Mitra, Ajoy and Chandra Ghosh, Asim and Anjana Ghosh, and Arindam and Susmita Mitra. I am incredibly lucky to have such a wonderfully supportive extended family in Kolkata and beyond. Thank you also to Kakoli, Ganesh-Da, and Laksmi-Di for making sure my time in India went so smoothly.

Of course, this research would not be possible without funding that has enabled me to spend time developing the project, conducting fieldwork, and writing this book. This research has been generously supported by the National Science Foundation Doctoral Dissertation Improvement Grant (#1022746), the Wenner-Gren Foundation Dissertation Fieldwork Grant, the Social Science Research Council International Dissertation Research Fellowship (IDRF), and the Dissertation Proposal Development Fellowship (DPDF), with funds provided by the Andrew W. Mellon Foundation. Graduate fellowships from Brown University, the Pembroke Center, the Cogut Center for the Humanities, and the Watson Institute have variously provided funding and space to pursue my research.

Versions of the book and chapters have been presented at the LSE Inclusive Economies/Economic Anthropology Seminar, the Director's Seminar at the Institute for Global Prosperity at University College London, the Anthropology Seminar at Brunel University, the India@King's Seminar at Kings College London, the Harvard Social Anthropology Seminar, and the Cogut Fellows Seminar at Brown. I am very grateful for the thoughtful questions and comments from these presentations.

I am grateful to the editorial team at Stanford University Press, including Marcela Maxfield, Kate Wahl, Olivia Bartz, and series editor Thomas Blom Hansen for taking on this project. Thank you to the reviewers, including Gustav Peebles, for their generous comments on the manuscript.

My final thanks are for my family. Thank you to Kaori, Siddhartha, and Sasha Kar. Siddhartha, my brother, has been my champion throughout the years. To my parents, Syamal and Rita Kar, thank you for always being there for me and your unflinching support and encouragement. Finally, to my husband, Jeremy Schmidt, thank you for making my everyday joyful.

FINANCIALIZING POVERTY

ENFOLDING THE POOR

SHIPRA HAD FAILED to turn up at the microfinance group meeting that morning to repay her loan.[1] After the meeting, her group's leader, Poornima, came to tell Putul and Amit, the microfinance staff, that she had gone to see Shipra. "Did you get the money from her?" asked Amit. "No," Poornima replied. "She's been drinking [alcohol]. There was probably something with her husband. She's saying she sent the money with a rickshaw driver. I don't understand what she's saying—you'll have to go talk to her." With that Poornima headed off to track down another borrower who had been absent.

Left alone, Amit, Putul, and I looked at each other, laughing awkwardly, uncomfortably. "Listen, you'll have to go," Putul instructed Amit. "Leave your bag here and go to her house." Amit was visibly troubled by this development. With both hands on the roof of a car, he rested his head against the top of the door, eyes shut. When he lifted his head, Putul repeated her instructions. Catching my eye, Amit laughed wryly and said, "You haven't seen this kind of thing yet, but now you see what really happens."

I had been accompanying Putul, the branch manager, and Amit, a loan officer, on their regular rounds of group meetings that morning in Kolkata's northeastern peripheries. The two worked for a commercial microfinance institution (MFI) that I call DENA and spent the mornings at group meetings where women repaid their loans in weekly installments. Microfinance is the business of giving small loans to poor borrowers that are paid back in frequent intervals with interest. Often these loans are targeted at women as a means of economic development and empowerment. In India, microfinance—including commercial or for-profit microfinance—has grown rapidly as a result of the government's expansion of its financial inclusion policy. Drawing capital from banks and private and public equity, these commercial MFIs have increasingly enfolded the poor into the circuits of global finance. This process of financialization has required extensive labor on the part of both borrowers, who seek out and constantly repay mounting debts, and MFI staff, who ensure this capital is continually in circulation by extending and managing its recovery. The morning's encounters between the borrowers and MFI staff reveal the complicated ways in which microfinance has enmeshed the urban poor of Kolkata into networks of formal finance.

Deliberating on what to do, Putul pulled out Shipra's passbook and examined the joint photograph of Shipra and her husband—the male guarantor required for her loan—attached to the front page. "Oh, she's elderly! Such an old person drinking?" she exclaimed. As she puzzled over the picture, another borrower from the group walked by. Recognizing her, Putul called out: "Do you know where Shipra-*Didi* lives?"[2] "Just near here; down the street and left." "Can you take us to where she lives?" "I know where she lives, but I couldn't tell you which one her flat is," the woman responded hesitantly, eager to leave. The creation of borrower groups is designed to reduce the risk of lending to poor individual borrowers who lack material collateral. MFIs require that women form small groups with their neighbors, usually living within walking distance of each other. This facilitates quicker meetings and easier monitoring of borrowers. Yet such moments of hesitation reveal the uncomfortable closeness these groups can cause when neighbors are called on to monitor each other's creditworthiness.

In the middle of this exchange, Poornima returned. "Did you get the money [for the other loan]?" asked Amit. "No. They don't have it ready yet. You'll have to go there [to get it]," replied Poornima. "You'll have to come with us," Putul told Poornima. We headed down the street, where Poornima pointed out the small roadside restaurant belonging to the second absent borrower. Amit approached the woman working over a large hot *karai* (a deep iron pan), frying up the day's lunch.

Microfinance is designed to help poor borrowers, typically women, start or sustain their own business and enable economic empowerment. As we waited, Putul wondered out loud: "They have a good establishment. They seem to be doing well; can you tell why she didn't pay today?" "They had to buy fish in the morning or something and used up all the money," explained Poornima. For borrowers such as the woman with the roadside restaurant, the regular repayments of microfinance intersect with the uncertainties of working in the informal economy. While there is little flexibility in the weekly repayment schedules of MFIs, the cost of buying fish can cut into the ability to make that day's repayment. Amit returned with the collected money. "What was the problem?" asked Putul. "Who knows?" said Amit. He was happy to have gotten the money and did not dwell too much on the reasons.

The detour over, we headed once more to find Shipra. Poornima pointed and said, "It's that building there." As we neared the entrance of the building, I was a little hesitant about continuing inside to accompany Amit and Putul on what was now a debt collection visit. But I remembered Amit's earlier comment that I had not seen what really happens; after all, this was as much a part of the reality of microfinance practices as the cheerful women in group meetings, who smilingly held up their passbooks for me to photograph on cue from the loan officer. I decided to at least go to the door and judge from there whether to go inside or not.

We entered an old building, with apartments built around a lightless courtyard. Poornima directed us up the stairs and to the first door. Standing back, she declared that she would not go in and would wait downstairs. Amit rang the doorbell, but there was no answer. He continued ringing the bell until the door cracked open. Standing in the doorway was a skeletal woman, appearing to be in her early fifties. "I'm unwell," she said in a shaky voice and started to close the door. "Shipra-

Didi?" said Amit, wedging himself in the open door. "Don't you recognize who this is?" asked Putul, indicating Amit. Shipra looked blankly. "It's Sir from DENA," said Putul curtly. A glimmer of recognition and embarrassment flashed across Shipra's face. "Of course, of course," she said. "I'm sorry, I've been sick from yesterday. I sent the money with the rickshaw driver. I don't know what happened. This has never happened before. You know that. I've always sent the money. I don't know what happened. Please, I'm not well; I'll get it to you later." "We have to get the money today," said Putul. "Please, you'll have to manage somehow." Even if Shipra were ill, there would be no reprieve from repaying the loan. To succeed and continue to attract capital, MFIs must maintain loan recovery rates well over 90 percent, for which MFI staff are responsible—sometimes with their own pay and promotions at risk. Only the death of a borrower or her guarantor will let them off from repaying, and even that risk is managed through mandatory life insurance.

Putul promptly went in, followed by the hesitant Amit. I hovered at the doorway, not knowing whether to go in or not, and finally decided to wait outside. Shipra, however, noticed me. "Come in, please, sit down," she called, slurring her words slightly. At the entrance of the flat was a pool of spilled liquid. "It's water," said Shipra quickly, as I stepped over the puddle. "My grandson spilled it." In close proximity now, I could smell the alcohol on her breath. There were vestiges of her grandson in the room: a deck of children's trading cards on the table, a digital collage photograph of Shipra and her husband with their son and grandson. On the dining table was a steel container with leftover rice and lentils. Compared to the one-room hut where the group meeting was held, this was a relatively nice flat, with a separate bedroom in the back and equipped with a television and DVD player. A few knick-knacks in the cabinets made for decorations.

The television was on, playing a popular Bengali serial, *Ma*, which centered on the matriarch of a family. "We'll stay and watch the serial," said Putul in a gentler tone. Sitting down on the green sofa, she gave Shipra time to figure out what to do. Clutching her mobile phone, which she had retrieved from underneath the sofa, Shipra disappeared into the bedroom. A few minutes later she emerged, smiling. "I'll be back. I'm so embarrassed. I don't know how this happened. It's never happened before," she repeated as she went out of the apartment.

"They have [lease] rickshaws," observed Putul. "I wonder why she didn't get the money. You know, the other women were saying that they don't let her into the meeting. Seems like she's like this a lot. . . . They just make her wait outside the house so that you [Amit] don't see her," she continued. The group to which Shipra belonged borrowed carefully and managed her presence in front of MFI staff. Her regular income through her husband's job as a baggage handler at the airport and from leasing out the rickshaws they owned meant that they had the financial resources for the loans. However, Shipra's drinking—something looked down on, particularly among women in India—counted strongly against her. The other borrowers did not want their own creditworthiness to be tarnished by Shipra's reputation. Despite claims to financial inclusion, microfinance requires loan officers deploy alternative forms of risk management, including assessing borrowers' creditworthiness through nonfinancial means such as lifestyle.

As we waited, Putul became engrossed in the serial, commenting now and then on the show. After a few minutes—growing uncomfortable with the situation—Amit said he would be waiting downstairs and stepped out. I asked Putul if this kind of thing happened often. "It happens," she replied. "But she [Shipra] won't do this again. See how embarrassed she was; she won't miss another payment. And it's good for Amit that I was here, because people will say even Madam [branch manager] had to go to her house." More than social capital among group members, MFIs rely on their staff to ensure the celebrated high rates of loan recovery. With moneylenders negatively marked in Indian society, loan officers have to struggle against their own stigmatization as debt collectors, while ensuring they complete their work. To emphasize their difference, they use powerful and coercive affective pressures such as embarrassment and shame rather than violence to make sure borrowers repay.

Fifteen minutes later, Shipra returned with Rs 300 (about US$6) for her week's installment, continuing to apologize. "I don't know what happened. You know I always pay back. I'm so embarrassed." Filling in her passbook to acknowledge the receipt of the money, Putul tried to assuage Shipra's humiliation: "It's okay, I won't think anything of it." As we were at the door, Shipra quietly added, "Poornima could have paid the money for me, you know. She owed me money. She could have not made me look small." Shipra's failure to repay stemmed not just from her absence but also from the fractures in her relationships with her husband, with whom she had argued, and with Poornima, who had refused to protect her reputation. Even as women forged relationships with other microfinance group members or with their guarantors, microfinance disclosed how neighbors, friends, and kin could both come together and fall apart because of debt.

Walking out of Shipra's place, Putul observed, "You know, we could have the meeting in Shipra-*Didi*'s place. It's quite spacious." "She's going to get another loan?" asked Amit, surprised. "No, but it would have been a good meeting place." Ever on the lookout to expand loans, Putul regretted the loss of an ideal meeting space.

As occurs with borrowers like Shipra and Poornima, debt has always been a part of poor people's lives in India, whether extended through informal moneylenders, kin, friends, or neighbors. The introduction of microfinance, however, structures debt relationships in new ways. As MFIs have proliferated across the country, women have access to multiple new streams of credit. While interest rates at these MFIs are lower than those of moneylenders, they are higher than those available from commercial banks so they can be profitable, meaning women are often paying annual interest rates of 25 percent or more for these small loans. MFIs offer little flexibility of repayment, creating new challenges for borrowers who must constantly keep up with these loans. Due to ongoing inflation, spiraling expenses, and poor social services, the loans have become necessary as "lump sums" to pay for various privatized services (e.g., schools and hospitals). Maintaining access to credit has become an invaluable part of women's domestic work. Meanwhile, the objective for loan officers, unlike that for informal moneylenders, is not to recover their own money; rather, capital extended and recovered must be circulated back into the financial system. MFIs can continue to profit only if they maintain their own lines of credit from commercial banks and other financial institutions and simultaneously profit these financial entities. The beneficiaries in this circulation are rarely the borrowers or the on-the-ground staff, working out of the branch offices.

Financializing Poverty discusses the ways in which financialized debt is extended to the poor and comes to shape people's lives in particular ways. Commercial microfinance, like other growing bottom-of-the-pyramid services for the poor, including health, education, and housing, is increasingly shaped by investment interests. Such financialization of poverty taps into the productive and consumptive capabilities of the poor to circulate more and more capital. Private firms can extract wealth from the poor through new financial products such as health or life insurance or new educational and housing loans. In the absence of good public services, the poor increasingly seek out loans and buy insurance to access services such as private education and health care. In both cases, the everyday precariousness of life for much of India's poor remains unchanged with these new financial flows.

THE PROMISE AND PITFALLS OF MICROFINANCE
With an estimated 60 percent of the Indian population historically not having access to formal financial services, successive Indian governments have promoted "financial inclusion" as a policy since the mid-2000s.[3] The policy—promoted by both the left-leaning Congress Party and the right-leaning Bharatiya Janata Party (BJP)—has aimed to bring those traditionally excluded from the formal economy into the formal financial fold through access to bank accounts and credit for the poor. Microfinance has been one such area in the promotion of financial inclusion for the Indian government. Often drawing on Muhammad Yunus's (2003) Grameen Bank model in Bangladesh, microfinance has expanded globally in the last two decades. In its early stages, micro*credit* referred to the provision of small loans to poor borrowers who lacked collateral to access credit from formal financial institutions. By forming small groups, poor borrowers could make up for the lack of material capital through social capital (e.g., group members

could guarantee each other's loans). In more recent years, micro*finance* refers to the more varied financial services that microfinance institutions offer to their customers, including savings and insurance, though credit remains predominant.

With microfinance capturing the popular imagination as a solution to the failures of state-led development, the United Nations declared 2005 the "Year of Microcredit," and in 2006 the Nobel Peace Prize was awarded to Muhammad Yunus and the Grameen Bank. Public figures ranging from journalist Nicholas Kristof to entrepreneur and eBay founder Pierre Omidyar and philanthropic organizations such as the Gates Foundation have lauded microfinance.[4] Major global financial corporations, including Citigroup, J. P. Morgan, and Deutsche Bank, have also invested in microfinance initiatives both as part of corporate social responsibility (CSR) programs and as profitable investment opportunities. With the tightening of credit in the United States following the 2008 financial crisis, microfinance—born out of developmental concerns in the global South—has become a source of credit for small businesses even in the global North.[5]

Proponents, both policy makers and academics, contend that financial inclusion mitigates socioeconomic disparities by incorporating the poor into more efficient and hence income-generating markets (Banerjee and Duflo 2011; Collins et al. 2009; Robinson 2001). Others have argued that even more than providing economic benefits, microfinance helps produce social capital, which in turn promotes women's empowerment in other domains, such as the domestic sphere (Moodie 2008; Sanyal 2009; Woolcock 1998). Yet as critics have pointed out, there are numerous problems in microfinance practices, including the creation of overindebtedness, unsustainable debt cycles among borrowers, reinforcement of gendered codes of shame, and extreme levels of peer pressure among group members (Brett 2006; Elyachar 2005b; Karim 2011; Lazar 2004; Rahman 1999; Rankin 2001, 2002; Schuster 2015; Stoll 2013).

In Kolkata, the outcomes of microfinance are ambiguous: it does not transform women into successful, financially independent entrepreneurs through access to credit; yet women continuously seek out these loans as a way to make ends meet in a situation of constant lack. Rather than mark it as unequivocally good or bad, it is perhaps more helpful to understand microfinance as a kind of working-class credit.[6] As noted earlier, debt itself is not new for poor and working-class borrowers, who have always been given loans from informal moneylenders, kin, friends, and neighbors. At the same time, what is new with commercial microfinance is the way in which this debt enfolds the formerly excluded into globalized financial networks. These financialized debts have come to reshape lives of both borrowers and lenders of microfinance, particularly through categories of financial risk and its management.

THE FINANCIAL FRONTIER

On August 16, 2010, five poor women, dressed in brightly colored saris, rang the gong to usher in the day's trading at the heart of India's financial world: the Bombay Stock Exchange (BSE). They were there to mark SKS Microfinance's (since renamed Bharat Financial Inclusion) public listing and initial public offering (IPO). Like Shipra and Poornima, the women were all poor microfinance borrowers, and they were there as invited representatives of SKS's borrower groups from around the country. Though the IPO offered hefty returns to its investors, it also demonstrated the extent to which finance capital had penetrated the everyday lives of the poor. In subsequent months, SKS and the microfinance sector as a whole in India experienced a crisis, partly triggered by the success of this IPO. As a result of the crisis, commercial banks that provided capital to MFIs became reluctant to extend further loans to the sector, creating a liquidity crunch for MFIs. Starved of cash, MFIs had to roll back their loans to the poor borrowers, many of whom now struggled to find alternative sources of credit. Through microfinance, poor borrowers have been enfolded into financial markets with systemic consequences in the larger economy.

Yet the eulogies for the Indian commercial microfinance sector came too soon. Though the crisis changed the situation for Indian microfinance, it had not dismantled it. By 2014, the industry had bounced back from the crisis (Kazmin 2014). On April 2, 2014, the

Reserve Bank of India (RBI), the country's central bank, announced that it had granted approval for the first time in ten years for two institutions to set up new private banks: IDFC Limited, an infrastructure finance company, and Bandhan Microfinance. The Kolkata-based Bandhan Microfinance beat out politically connected corporate heavyweights for the coveted licenses. In 2015, the RBI offered eight additional MFIs small finance bank licenses, a new type of bank enabling MFIs to offer multiple financial products (Kazmin 2015). Investments in the sector have also kept apace, with Indian MFIs raising around US$470 million from investors such as Morgan Stanley Private Equity and Citi Venture Capital International. Even the crisis-hit SKS Microfinance has bounced back, with foreign investors appearing bullish on its stocks, raising their stakes from 36.9 percent in September 2013 to 44 percent in September 2014 (PTI 2014a). In fact, it seems that microfinance has become part of the boom-and-bust cycles of financial crisis (see Kar 2017b).

Ethnographic examinations of microfinance have provided key insight into the local relationships between borrowers and lenders, including the creation of unequal patron-client relationships (see, e.g., Ito 2003; Karim 2011; Rahman 1999). Yet the growth and development of commercial microfinance has extended far beyond the dyadic relationship between a borrower and a local nongovernmental organization (NGO). Microfinance's popularity over the past two decades reflects its inherent coherence with neoliberal modes of governance, relying not only on freer capital flows but also on the promotion of self-reliance rather than welfare, and private- rather than public-sector involvement (Ananya Roy 2010; H. Weber 2004). With the growth of for-profit microfinance, commercial bank lending, private equity, securities, bonds, securitized debts, and investment vehicles have all flooded the sector. DENA, for instance, raised capital not only through commercial debt from banks but also through investments from a Dutch pension fund and, more recently, a 10 percent ownership by a commercial bank. Far from the simple transaction between the borrower and lender, microfinance has become an intricate network of financial flows (see Figure I.1). This process of financial-

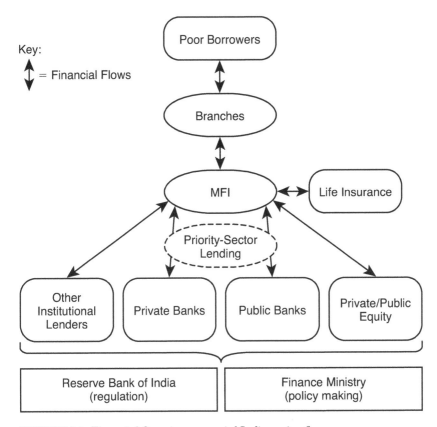

FIGURE I.1 *Financial flows in commercial Indian microfinance*

ization has significant consequences not only for the MFI but also for borrowers, who suddenly find themselves tied into much wider networks of finance with limited ability to understand or influence them.

Financial markets have expanded rapidly across the world since the 1970s, as profit-making activities have increasingly focused on financial channels rather than production (Krippner 2011). In India, for instance, the BSE index, the S&P BSE SENSEX, went from closing at 3,055 points in 1997 to closing at 26,626 points in 2016. At the heart of this expansive financial system has been credit.[7] From consumer credit (e.g., credit card, home loans, education loans) to debt capital (i.e., loans taken out by businesses), credit is a key source of capital for the functioning of the financial markets. It is not surprising that, according to the RBI, the outstanding credit in the Indian economy also expanded to ten times the amount between 1991 and 2006, and credit to GDP ratio increased from 34 percent in 1991 to 54 percent in 2006 (RBI 2011).

Financial markets inform not just corporate decisions but also fiscal and monetary policy and affect individuals through systems of credit, pensions, and savings (Knorr Cetina and Preda 2005). Our everyday lives are increasingly suffused with financial technologies, from the securitization of debt to the creation of increasingly more complex derivatives. Finance is no longer relegated to stock exchanges and investment banks but informs and shapes everyday life and finds cultural expression in popular culture and media.[8] The expanding process of financialization requires "the capitalization of almost everything" (Leyshon and Thrift 2007) with the constant search for new assets that can be mined for financial circulation.

Social scientists have also begun to explore the impact of this complex phenomenon of financialization. Research into the social studies of finance has examined the performative nature of finance: that is, how economists and finance theorists "contribute toward enacting the realities they describe" (Callon 2007, 315).[9] The social studies of finance demonstrates the ways in which seemingly abstract theories and technologies come to shape the very objects they are supposed to describe.[10] An emerging body of literature on the anthropology of finance, meanwhile, has demonstrated not only the social embeddedness of banking and finance but also the ways in which it is suffused with power relations, ideology, and faith and shaped through language and practice.[11] Contesting the ways in which finance has been taken to be a "natural reality," these works show that financial discourses are "historically contingent, and dependent on cultural practices of valuation" (De Goede 2005, xv; Poovey 2008). The universalizing abstractions of financial tools and products often belie their social and cultural constructions.

While providing critical insight into the process of financialization, these ethnographic studies tend to remain concentrated on the experiences of finance practitioners in the global North. Financialization is, however, a global phenomenon, often radically transforming the lives of people in the global South. Indeed, financialization has further deepened inequalities, with speculative raiding by major financial institutions at the cutting edge of what David Harvey terms "accumulation by dispossession" (2003, 147).[12] As capitalist social relations are increasingly mediated by speculation and risk rather than labor, people come to experience the crises of capitalism more acutely in everyday life.[13] This "hypertrophy of 'fictitious' financial capital" (Lutz and Nonini 1999, 93; Marx 1993a) has often violently marginalized and dispossessed populations. Financialized credit to the poor has frequently served the interests of investors rather than borrowers. The "frontiers of capitalism" (Tsing 2005, 27) include the populations that remain outside the mainstream of finance, the financially excluded.

The 2008 crisis and subsequent turmoil in the global economy have revealed both the dominance of and fractures in the current financial system. Backlash against the bailout of banks at the expense of citizens and growing inequality in a financialized economy inspired the transnational Occupy movement, politicizing what has long been the depoliticized arenas of finance and economics.[14] For some, the crisis signifies the end of American financial hegemony and a shift toward a multipolar world with emerging economies such as those of China, India, and Brazil at its core (Duménil and Lévy 2011). As finance is normalized in the global South, their discourses and practices have to be understood and analyzed within the context of these shifts in the global political economy. Microfinance is an example of the way in which the lives of those at the periphery are incorporated and shaped through finance capital. It is not, however, a simple story of top-down imposition; rather, there are multiple negotiations at various levels through which financialization is experienced, accepted, and contested.

THE LABOR OF DEBT

While credit to the poor in India has become a new pool of abstract finance capital, it is nevertheless always mediated by individuals. This book examines how such abstracted notions of creditworthiness and financial risk are constructed and negotiated in the everyday interactions between loan officers and borrowers and how they are informed by existing local social and cultural beliefs and practices. Though emergent forms of capitalism have increasingly profited from speculation and abstraction, labor has not disappeared. Poor women have absorbed the work of seeking out and repaying credit into existing regimes of domestic labor. Meanwhile, MFI staff labor to produce and alienate debt relations with borrowers to sustain the circulation of capital. Before it can be speculated on, there is the labor of both borrowers and lenders that sustains the extraction and circulation of capital.

On the one hand, usury, or lending on interest, has negative connotations historically and cross-culturally. Lending on interest and the profit motive represent the point at which money both begets money and "short-circuit[s] the networks of reciprocity" (Henaff 2010, 66). On the other hand, anthropologists have consistently shown the relationality inherent to debt and the ways in which debt binds people across time and space in obligations of reciprocity.[15] The proliferation of credit markets has been one of the cornerstones of financialization, but it has required increasing abstractions and social distance of debt relationships (Shipton 2010). Given this expansion of formal credit, what happens to the inherently relational nature of debt?

The emergence of financial technologies such as complex derivatives reflects the increasing abstractions in the market. Money, however, in both its physical sense and its abstractions, remains socially constructed and interpreted. While recognizing how new financial forms transform societies, market and monetary relations remain socially embedded.[16] Challenging the reductionism of scholarship on finance to quantification and mathematical modeling, anthropologists have demonstrated how nonquantifiable elements (e.g., social relations, ethics) continue to define money and finance and not just "traditional" economies.[17] Tracing the genealogical development of ideas about money, Jonathan Parry and Maurice Bloch argue that in its representation as an abstraction that destroys sociality, money is in "nearly as much danger of being fetishised by scholars as by stockbrokers" (1989, 3). What is needed is closer scrutiny of money in the entire transactional system and within the context of the local cultural matrix. Indeed, the ethnographic inquiry into money and monetary forms has complicated the picture of the "great transformation" and the perceived loss of sociality in economic relations in modernity (Maurer 2006).[18] In the era of financialization, where money is increasingly abstract, it is hard to locate the relational aspects. Yet finance, too, requires the labor of various actors, not just in the spaces of high finance but also in the everyday interactions of loan officers and borrowers in Kolkata.

Access to microfinance loans requires work on the part of borrowers: women have to seek out and maintain neighborly relations to belong to a borrower group; they have to ensure they have the right documents; they have to attend each of the weekly group meetings for the MFIs from which they have a loan. Over time these tasks have become everyday forms of domestic labor. Loan officers, meanwhile, have to navigate the complicated demands of ethical practice and financial sustainability. Constantly trying to create distance from the reviled cultural figure of the moneylender, loan officers have to sustain high levels of financial return for the MFI as well as their sense of an "ethical selfhood" (Pandian 2008, 16). The loan is therefore not a singular financial transaction but one that has to be sustained through various forms of sociality. Moving beyond just looking at high rates of loan recovery, this ethnographic project recognizes these forms of labor and sociality as being at the heart of financialization and emergent processes of capitalist accumulation.

SYSTEMIC ENFOLDING

The discourse of financial inclusion and development occludes the ways in which certain groups are still not deemed valuable or profitable as customers. MFIs spend significant time and effort to mitigate the risks of lending to the poor. For financial institutions this is not surprising; it is encouraged and desirable for sustainability, as extensive lending to high-risk borrowers could destabilize the financial system and lead to crisis. Practices of reducing risk include implementing methods such as house verifications to assess the creditworthiness or to require borrowers to buy mandatory life insurance with their loans.

These measures of assessing and managing financial risk are not without consequence for borrowers. First, categories of risk are shaped by the judgment of MFI staff, who bring their own worldviews of class, caste, religion, and gender into their assessment. Practices of due diligence can ultimately bolster unequal social structures rather than challenge existing hierarchies. Everyday practices reinforce these differences between groups of people, creating mundane forms of oppression or violence.[19] In Kolkata, women, Muslims, and non-Bengali migrants are all subject to forms of structural inequality, whether through patriarchal norms or through discrimination against minorities and migrants. These everyday forms of inequality are reproduced and reinscribed when some are deemed less creditworthy than others, not on a financial basis but on existing social and cultural evaluations of worth.

Second, the bundling of life insurance with credit produces a complicated relationship between precarious life and insured death. In the absence of material collateral, life insurance collateralizes life itself, becoming the last resort for MFIs to recover loans from borrowers with higher rates of mortality. While countering risk on the part of lenders, life insurance tends to obscure the uncertainties of everyday life, where health and work can be precarious. Thus, even though loans are protected, there is little attention to the difficulties of everyday life at the margins. Finally, the use of life insurance in microfinance has also led to the proliferation of even more financial technologies into the lives of the poor.

MFIs engage in risk management not only because of their interest in maintaining good returns but also because of the increasing incorporation of microfinance into the global financial networks and systemic risk. Systemic risk is an economic concept where "a trigger event, such as an economic shock or institutional failure, causes a chain of bad economic consequences—sometimes referred to as a domino effect" (Schwarcz 2008, 198). Because of the interlinkages between financial institutions, an adverse event can lead to a systemic crisis. The 2008 subprime crisis in the United States demonstrates how systemic crises can not only bring down financial institutions (e.g., Lehman

Brothers) but also drastically trigger a wider economic downturn, affecting the lives and livelihoods of millions worldwide.

In India, the 2010 microfinance crisis revealed the extent to which credit bound together the lives of the urban poor with banks and financial regulators in new and unprecedented ways. Even as borrowers found it harder to get new loans, the effect was not simply in the financial "downstream" of borrowers.[20] For example, in 2008, L&T Finance—a subsidiary of the Indian engineering and construction corporation Larsen and Toubro—entered the microfinance sector, and by 2011, microfinance accounted for 5 percent of its total loan book (*Economic Times* 2011d). In 2011 L&T Finance repeatedly delayed its IPO because of instability in the stock market, including the effects of the microfinance crisis. In other words, a crisis in lending to the poor had systemic consequences for a large financial institution. The extent to which microfinance constitutes a systemic risk is still debated by the Indian central bank.[21] Nevertheless, as more and more people are incorporated into the formal financial sector through a process I call "systemic enfolding," they are tied into these concerns over systemic risk.

If inclusion—the formal policy—suggests incorporation into a formal financial system, enfolding marks the way in which financialization captures everyday life. Poor microfinance borrowers are offered new financial services that are increasingly necessary to the systemic expansion of finance. Conditions of poverty produce the demand for credit, and it is this demand that allows financial institutions to further capitalize on poverty.

Like systemic risk, structural inequality also depends on the systemwide interlinkages that perpetuate hierarchies. In other words, systemic risk and structural inequality both maintain an existing system. To avoid an adverse event, systemic risk management requires adherence to a certain status quo, whether it is the exclusion of people deemed high risk or the constant threat that systemic crisis will wreak havoc in our social world. In effect, the entrenchment of existing ideologies is often sustained by the fear that a collapse of such a system will lead to crisis. Systemic risk is a powerful argument for maintaining stability in the financial system. However, it is perhaps also a powerful argument for maintaining an unequal status quo.

With systemic enfolding drawing in more and more of the world, is there now a system that is "too big to fail"? As Janet Roitman argues, "Systemic risk is now cited as a primordial agent in contemporary crisis accounts" (2014, 72).[22] Yet the very discourse of crisis becomes a limiting terrain of what is possible. Kath Weston (2013) has observed that metaphors that compare the financial system to the circulatory system of the body demand that this body be saved, particularly at times of crisis.[23] An alternative economic system seems unimaginable. Likewise, managing risk means containing the unexpected or the uncertain, or "conceptually translat[ing] uncertainty from being an open-ended field of unpredicted possibilities into a bounded set of possible consequences" (Boholm 2003, 160). François Ewald has argued that the management and even avoidance of risk becomes "an exhaustion in innovation and therefore to a revolutionary change in society with even more unfortunate consequences" (2002, 299). More radical change is foreclosed on by what is known and knowable through practices of risk analysis and avoidance of systemic crisis. As more and more people are enfolded into the networks of finance, its risk management necessarily stabilizes an unequal system. The systemic nature of finance and the structural form of inequality then call for rethinking risk management.

As financial inclusion is pushed forward as development policy, banks and financial intermediaries such as MFIs manage the risks of lending to the poor. They do so by continuing to exclude those deemed unworthy of credit and through the proliferation of other financial products, including securitized debt and insurance. With attention to risk, bottom-of-the-pyramid finance becomes more a strategy for capitalizing on poverty and less one for social change. For borrowers, however, credit does not resolve the problem of lack; rather, it displaces it temporally. In the everyday struggles to make ends meet, access to credit can fill gaps in income, but it is only a temporary solution and one that both accrues monetary interest and accumulates social obligations, often adding to the burden. Microfinance rarely fills the income gaps, the gaps in adequate employment, or the gaps in paying for increasingly costly bills and fees under inflationary conditions.

This is not to advocate a banking system without regulatory oversight or risky lending that can lead to crises; indeed, due-diligence measures are necessary to avoid predatory lending to the poor. Rather, it is an argument to rethink microfinance as primarily a form of working-class credit. It is an argument to demand less of microfinance as a tool of development and to regulate it with the same considerations as other financial institutions, perhaps with greater attention to the fact that this is high-interest credit extended to those who are least able to afford it. Ultimately, it is an argument that the state has to be the one to *take the risk* of including those who otherwise are excluded by practices of risk management. This can be achieved only through policies of redistribution and by continuing to provide forms of welfare and social support that do not depend on market forces.

SETTING THE SCENE: KOLKATA

The city of Kolkata (formerly Calcutta), the capital of West Bengal, sprawls from north to south on the eastern bank of the Hoogly River. In 2001 the city's name was officially changed from the anglicized Calcutta to the Bengali Kolkata. I use Kolkata in contemporary usage but refer to Calcutta in the historical context. Despite its centrality under colonial rule, since independence the city has been described in terms of its decline, decay, and poverty (Fruzzetti and Ostör 2003; Hutnyk 1996; Ananya Roy 2003; Thomas 1996). While some dispute its origins, the general consensus is that Calcutta was established as a port, including fortifications, in 1690 when Job Charnock of the East India Company leased three villages from the Mughal emperor. However, as territorial claims of the English traders expanded, they came into conflict with local rulers. The defeat of the ruling Nawab Siraj-ud-daullah in the 1757 Battle of Plassey turned control of Bengal to the East India Company. Calcutta remained the "second city of the British empire" (Chakravorty 2000, 61) and a thriving center of cultural, political, and economic life until the capital was moved to Delhi in 1911.[24]

Industrial growth began with the establishment of jute mills in Calcutta in 1855. By 1919, there were seventy-six operating jute mills there, which recruited migrant labor from the north, what are now the states of Bihar and Uttar Pradesh (Chakrabarty 1989; L. Fernandes 1997).[25] Many of the migrant laborers resided in slum settlements (*bustees*) that formed around the mills. Jute remained a mainstay of the city's industry into independence, but demand for jute was in decline globally. Partition in 1947 effectively cordoned off the jute-producing region (in East Pakistan, now Bangladesh) from the mills in Calcutta. Moreover, postindependence economic policy was driven by import-substitution industries, often based in smaller cities. Core cities such as Calcutta served as "centers of regional and/or national administration (with increasingly large bureaucracies in the public sector, and expanding offices of the private sector), trade and commerce, small scale industry, and services in general" (Chakravorty 2000, 62). The hinterland outside Calcutta remained unindustrialized; thus, industry stagnated in the city, providing few employment opportunities for the city's expanding working class.

Kolkata has also had a unique political situation in India: the Communist Party of India (Marxist) (CPM) has been in power with a leftist coalition (Left Front) for thirty-four consecutive years from 1977 to 2011. The success of the Communist Party depended in part on growing labor militancy in the jute industry in the 1960s and 1970s. Although the CPM came into power in 1977, by the early 1980s the labor movement was facing a backlash from mill owners, who threatened closure and forced workers to accept whatever terms they dictated, including the increasing casualization of labor. Rather than defend workers' rights, trade unions "appeared to be more and more complicit with employers and as mere appendages of political parties" (Gooptu 2007, 1925), ensuring electoral success for the CPM.

The industrial sector in West Bengal has been in decline since independence because of partition, national policies such as import substitution, pricing policies, the labor movement that discouraged private investment, and the CPM's prioritization of rural areas.[26] Moreover, while brought to victory by the labor movement, the party soon moved to temper its radicalism to attract industrial investment to the state. Liberalization of the Indian economy in 1991 further impacted the stagnating industrial growth in West Bengal. The reforms also led to "the rise of 'competition States' within India's federal democracy" (Corbridge and Harriss 2000, 158). With the demise of the central state-led development model, individual states tried to attract investment in competition with each other. The political response was a move to what Ananya Roy calls "New Communism," which sought to be "as comfortable with global capital as with the sons of the soil" (2003, 10). A number of high-profile cases of the state's accommodation of industry in Nandigram and Singur highlight this tension between private investment and populist demands for redistribution.[27] These conflicts culminated in the defeat of the CPM by the populist Trinamool Congress Party in the state assembly elections in May 2011.

In addition to ongoing rural-urban migration from the hinterlands, Calcutta encountered two waves of mass migration: first at partition and the creation of East Pakistan; and second in 1971 during the Bangladesh Liberation War. In this "city of refugees and migrants" (Ray and Qayum 2009, 36), an estimated 4.2 million people entered West Bengal as refugees between 1946 and the mid-1970s, mostly settling in the urban center of Calcutta. Both forms of migration have provided a steady stream of labor to the city. The 2011 national census recorded 14.1 million people in the Kolkata urban agglomeration, with a decadal growth rate from 2001 of 7 percent.[28] As the city expands, the influx of migrants has intensified Kolkata's urban problems, including the provision of housing and sanitation, potable water, and employment (Figure I.2).

In Kolkata, as in much of India, there is also growing middle-class activism toward creating a "world-class" city, demanding beautification projects that pit the middle class against those who live in slums and work in the informal economy (e.g., as sidewalk hawkers).[29] This bourgeois idea of the postindustrial city, developed in the West, argues Partha Chatterjee, "is driven not by manufacturing but by finance and a host of producer services" (2004, 142). The landscape of Kolkata has been shaped by these new financial flows, with the development of ar-

FIGURE I.2 *Neighborhood in eastern periphery of Kolkata*

eas in the northeast of the city to attract investment and create hubs
for IT and financial services. While such sectors provide employment
for the middle class, there are fewer new jobs for the working class,
with the exception of construction labor. The political cost of this new
model of urbanity is that it does not offer opportunities to the working
class and that "unlike the middle class produced by state-led industrialization is unlikely to produce an expanding middle class" (ibid., 144).
In the absence of such formal-sector work, the informal sector remains
central to Kolkata's working class.

The particularities of local culture and society are also reflected in
the city. In Kolkata, the hegemony of the Bengali upper- and middle-
income *bhadralok* class has shaped the city's identity.[30] By the nineteenth century, the British, followed by the Marwari community from
Rajasthan, controlled much of the city's commerce. The Bengali upper-
and middle-income groups came to fill the administrative sector but
also controlled much of the city's intellectual and cultural life, domi-
nating Bengali gender and work ideologies. These social, cultural, po-

litical, and economic conditions have continued to shape Kolkata's urban development today, including its relationship to the urban poor).

ON URBAN MICROFINANCE

While there are numerous studies on microfinance in rural India (e.g., Karmakar 1999; Moodie 2008; Sanyal 2009, 2014), the effects on the urban sector remain understudied. In microfinance and financial inclusion more broadly, the focus has largely been on the rural sector due to the government's focus on agriculture, creating a "rural bias" in credit to the poor (Nair 2009). As identified in the National Bank for Agriculture and Development's (NABARD) report on financial inclusion, "There are no clear estimates of the number of people in urban areas with no access to organized financial services. This may be attributed, in part at least, to the migratory nature of the urban poor, comprising mostly of migrants from the rural areas. Even money lenders often shy away from lending to urban poor" (Rangarajan 2008, 17).

Since the 2000s, however, urbanization has increased rapidly in India, bucking the slowdown of urban growth in the 1980s and 1990s (Bhagat 2011). As projected by the consulting firm McKinsey, with 40 percent of the Indian population living in cities by 2030 and expected to account for around 70 percent of gross domestic product (GDP), the urban sector has also attracted private-sector investment.[31] Given the growing importance of India's cities in size and economic influence, both the government and private sector have focused on urban policies and markets, particularly as they relate to the urbanization of poverty. In 2005, for example, the central government announced the Jawaharlal Nehru National Urban Renewal Mission (JNNURM) targeted at improving urban infrastructure and basic services to the urban poor and at reforming urban governance.

As a category, the urban poor encompass a wide range of socioeconomic groups. In 2014, for instance, the Indian government designated the poverty line to be Rs 1,407 (around US$22) monthly expenditure in urban areas and Rs 972 (around US$15) in rural areas (Press Information Bureau 2014). People with expenditures lower than this amount are categorized as below the poverty line (BPL), and those above, as above the poverty line (APL). MFI staff at DENA explained that they typically targeted APL families for lending, while other MFIs such as Bandhan have the "Hard-Core Poor" program for rural BPL house-holds.[32] Microfinance borrowers, however, encompass a diverse range of urban poor, from daily wage laborers and women who roll *bidis* (cig-arettes), to owners of small informal factories and schoolteachers. Fur-ther, MFIs such as DENA distinguish between neighborhoods based on economic capacity, and borrowers also identify variously with class categories.

While the urban poor are not homogeneous, urban microfinance poses its own set of problems. This book emphasizes these urban con-cerns, particularly given the overdetermined nature of microfinance geared toward rural areas. Existing models of microfinance can fail to address the particular needs of the urban poor. For example, in the crowded slum settlements, there is often little space to conduct group meetings that lead to positive impact of social capital. Further, uni-form regulatory caps on household income for microfinance loans in rural and urban areas do not account for the fact that urban households may have higher incomes but also higher expenditures. Finally, urban poor populations are also seen as higher risk because many are mi-grants or simply as less deserving than the rural poor.

METHODOLOGY

Financializing Poverty takes credit as a "site of encounter" (Faier 2009) between global finance, state and institutional norms and regulations, and the situated everyday practices of people whose social worlds would not otherwise intersect. It examines the ways in which both borrow-ers and lenders of microfinance negotiate the often-divergent ethics of financial sustainability and the demands of everyday social obliga-tions. The book draws primarily on fourteen months of ethnographic fieldwork in Kolkata, India, between 2009 and 2011. I conducted two months of fieldwork in the summer of 2009 and twelve consecutive months of fieldwork between August 2010 and July 2011.

The majority of the fieldwork was conducted working with a

Kolkata-based MFI that I call DENA. Accompanying MFI staff on their daily rounds, I attended the weekly meeting of borrower groups as a participant-observer. The borrower groups are the units through which MFIs operate: Individual women belong to groups consisting of ten to thirty borrowers. Each group has a leader, secretary, and cashier. These group officers (which can rotate among members) assist the loan officer in the weekly collections. Each group meets once a week in the morning during which loan officers collect weekly loan repayments. To gain a comparative perspective, I visited three different branch offices of this particular MFI in different parts of city, spending about three months at each.

The branch offices were not chosen randomly or based on my own choice but in consultation with the head office, which granted permission for my fieldwork. One loan officer mentioned during the course of my visits that the MFI had selected the better branch offices (i.e., ones with lower rates of overdue loans). Two of the branch offices were located on the eastern peripheries of the city, which contain a mix of old and new slum settlements. One branch was located in the heart of North Kolkata, which consists of mostly older settlements. The three branch offices also provided variance in the staff: one (A) had a female branch manager, with mixed-gender loan officers, while the other two (B and C) had male branch officers. However, while B had all male loan officers, A and C had mixed-gender loan officers. All required loan officers to work in the branch office six days a week.

Through DENA, I visited ninety-two different groups, some repeatedly. Participant observation during these meetings provided important insight into the everyday practices of microfinance (e.g., the technicalities of what actually happens during the meetings), the social networks (e.g., husbands, children, parents, in-laws, neighbors) on which women rely and navigate to maintain current and ensure future loans, and the problems associated with maintaining creditworthiness. These interactions with the borrowers also provided opportunities to interview borrowers and learn more about their experience of microfinance. Interviews with borrowers in Bengali were often conducted on the side during the meetings. Although the meetings were an institutional space, borrowers often expressed their grievances about microfinance during these conversations and asked me to express their concerns to the MFI head office.

I also accompanied MFI staff—a total of fourteen loan officers and four branch managers—during loan applications and house verifications. Attending to these practices helped elucidate the process of determining creditworthiness of urban poor borrowers. For example, in addition to the formal application in which the borrower states her gross and net income and the intended purpose, the potential borrower is judged by a two-step house verification—one by the loan officer and one by the branch manager—as well as confirmation from existing group members. This second process includes informal assessment of a person's creditability that is not immediately apparent in the formal application form. I also conducted in-depth interviews with loan officers and branch managers, often in between meetings and verifications.

I also visited head offices, branch offices, and group meetings of two other MFIs in Kolkata. Additionally, I spent some time with a nonprofit organization that provides microfinance as a self-help group (SHG). The SHG model is the alternative to the for-profit MFI and is also subsidized by the Indian government, and investigation of this model provided comparative insights. For example, while the MFIs are able to offer lower interest rates through scale, they rarely offer alternative forms of support such as livelihood training or women's rights advocacy.

Over the course of the year, I attended workshops and a national conference in New Delhi organized by Sa-Dhan, the largest industry association for microfinance in India. In addition to being a way to meet various people associated with microfinance, these meetings provided important insight into the major concerns faced by the microfinance industry. Through this participation, I was also able to interact with scholars who work with the association and speak with them and share some aspects of my research. Alongside continued monitoring of news, including the release of a number of key reports, I conducted interviews with MFI staff, policy makers, and representatives from commercial banks that lend to MFIs. These interviews helped develop the background for understanding microfinance in India and the linkages that connect urban poor borrowers in Kolkata to the financial flows of global capital through banking.

CHAPTER OVERVIEW

The first two chapters examine the political economic context and historical legacy under which commercial microfinance has grown in India. In Chapter 1, I examine microfinance in the context of an emergent form of capitalism. Given the popularization of "social businesses" and "bottom of the pyramid" as a viable market opportunity, this chapter traces the development of what is considered a more ethical form of capitalism. Social entrepreneurs, such as the founders of MFIs, who serve a double bottom line of financial profit and social welfare, are celebrated as the future of development. However, even as the poor are encouraged to become entrepreneurs themselves, work in the informal economy remains precarious. While the culture of entrepreneurship encourages the poor to become increasingly self-sufficient, it simultaneously ignores the desire of many to attain more secure forms of livelihood and access to social services.

Chapter 2 traces the history and politics of microfinance in India. Microfinance and financial inclusion more broadly have to be situated within a longer history of banking practices in India rather than simply with the origins of the Grameen Bank in Bangladesh. This history includes the role of moneylenders under British colonialism, the development of social banking postindependence, the liberalization of the banking sector in the 1990s, and the shift to the paradigm of financial inclusion. This history has led to the creation of multiple models of microfinance in India, including the SHG movement, the commercial MFIs, and new business correspondent (BC) model, with different political stakes. It concludes with an analysis of the 2010 microfinance crisis in India, which highlights the intersecting political interests and commercial expansion of MFIs.

Chapters 3 and 4 turn to the labor of debt, demonstrating how abstractions of finance are caught up in the everyday lives of borrowers and lenders. Chapter 3 shows how MFI staff, particularly loan officers and branch managers who interact with borrowers regularly, collect repayment and determine creditworthiness. Loan officers try to distinguish themselves from the culturally negatively marked but socially embedded moneylender as employees of the formal banking sector. However, as "proxy creditors," they must produce and alienate debt relationships to create abstracted loan products. Because debt is inherently relational, loan officers navigate and negotiate the ethical demands of such relationships by enacting forms of care and desiring respect. As microfinance becomes increasingly financialized, including through processes of securitization, loan officers must make sense of the traces of relationality that remain even when the debt is passed on as a loan product.

Chapter 4 discusses how microfinance practices have been enfolded into the everyday domestic labor of poor women. Proponents of microfinance have often pointed to social capital as enabling women to overcome gender discrimination both by serving as a form of collateral and by creating social networks for women to rely on. Access to credit, however, requires the labor of women who must not only build and maintain these networks but also manage the time taken by weekly meetings with other forms of domestic labor. Moreover, I argue that this perspective undervalues the power of the hegemonic Bengali middle-class ideology that encourages women to be good wives and mothers. Thus, despite the promise of addressing gender inequality, microfinance can create conservative outcomes as loans are enfolded into existing social and cultural norms of middle-class patriarchy.

The next two chapters explore how MFIs manage the risk of lending to the poor through credit risk assessments and life insurance and the consequences of these practices. Chapter 5 argues that the conservative outcome of microfinance is also tied to the need to minimize risk for the creditor. Beyond the financial reasoning, loan officers also rely on the moral economy to determine who ought to get loans. While appearing objective, risk analysis enfolds multiple forms of social discrimination and hierarchies, including caste, class, language, and religion. Even as MFIs turn to more formal credit risk management systems such as credit bureaus, I show that these data are always already produced through these existing and exclusionary forms of social and cultural knowledge.

Chapter 6 traces the intimate link between debt and death. Analyzing the requirement for microfinance borrowers to buy life insurance, I argue that MFIs are able to collateralize the loans against the lives of borrowers. While higher mortality rates are used as justification for requiring life insurance, this system of risk management can have unexpected outcomes for borrowers. In particular, as borrowers face enormous pressure to repay their loans, death—including suicide—can become perceived as the only way to escape debt. However, the discourse of debt-related suicide in India is often overdetermined by the farmer-suicide problem. While recognizing the tragedy inherent in debt-related suicide, I argue that the political and media focus on death obscures the reality of living in increasing conditions of precarity. One such area is the increasing costs of health care. Many borrowers have loans to pay for health care or find that sudden medical expenses can impede the ability to repay existing loans. These events and expenses require attention not at the moment of death but throughout the everyday struggles in which people attempt to make ends meet. The Epilogue considers microfinance in light of emerging trends in financial inclusion in India and its potential impact on poverty alleviation and development.

CHAPTER 1

ENTREPRENEURSHIP AND WORK
AT THE "BOTTOM OF THE PYRAMID"

"ONE DAY, Mr. Bose dreamt that his father—who had passed away when he was very young—came to him and asked what he had accomplished in his life. When he recounted everything he had done, including his successful banking career, his father asked, 'So what?' That," explained Mr. Ray, "was the question leading to the microfinance project." Based in Kolkata, Mr. Ray, the regional chief operating officer (COO) of a Bangalore-based MFI, was telling me of his entry into microfinance after thirty-five years in commercial banking. In narrating his own journey, he traced that of Mr. Bose.

"I met my guru while working at Citibank," explained Mr. Ray in the small, windowless MFI office—a world away from the sleek offices of global finance. He had left his comfortable job at a multinational bank to follow Mr. Bose, his mentor, into microfinance. Mr. Bose had been a successful international banker with a prestigious American master of business administration (MBA). He had worked in retail banking for a long time but became tired of the corporate "rat race." Soon after the dream of his father, Mr. Bose met with Muhammad Yunus of the Grameen Bank and set about establishing his own MFI in India.

In this narrative, the transformation from a commercial banker to MFI founder is precipitated by an ethical encounter. The moral voice of

Mr. Bose's father, denouncing his achievements in commercial banking, turns him from the rat race to the more virtuous path of microfinance. Going into the business of microfinance is not just a matter of
economic rationality (i.e., the poor are profitable) but is inspired by the
ethical dimensions of "doing something for the downtrodden."

Yet throughout our conversation, Mr. Ray was careful to distinguish commercial microfinance as being part of the financial services
industry, not simply a development-oriented NGO. This, Mr. Ray explained, enables borrowers to depend on the MFI as a sustainable institution. Moreover, investors support the MFI precisely because of
Mr. Bose's reputation as a banker, as now "many big names in banking are affiliated with [the MFI]." "Doing well" (financially) and "doing good" (socially)—the mantra of social enterprises—are inextri-
cably linked in this narrative of microfinance. "The goal of the MFI
is to make a profit, because," noted Mr. Ray, "why would people invest in a company that is not profitable?" In fact, to keep the distinctions clear, and rather than attempt to do more social work through
the commercial arm, Mr. Bose had established a separate NGO to
take on these tasks. So, Mr. Ray explained, "there is the business side
of microfinance, which requires cautious steps, and the other side is
that of helping people." As social enterprises, MFIs have to incorporate a double bottom line: economic and social.[1] As demonstrated in
the conversation with Mr. Ray, the pursuit of these dual goals is often
complicated. Further, there is ambiguity in how to account for the social side of the ledger. The moral duty to help the poor is shot through
with concerns for a sustainable and profitable business, attendant to
the risks of lending to the poor.

This chapter discusses the emergent culture of entrepreneurship as
it undergirds both the popularization of social businesses and the idea
that micro-entrepreneurship can serve as a means to escape poverty. It
interrogates the extent to which the practices of both MFIs and poor
workers intersect with the ideological premise of entrepreneurship.
First, I examine how the stories that social businesses tell, especially
foundational narratives—official and unofficial—sustain the ideological premise that these companies are doing good socially while doing

well financially. Centering on the founders, these narratives also celebrate an emergent entrepreneurial spirit in India. Effectively, this culture of entrepreneurship ideologically bolsters the current growth of social enterprises.

Second, I explore how social entrepreneurship has coincided with the explosion of "bottom-of-the-pyramid" (BOP) capitalism. Under this paradigm, the poor are no longer considered just passive objects of state-led development but active market participants as consumers and entrepreneurs themselves. The BOP goods and services, stretching from consumer goods to banking, have transformed the poor into new sources of capitalist accumulation. The extent to which the poor have benefited through BOP finance, however, remains unclear. Finally, I look at the precarious conditions of labor, now coded as micro-entrepreneurship, in the informal economy.

FOUNDATIONAL NARRATIVES

One morning, as we went from one group meeting to another, Dinesh, a loan officer at DENA, recounted the story of Mr. Basu, the founder of an MFI where Dinesh had previously worked. Mr. Basu, explained Dinesh, had started with about Rs 18,000 to begin doing business in the district of Howrah, neighboring Kolkata. When he began, there was such demand for money from the people and pressure to provide loans that he did not know what to do. At the eleventh hour, his wife gave him her wedding jewelry to get more money to give loans. When Mr. Basu hesitated to take her jewelry, his wife said, "If you can make people smile with this, then that is an ornament enough for me." Dinesh had come to microfinance by chance when, while waiting to take the examinations for the much coveted civil service jobs, he had applied to and gotten a place at Mr. Basu's MFI. For Dinesh, the foundational narrative offered a way for him to make sense of and give meaning to his job as a way of doing good for others.

As did Dinesh and Mr. Ray, people working in various levels of the business recounted their narratives about the foundational moments of microfinance. While a version of Mr. Ray's narrative is publicly available in a newspaper interview, Dinesh's retelling is not officially documented.[2] However, rather than attempt to verify these stories, I am interested in understanding how these and other foundational narratives shape employees' and popular perception of microfinance.

In these two narratives, the protagonists—Mr. Bose and Mr. Basu —have significantly different personal and institutional origins: the former comes from an elite international education and work experience in a multinational bank, while the latter is from a middle-class background with a grassroots experience in microfinance. However, the two narratives have similar structural elements: both protagonists are pushed by close kin to further pursue their work to do good for the poor. These are key turning points for the two men in the foundation and development of their MFIs.

The transformative moment is also present in official foundational stories. Two autobiographical works, Muhammad Yunus's *Banker to the Poor* (2003) and Vikram Akula's *A Fistful of Rice* (2011) describe moments of revelation and transformation that lead to the founding of the Grameen Bank and SKS Microfinance, respectively. For Yunus, an encounter with a young woman in rural Bangladesh who was unable to buy supplies in bulk pushed him to think about microcredit.[3] For Akula, it was a woman who was turned away by the NGO where he worked that drove him to scale up lending through his for-profit MFI.[4] The figures driving the transformation in these two cases were poor women rather than close kin. Like the popular narratives, these autobiographical accounts of foundational moments demonstrate how deeply moral and financial rationalities are entangled in shaping the corporate histories of microfinance.

All four of these narratives draw on a form of sentimentality, or "the emotionally suffused experience of sympathy for others"; sentimentality implies a form of selfhood that "takes shape through its immersion in the well-being of others" (Black 2009, 270). As in the stories of poor borrowers that Shameem Black examines on the peer-to-peer lending site Kiva, foundational narratives rely on sentimentality to drive the development of MFIs.[5] Each founder is inspired by a sentimental connection to do something for the poor, and it is sentimentality that structures the ethical dimension of the MFI. As Black contends, however, sentimental accounts can gloss over structural forms of inequality.

The sentimental narrative, moreover, masks a subtler ideological move: Yunus does not simply give money to the poor woman. In his account, he explains that she does not want charity (Yunus 2003, 48). Similarly, Akula wants to find a way to end poverty through profitability. He writes that to help poor women like the one he encountered, he needed to bring more money into microfinance. His solution is to focus on investment: "Why not bring the circle around, making it possible for donors—or investors, as the case would be—to make money from supporting microfinance?" (Akula 2011, 53). Both Mr. Bose and Mr. Basu also turn to establishing for-profit institutions as their primary focus. In effect, what emerges from each of these encounters is a reinforcement of capitalist market logics that implicitly critique welfare as handouts and as unsustainable. Sentimental narratives then require disentangling in terms of their ideological work in sustaining a culture of entrepreneurship that celebrates self-sufficiency over dependence on the state's provision of services for the poor.

Through the use of sentimentality, narratives of social businesses are not just stories that blatantly celebrate the free market, but they do so in ways that can be harder to disentangle from other discourses. Corporations are "deeply invested in their stories in telling their histories" as part of their social identities, and these stories often invoke tropes that "obfuscate the actual relations of production and division of labor that they must organize and regulate" (Bose and Lyons 2010, 8–9). Investment in this narrative is particularly important for social businesses such as microfinance that must sustain their identity of doing well and doing good.

THE CULTURE OF ENTREPRENEURSHIP
Social businesses, however, have emerged amid a larger social and cultural shift in the celebration of an entrepreneurial disposition and ethos. In India, a growing number of television channels are dedicated to twenty-four-hour news coverage of business and finance, from the

English-language NDTV Money, CNBC-TV18, and ET Now, to the Hindi-language Zee Business and CNBC-Awaaz. Additionally, there is a growing popularity of business degrees and valorization of business figures. All of these examples mark a palpable transformation of the Indian middle class into what Arjun Appadurai, in the American context, has called "business junkies" (2015, 65), where everything from home ownership (mortgages, financing) to sports (franchising, trading players, team ownership) has become increasingly subject to business analysis, while start-up entrepreneurs have become heroes.

The dissemination of business knowledge in Indian everyday life, however, happens in its own social and cultural context. A form of entrepreneurial personhood has always existed within South Asia, where mercantile ethnic groups and castes often structure the identity of the individual engaged in business (e.g., Fox 1967; T. Roy 2010; Weeratunge 2010). Members of the mercantile castes have an advantage over other castes by mobilizing capital through existing social connections (Damodaran 2008). Though professions can no longer legally be predetermined by caste, caste-based and ethnic networks continue to influence everyday economic and professional life in India.[6]

Lining the shelves in bookstores and on sidewalk stalls across India are books and magazines hawking knowledge about how to succeed in this new economy through business and entrepreneurship. One such nonfiction bestseller in India is journalist Rashmi Bansal's (2011) *I Have a Dream: The Inspiring Stories of 20 Social Entrepreneurs Who Found New Ways to Solve Old Problems*. The introduction of the book documenting successful social entrepreneurs consists of short paragraphs almost poetic in form. Bansal identifies the traits of social entrepreneurs as "a new breed of people" who "think like entrepreneurs but feel and work for the cause of society" (ibid., author's note). There are, according to Bansal, two kinds of people: "thinkers," who do not do anything about poverty or inequality because they "believe the world is a neat place, with boundaries"; and "feelers," who will give something, "if not a coin, at least a moment of compassion." Social entrepreneurs are "thinking-feeling individuals"; they are able to transcend this divide to help bring about change by applying the principles of business. Social entrepreneurs, for Bansal, are neither demanding radical social change, nor are they iconic figures themselves; social entrepreneurs are not like Mother Teresa but are "people like you and me . . . using the principles of business, to create a better world" (ibid.). In other words, social entrepreneurs can be a bridge between the sentimental and free-market rationale.

Bansal concludes in the introduction that while "the bank balance you have on earth will remain, when you depart[,] your *karma*, you carry forward" (2010, author's note; emphasis in original). Using the somewhat ironic analogy of a bank balance, she draws on the popular understanding of the Hindu and Buddhist concept of karma—that present circumstances are predetermined by previous actions and that current action can shape future ends—to make a case for social enterprise.[7] In making this argument, Bansal assumes the legitimacy of making profit. Thus, she writes of a world where "profit does not equal greed" or "where 'I' does not mean crushing 'them'" (ibid.). The argument stands that profit *can* be good as long as it does not crush "them." Forget class struggle—the message suggests—accumulation can exist without exploitation due to the thinking-feeling social entrepreneur.

While Bansal works karma into the entrepreneurial disposition, others have adapted independence leader and critic of Western capitalism Mohandes K. Gandhi as a model leader, strategist, and innovator.[8] For instance, Arun Maira, the former chairman of Boston Consulting Group in India, who has served as a member of the Indian Planning Commission, turns to Gandhi in his argument for a more local model of business management. Speaking to the online news site *Rediff,* Maira notes, "We keep feeling that models of people in the West are the ones we should follow. In a way, we remain subservient to the leadership values and models of the West" (quoted in Ganapati 2003). Maira—strangely echoing postcolonial critiques—is insistent that Western corporate models cannot be used in the Indian case. Rather, he suggests, we need to turn to Indian leaders as a model for business leadership. He argues, "In business, empowerment is all about making sure everyone is connected to the organization's goals. Gandhi has a way of doing that: making sure that everyone in the cause is connected to the goal" (ibid.). Finally, Maira turns to aligning capitalism with Gandhi's vision of India:

> In the last few years, there is a thinking that capitalism is not just about cre-
> ating wealth, but you have to take care of the shareholders and stakeholders,
> too. Many years ago, this emphasis on the interests of the stakeholders was
> labeled socialism. So, Gandhi's ideas and the lessons learnt from him are not
> totally different from what corporate India would like to do. (Ganapati 2003)

The corporation's wealth creation cannot occur apart from wider social concerns. In identifying the populace as shareholders and stakeholders rather than citizens, Maira simultaneously reworks the relationship between the state, its citizens, and corporations, and indeed between capitalism and socialism. Businesses have to be concerned as part of management strategy with doing good and balancing the interests of both the corporate shareholders and the stakeholders of society more broadly.[9]

Rather than a singular teleology of capitalist development, Luc Boltanski and Ève Chiapello define the spirit of capitalism as *"the ideology that justifies engagement with capitalism"* (2005, 8, emphasis in original; see also Weber 2001). Thus, the culture of entrepreneurship in India is a distinct ethos, not necessarily a globally legible one. Capitalism absorbs its critiques, but in a distinctly Indian way, drawing together existing notions of mercantile castes and ethnicities, Gandhi, and ideas of karma. Anthropologists have long examined the capitalist encounter with noncapitalist societies and the process of enfolding greater parts of the world into the capitalist system (Nash 1994; Taussig 1980). Other scholars have subsequently argued for the need to study the hybrid forms of capitalism that emerge in these encounters rather than privilege the "Eurocentric assumption that the Midas touch of capitalism immediately destroys local indigenous economies and cultures" (Yang 2000, 481; see also Bear et al. 2015; Li 2014; Tsing 2005). Historical analyses of economies in the colonial encounter challenge universal models of capitalist transformation, demonstrating the role of indigenous capitalists in the process of transformation (e.g., Birla

2009; R. Ray 1995). Rather than reproduce a singular grand narrative of global capital, attention to the local particularities and historical contingencies reveals the dialectical processes through which global capital interacts and intersects with vernacular capitalisms, competing elites, and local politics.

That the expansion of capital has not been homogeneous is not to say that capital has not been triumphant; rather, it is to suggest that its forms of expansion have often been more complex and absorbed into the social fabric of everyday practices and local ideologies. May 2011 marked the opening of the Mumbai chapter of the Dalit Indian Chamber of Commerce and Industry (DICCI). Held at the exclusive Taj Mahal Hotel, the organization was feted by Dalit entrepreneurs, as well as members of Mumbai's business world and officials of the BSE. While some heralded this as "Dalit capitalism" or "capitalism with a social face," others wondered if a few elite, successful entrepreneurs could really make a difference for the millions of Dalits who continue to face caste discrimination in India (*Economic Times* 2011b; Karunakaran 2011). Entrepreneurship, it would seem, could be brought to bear on one of the harshest forms of social exclusion in South Asia, if only those who are oppressed are entrepreneurial enough to escape their exclusion.

SOCIAL BUSINESSES AND THE DEVELOPMENT OF THE BOTTOM BILLION

Speaking to the *Economic Times*, K. C. Chakrabarty, the former deputy governor of the RBI, observed, "Our dream of inclusive growth will not be complete until we create millions of micro-entrepreneurs across the country. . . . While much of social capital creation has been driven by idealism and the non-profit sector, a view that is fast gaining ground is that creating access to essential services and products for under-served communities—rural or urban, below or above the poverty line, can be profitable" (*Economic Times* 2011c). For Chakrabarty, the dream of inclusive growth is equated with the creation of self-sufficient micro-entrepreneurs. Ultimately it is the appeal of profitability, not idealism of the nonprofit sector, that drives this dream. Thus, the movement toward social businesses depends not on an alternative to capitalism but on a shift that operates very much within its logic.

In 2004, C. K. Prahalad, a professor of management at the University of Michigan, published *The Fortune at the Bottom of the Pyramid: Eradicating Poverty through Profits*. The book is a critique of "the paternalism toward the poor" (2010, xiv) not only by the state but also by NGOs and multinational corporations (MNCs). The BOP model is not a call for greater CSR. Rather, it is an argument for what Prahalad calls "inclusive capitalism" (ibid., xiii). With dignity tied to consumer attention and choice, the BOP model advocates a shift from thinking of the poor as victims to considering them "resilient and creative entrepreneurs and value-conscious consumers" (25). Note here the transformation of the poor from proletariat with nothing but their labor to sell to both entrepreneurs and consumers. The bottom line, writes Prahalad, "is simple: It is possible to 'do well by doing good'" (26).

For corporations, the bottom billion offers an immense, untapped, or unsaturated market of potential consumers. This concept of the bottom billion has been widely picked up in mainstream business and investment practices. From tailoring fast-moving consumer goods, such as sachets of shampoo or detergent, to investment in banking services such as microfinance, corporations looking to expand their markets have increasingly embraced the poor. There are opposing views of whether profit from social businesses should be accumulated by capitalists or only reinvested in the company. Within microfinance, for instance, the sides are represented by Muhammad Yunus, who sees social businesses as a "non-loss, non-dividend business" (2007, 24), and Vikram Akula (2011), who argues that investor returns are necessary to scaling up.[10] Nevertheless, for both sides, profit is the hallmark or symbol of a sustainable business and therefore absolutely necessary. Thus, even as the BOP approach is seen to restore the dignity of the poor as consumers and to reaffirm the notion that businesses and their leaders are not driven by the singular pursuit of amassing wealth, it still operates within the framework of capitalism.

As corporations have expanded their social influence, the growing focus on "business ethics" in management studies reflects a larger shift toward considering the role of the corporation within society at large (Das Gupta 2010). With the popularization of social businesses emerges a new conceptualization of capitalism as ethical (see also Barry 2004; Dolan, Garsten, and Rajak 2011). I use the term "ethical" here without normative judgment. In other words, it is not that ethical capitalism is "good" as opposed to other forms of capitalism. Rather, the term connotes the way that individuals involved in social businesses understand their work as being particularly morally inflected, particularly with social ideals of poverty alleviation. The shift to the BOP is, as Ananya Roy suggests, the *"ethicalization of market rule"* or the "struggle to retool practices of calculation and rationalities of risk that take account of, and even mitigate, the exploitative character of bottom billion capitalism" (2012, 106; emphasis in original). This is not trickle-down economics where benefits of the free market will eventually get to the poor; rather, the poor are central to the economic and ethical dimensions of businesses and the future of capitalism.

One aspect of the turn toward ethical capitalism has been the growing emphasis on CSR and fair trade. The CSR framework does not provide corporations with regulations around what to do but, as Dinah Rajak (2011) argues, enables businesses to reframe social problems to align with corporate interests.[11] Meanwhile, fair-trade movements have moved producers, sellers, and consumers to imbue products with ethical meanings as they circulate, though never questioning the basic premise of capitalist production and circulation.[12] Rather than a simple and crude adherence to free-market logics, both CSR and fair trade offer the possibility of a *more ethical* capitalism. Social businesses, like CSR and fair trade, attempt to explicitly link the ethical and economic in their business model. Unlike CSR and fair trade, however, social businesses are directed toward both providing services to and profiting from the poor or underserved populations. The poor are seen as a potential market for businesses, not as objects of charity or beneficiaries in a supply chain.

Such moralization of the market is a complicated process that intersects with existing ideas of development, the role of the state, and corporations. On the one hand, economic relations are not themselves driven purely by rational choice calculations of individuals. Local ideologies and cosmologies, social obligations, forms of reciprocity, and hierarchies have always shaped economic relations (Graeber 2001, 2011a; Malinowski 2002; Mauss 2000). On the other hand, the rise of neoliberal economics since the 1970s has given way to a conception of the market as a calculative logic that is applied to social spheres beyond the economy (Brown 2005, 2015; Ong 2006). While grand narratives of free markets have relied on the concept of the invisible hand of the market, movements toward an ethical capitalism demonstrate "the rise of a new *visible* hand, which conjures morality at the heart of corporate capitalism" (Rajak 2011, 16; emphasis in original). Here, not only is the failure of free markets to address poverty acknowledged, but private corporations are actively endowed with new meaning: to incorporate development goals into their missions as a profitable practice.

Ethical capitalism, particularly through social entrepreneurship, marks an attendant shift in the ideologies and practices of development. Anthropologists have variously critiqued development discourses and interventions in the global South, often focusing on the discursive production of development as a technology of power (e.g., Escobar 1995; Ferguson 1994). Yet, as Julia Elyachar argues, the very problem of development is reformulated with the introduction of BOP capitalism. The discovery of the wealth at the BOP and of the ability to do well while doing good has meant "there is no need to try to change poor people. Nor is there a need to change the institutions in which poor people are educated and work. There is no need, as such, for development" (2012, 113). Development, including the provision of social welfare, is no longer conceptualized as a means of reducing poverty but more aptly is expected to be a positive externality of corporate enterprise.[13]

Deconstructionist critiques of development aimed at centralized planning emerged at the very moment that neoliberal policies (e.g., structural adjustment and economic deregulation) were changing the terrain of development and the role of the state (Smith 2008). Ironically, then, critics of development—including, perhaps unwittingly, anthropologists—have rejected the assumption that the state or development agencies "could know the poor and their needs" (Elyachar 2012, 119). Corporations can now imagine the poor as agentive consumers in a new or underserved market rather than as citizens deserving basic provision of services. In effect, it is the bottom line—not the state's obligation—that provides poor people with affordable access to education, housing, or health care.

With the growing privatization of everything from education to health care, including through the socially inclined businesses, it is purchasing power that increasingly determines access and availability of basic services for the bottom billion. This shift has also aligned with financialization. Thus, in addition to taking the poor as a potential market, public services have become sites for investment. For example, a report from J. P. Morgan on "impact investing" explains how "in a world where government resources and charitable donations are insufficient to address the world's social problems, impact investing offers a new alternative for channeling large-scale private capital for social benefit" (O'Donohoe, Leijonhufvad, and Saltuk 2010, 5). Impact investing, following the BOP model, is expected to generate social benefits beyond the financial return. The authors of the report explain that this "emerging asset class" offers a vast market opportunity for investment, estimating "a potential over the next ten years of profit ranging from \$183bn to \$667bn and invested capital ranging from \$400bn to nearly \$1 trillion" (ibid., 11). Potential areas for impact investing include agriculture, health, water, energy, housing, education, and financial services.

As a financial service, microfinance also falls into this category. Access to credit is formulated not only as part of inclusive growth but also as a profitable business. From the perspective of the critiques of development, there is something ironic in the conceptualization of the poor as now free from the paternalistic and disciplinary powers of NGOs or state-run development programs. With the new avatar of the poor who can pull themselves up by their bootstraps with access to credit and a little bit of entrepreneurial ambition, even critiques of the development discourse can fail to acknowledge the structural inequalities of everyday life at the margins in the absence of the state's services. Debt becomes a means for the poor to pay for these privatized services, so more capital is extracted from the poor and circulated to pay for these now private social services.

THE MICRO-ENTREPRENEURS OF KOLKATA

The culture of entrepreneurship not only promotes businesses to fix social problems; it also envisions citizens, including the poor, as potential entrepreneurs. While the discursive emphasis in microfinance of creating millions of micro-entrepreneurs may cultivate a culture of entrepreneurship (i.e., a social and cultural context in which the traits of the entrepreneur are celebrated and embraced), does it actually succeed? Moreover, how does this new form of the entrepreneurial poor fit into the existing notion of the informal economy?

Ajanta, a DENA borrower in her thirties, ran a sari business and offered to show her stock one morning after the group's meeting. She had taken a loan from DENA most recently to buy a new stock of saris in anticipation of the increased demand ahead of the upcoming Durga Puja festival, the biggest festival in West Bengal, celebrating the goddess Durga's annual return to the Himalayas, her natal home. People wear new clothes over the ten-day celebrations. For the wealthy of Kolkata, this might mean multiple new outfits; for the poor, it might mean one or two. Regardless, Durga Puja signals the busiest shopping season in the city, a time of intense business for sellers.

Up the narrow set of stairs in a concrete building with a communal courtyard, we arrived at the small room where Ajanta lived with her family. Climbing on top of the bed, she retrieved the bags on top of the steel *almirah* (wardrobe) containing the stock she had just picked up from the wholesale district of Burra Bazar and pulled out the saris that were still crisply folded. She explained that the more expensive saris cost about Rs 800 for her to buy, and she sold them at about Rs 1,300 for a profit of about Rs 500. In addition to selling to neighbors and friends, she had found certain places where she went round to sell the saris, such as a nursing home nearby. Most of the women who formed her clientele, however, could not afford to buy a sari upfront. Rather, they paid for it most often on credit: a deposit of Rs 300 and the rest repaid in increments. Thus, Ajanta's debt to DENA had produced new networks of debt. Ajanta was the exemplary borrower for DENA: a true micro-entrepreneur. She had taken a loan to build her small sari business, but indebtedness now extended outward from her, as she sold her goods on credit to those who could not afford them outright.

Yet in many ways Ajanta was also an outlier, precisely because she did run a sari business. During another group meeting, I was asking all the members for what kind of businesses they had taken loans. As several of the women responded "sari business," Mukul, the branch manager, who was familiar with my research ritual, joked to muted laughter from the borrowers: "I've always wondered; you all take loans to sell saris. Who is buying and who is selling?" Certainly, a striking number of borrowers (143 of 625 borrowers or 23 percent; see Table 1.1) told me they had a "sari business."[14] On a number of occasions, loan officers explained the prevalence of the sari business among borrowers in terms of the relative ease in providing evidence during the verification process. Women would often keep one or two new saris at home, and when the loan officer asked to see evidence of their business through inventory, the potential borrower could bring out these saris. Similarly, others claiming to sell cosmetics, usually from catalogs (e.g., Oriflame, a Swedish multilevel marketing company), would bring out an old and out-of-date catalog—one that could be circulated among other group members—as proof of a business.

This is not to say that there are no legitimate sari business owners among the borrowers, such as Ajanta. In contrast to the rhetoric of women's empowerment through entrepreneurship, borrowers most often described their businesses as belonging to the family or, more specifically, to a husband or son. In particular, these were the service jobs (e.g., taxi, rickshaw), small manufacturing work (e.g., leatherwork, plastics recycling), and construction (see Table 1.1). Women did run many of the retail businesses, such as selling fruit and vegetables or running food stalls, but these were considered more to be family run, rather than singularly owned by the woman. While the loans were often used for nonbusiness purposes (e.g., education, health, household

TABLE 1.1 *Businesses of borrowers from DENA*

Retail		*Services*	
Clothes/sari	143	Car/taxi	30
Grocery store	35	Tailoring	23
Food stall	33	Rickshaw	22
Tea stall	21	Auto-rickshaw	15
Fruit/vegetable	18	Electrician	12
Fish	13	Beautician	8
Cosmetics	11	Cycle repair	6
Meat	10	Laundry	3
Medicine shops	10	Photo studio	3
Bidi/paan stall	9	Photocopy	3
Jewelry	9	Plumbing	3
Coal/cooking gas/kerosene	8	Rental property	3
Electronics	8	Travel agency	2
Miscellaneous	8		**133**
Direct seller	6		
Flowers	4	*Production*	
Milk	4	Leatherwork	45
Newspaper	4	Plastics	18
Shoes	4	Clothing workshop	5
Stationery	4	Embroidery	3
Spices	3	Bookbinding	2
Mobile phone	3	Printing	2
Poultry	3		**75**
Tableware	3		
Chemicals	2	*Construction*	
Eyeglasses	2	Construction	22
	378	Furniture/carpentry	12
		Marblework	3
		Painters	2
Total respondents: 625			**39**

repairs), on paper, at least, they were for businesses that reflected not an emergent entrepreneurial culture but the existing informal economy.

During a house verification for a new loan, Putul, the branch manager, asked the husband of a borrower—she was out when we visited—what he did. "I drive a bus," he replied. "But I also run a business delivering Bisleri [filtered water]." Asked what he did for this delivery business, he explained that he had to pick up the twenty-liter jars of water from the Bisleri dealer, for which he put down a deposit. For these deliveries, often up several flights of stairs in apartment buildings without elevators, he received a small delivery charge. Looking through the loan application forms, Putul noted that for the last loan, he had listed a business selling fish. "Yes, but that didn't work, and now I'm working in water," he replied. If the expectation of microfinance is that the poor, with the small loan, will be able to grow a sustainable (and profitable) small business, this borrower reflected the realities of working in the informal economy, where people constantly move between jobs and sources of income. Further, the borrower who delivered water for Bisleri made very little from the deliveries, while his labor enabled greater supply networks for the private bottled water company.

Almost 90 percent of the Indian population is estimated to work in what is categorized as the informal economy.[15] Liberalization of the Indian economy has led to its further informalization, with privatization leading to fewer public-sector jobs and increasing efforts on the part of private firms to reduce costs of production through labor cuts (Harriss-White 2002). The ongoing industrial decline in West Bengal and the "flexibilisation of production" (Raychaudhuri and Chatterjee 1998, 3062) have also contributed to this process of informalization of labor, particularly in the urban center of Kolkata.[16] It is difficult to differentiate between micro-entrepreneurs and the millions who already work in the informal economy, sustaining their incomes through multiple ways other than or in addition to waged labor.

Even in cases where a borrower or her husband might have a job in the formal economy, they were often supplementing incomes through informal work (e.g., small businesses, domestic work). Yet the designation of the informal economy has effectively removed the obligation of the state to help those who seem to have "made their own way, depending on themselves or their communities to survive" (Elyachar 2005b, 172). Informal work is no longer seen as an issue for the government to address but is simply assumed to be part of a functioning economy. This is not to deny the centrality of the informal sector in the economy as a whole.[17] Informalization of the economy can, however, be seen as the process by which people are increasingly held responsible for their own well-being, a process that resounds with the microfinance goal to create millions of entrepreneurs who are responsible for their own fate, but without much attention to what this might look like or how it might be experienced by borrowers.

Quite in contrast to what is recommended in the management books and courses that have become so popular in India through the culture of entrepreneurship, making do in the informal economy often requires constant movement between multiple or on to new projects— the "*jugaad* ways of development to fulfill their basic needs" (Singh, Gupta, and Mondal 2012, 88). *Jugaad* is a Hindi word for "making do" or a "quick fix." At the bottom of the pyramid, *jugaad* "is not just an innovation system, but a strategy for survival, by stretching resources of the poor, to extract more value from smaller resources" (ibid., 104; Jeffrey and Young 2014). Small businesses owned by the urban poor rarely follow a structured plan. Rather, under conditions of chronic un- or underemployment, people constantly try to make ends meet by hustling between subsistence strategies.[18] Such informal workers in the slums are unlikely to accumulate capital in the long term.

ENTREPRENEURSHIP AND INFORMAL LABOR

The tiny windowless hut was the bookbinder's workshop. On our way, Saurav, the branch manager who was introducing me to them, explained that Purnima and her husband, Arijul, had gone to six other microfinance institutions before finally getting a loan from DENA, which he had sanctioned. We came to the door, where the middle-aged couple sat in the dark room, squatting on the floor with a bucket of glue, surrounded by piles of completed and incomplete books. During the interview, Arijul answered most of the questions, even though it was Purnima who was the official borrower.

When they had decided to set up the bookbinding workshop, Arijul and Purnima had rented the room but could not afford to buy the equipment they needed. Arijul explained that they first had taken a loan of Rs 8,000 from DENA two years ago to buy special equipment for binding, indicating a heavy green metal contraption in one corner of the room. The press helped bind the books with the glue, a bucket of which Purnima was mixing by hand when we arrived. Since then, the loan amounts had increased, and they were now on their fourth loan of Rs 17,000. But how well the business did depended on the season. Usually, they managed the work between husband and wife, but during the busy seasons, such as around Durga Puja, they had to hire additional labor. During these times, they needed at least two more people to complete the work. Even during these busy seasons, once the costs of labor had been accounted for, they made about Rs 10,000 per month.

Arijul explained that the weekly repayment to DENA could sometimes be hard, and at times they did not have the money to repay the loan (around Rs 360 per week). On those occasions, they had to get the money from elsewhere (e.g., moneylenders). Sometimes they did not get paid by their customers and would have to wait a while for payment. They now hoped for another loan to buy equipment to make the binding process faster. For Purnima and Arijul, their business meant managing a constant set of risks: seasonal demand, extra labor, and managing multiple loan repayments.

In an interview with Mr. Maity, the deputy director of the Enterprise Development Institute (EDI) in Kolkata, I asked what constituted an entrepreneur. An entrepreneurship promotion organization, EDI was founded in 1999 through joint collaboration between the Bengal National Chamber of Commerce and Industry (BNCCI) and the Government of West Bengal. EDI offers training and support to develop entrepreneurship in the state. Among its activities, it works to create awareness about entrepreneurial activities and runs workshops and courses on entrepreneurship for small-business owners, unemployed youth, retired military servicemen, women, and minorities. In response to my question, Mr. Maity distinguished entrepreneurs from managers: "[The] entrepreneur, he is the owner of his enterprise. He started his venture. It is *his* venture, and he is the owner." Here, the distinguishing feature of the entrepreneur is ownership. Beyond proprietorship, however, the distinguishing disposition or traits of the entrepreneur, according to Mr. Maity, are "independence, risk-taking ability—should be moderate risk taking, not high risk, not low risk—perseverance, problem-solving attitude, flexibility, communication and interpersonal skill, hardworking." While proprietorship reflects the need for ownership of capital or the material dimension of the business, the entrepreneurial habitus is marked by the ability or willingness to take appropriate risk.

Can poor, informal-sector workers really be considered to be entrepreneurs? As proprietors and risk takers, Purnima and Arijul could, of course, nominally fit into Mr. Maity's definition of the entrepreneur. They even hire labor at certain times of the year. Yet the choice to enter this kind of work remains structurally conditioned for the poor. The material conditions—the equipment, stock, or capital—that allow the bookbinding couple to stay in business are tenuous. Moreover, earning Rs 10,000 per month (approximately US$2 per day per person, with the family unit being just the couple), and with debt payments to one MFI alone being around Rs 1,440 per month, does not allow for much accumulation of capital—not, at least, enough to get them out of poverty. A culture of entrepreneurship celebrates those like Purnima and Arijul, with their small bookbinding business; it renders these small businesses into the goal of development policy. What it does not do is acknowledge their difficulties and structural constraints. Once the poor have credit from an MFI, it is assumed they will be able to harness the market to pull themselves out of poverty. Yet such a formulation fails to account for the everyday conditions of labor of the "self-employed." Without a labor movement to draw attention to such conditions, the toil of small businesses is effectively erased.

Aneel Karnani argues that rather than romanticize the idea of entrepreneurs, focusing on creating "opportunities for steady employment at reasonable wages is the best way to take people out of poverty" (2007, 31). Arguing that most informal-sector small-business owners are not necessarily so by choice, given higher and regular wages in the formal sector, Karnani suggests the International Labour Organization's (ILO) term "own-account worker" is more appropriate than the romanticized notion of "poor entrepreneur." In other words, while "entrepreneur" comes to mark the ideological valuation of self-sufficiency and market efficiency, "own-account worker" refers to the basic definitional category of people who are self-employed without having employees.

Of course, the definitional change from entrepreneur to "own-account worker" does not necessarily reflect the realities of working in the informal economy. Consider, for example, the case of Rekha and her husband, who drives a taxi. They lease a taxi, paying the owner Rs 400 every day that it is driven. The taxi would be theirs when or if they ever paid up the Rs 3 *lakhs* (about US$5,000) for it.[19] Rekha estimated that they made about Rs 8,000–10,000 per month as income, but after accounting for fuel, car repairs that seemed to constantly add up, and necessary household expenditures for their family of four, there was never quite enough to pay off the lease. Certainly "own-account" is not as romanticized as "entrepreneur," but it still tends to individualize the informal-sector worker rather than recognize the structural conditions and social networks of obligations (leasers, moneylenders, etc.) under which they work.

IN SEARCH OF LESS PRECARIOUS WORK

It was July, and the monsoon rains had flooded the streets of North Kolkata. Tania, the loan officer; Mukul, the branch manager; and I waded our way through the murky water to the group meeting. When we arrived, the meeting center, adjoined to a temple for the goddess Sitala, was bustling with preparations for the *puja* that was to take place in the evening. As we waited for the other members of the group to show up, one of the borrowers, Kalpana, spoke of her son. "He's finished college, but he doesn't have a job," she sighed. "He's taken all the [civil service] exams, but nothing came of them. Do you know where he can get a job?" she asked the DENA staff, desperate for information on how to secure a position for her son. Despite the rise of the culture of entrepreneurship, Kalpana's plea for DENA to help her son find a job marked its limits. As India celebrates its newly minted millionaires and billionaires in the new economy of entrepreneurship, many still wait for jobs that will offer stability in their everyday lives.

Caught up in a process of what Craig Jeffrey has called "long-term waiting" (2010, 3), many—particularly youth—in India are forced to defer dreams, goals, and life projects as they wait to enter stable employment. That Kalpana desires a job for her son with stable wages and benefits is understandable under conditions of insecurity. As people wait for these seemingly unattainable jobs, however, they continue to hop between the precarious ones, hoping to find ways of making do, in conditions increasingly familiar across the world. Following neoliberal reforms of the 1970s, much of the world has experienced a shift from stable, long-term employment to temporary or contractual labor conditions as the norm (Allison 2012; Molé 2012; Muelebach 2011; Muelebach and Shoshan 2012; Weston 2012). Globalization has entailed the movement of manufacturing jobs from the global North to the South, albeit with lower wages and markedly less security. On the one hand, Fordism in the industrialized world has provided "powerful images for a social order of mass inclusion and citizenship through labor" (White 2012, 400) and the hope of more secure lives in the industrializing world. On the other hand, despite growing precarity in the global North, Fordism remains an imagined future for the global South.[20] It is imagined that the new regimes of labor will enable the kind of security offered by Fordist promise.

In India, the transition from the developmental to liberalized state reflects this duality, with the dismantling of state-owned industry. Whereas the postindependence Nehruvian model of large-scale industrialization was once the perceived way forward for development, liberalization has led not only to privatization of these industries but also to growth in service-sector jobs (e.g., call centers) that have helped a growing new middle class rather than the working class.[21] Of course, informal labor has always been precarious for the poor in India and is not simply the result of neoliberalism (Cross 2010). Nevertheless, the neoliberal state and business have increasingly weakened organized labor and undermined workers' rights, including blocking demands for greater employment security.[22] Further, with the ongoing process of urbanization, there is a steadily expanding population of precarious labor in the cities of the global South and a pressing need to address mass under- and unemployment in these metropolises.

Despite exploitation and alienation of labor in Fordist disciplinary regimes (Fraser 2003), its passing has engendered nostalgia for a past that guaranteed employment and security, or what critical theorist Lauren Berlant calls "cruel optimism." People grasp for stability through attachment to a "problematic object *in advance* of its loss" (Berlant 2006, 21). Here, attachment to labor, whereby changing economic conditions, including the flexibilization of labor and the privatization of services, has engendered a desire for industrial capitalism despite its exploitative dimensions. How do we think of alternatives when the resistance to the new culture of entrepreneurship is expressed as the desire for another form of exploitative industrial labor?

DOING SOMETHING FOR YOURSELF

Aditi, dressed in a maroon *salwar kameez* (loose-fitting pants and tunic) and her black hair in a long braid, sat bouncing a small child in her lap during the meeting. When asked what she used her loan for, she stated quietly that she gives the money to her husband for his vegetable stall. It was early in my fieldwork, and the regional manager of an MFI (not DENA) was taking me to visit group meetings. With a visitor in the midst, the regional manager glanced up sharply and admonishingly pressed her: "You don't do anything yourself?" "No," she responded. "But you're supposed to do something for yourself," he persisted. "With the child to take care of now and all, I can't really do anything," she responded half defiantly, rocking the young child on her knee, refusing to further explain her not "doing anything."

In this exchange, while the question "Don't you do anything *for yourself*" is a highly individualizing statement, Aditi locates herself within the social world of familial obligations. Although she references her husband's vegetable stall, her apparent dismissal of doing something struck me as a kind of disavowal of the ethos of the culture of entrepreneurship. Aditi not only recognizes the value of her own labor in providing child care; she refuses to engage with the conversation that she must do something to prove that she deserves the loan.

Political theorist Kathi Weeks, writing of antiwork politics, notes that "the willingness to live for and through work renders subjects supremely functional for capitalist purposes" (2011, 12). In the case of the borrower delivering Bisleri water, in his hustle to find work, he expands the networks of a major water distributor while making only a fraction of the capital the company accumulates. This is not to deny that those like Ajanta or Purnima and Arijul may truly enjoy or find pleasure in work. Moreover, they must work in these various spaces to survive and to ensure the well-being of their families. The unqualified valorization of those who make do in the informal economy without recourse to the state, however, makes it very difficult to critique structural conditions of capitalism and of the impact of structural transformations in the Indian economy on lives and livelihoods.

This chapter began with a discussion of the notion of ethical capitalism and social businesses serving the bottom billion. Both contradict classical liberal economic theories of free markets while still holding to the tenets of capitalism as a social good. The ideological power of ethical capitalism reveals what Boltanski and Chiapello (2005) observe is the ability of capitalism to absorb critique. Critique, in effect, is enfolded into the possibilities of capitalism itself rather than in the development of alternative social and economic systems. Rather than simply celebrate the entrepreneurial spirit of social businesses such as MFIs or micro-entrepreneurs themselves, or alternatively turn to nostalgia for industrial capitalism, it becomes necessary to recuperate the nonsentimental utopia from its capitalist co-optation and to consider the possibilities of alternative economic arrangements.

In conditions of precarity, informal labor—coded as entrepreneurship of the poor—is celebrated while ignoring the structural conditions of poverty. The culture of entrepreneurship calls forth and celebrates a particular disposition; it enfolds the entirety of the person into the goal of building a business: "every subject is rendered as entrepreneurial no matter how small, impoverished, or without resources, and every aspect of human existence is produced as an entrepreneurial one" (Brown 2015, 65). Resisting the demands of such all-consuming work, Weeks recommends resisting "the work ethic's ideals about labor's necessity and virtues" (2011, 15). As Kathleen Millar (2014) argues, such resistance can, for example, be found among *catadores* in Brazil, who counter the demands of wage labor and seek out greater autonomy to balance the precarious demands of everyday life through work on Rio's trash dumps. Beyond the refusal to work under conditions of Fordist or precarious labor, however, is the need to consider new politics of redistribution. For instance, basic income grants can disrupt the existing normative work-based programs in development by bringing the right to income *before* work to the world's poor (Davala et al. 2015; Ferguson 2015; Standing 2009). Such transformations, however, would not be wholly new in India; rather, they would be part of an ongoing process by which money and banking have been part of the state's project of development, which is explored in the next chapter.

CHAPTER 2

FROM SOCIAL BANKING
TO FINANCIAL INCLUSION

ON AUGUST 28, 1969, Indira Gandhi, then prime minister of India, addressed the Bankers' Club in New Delhi, a group, she conceded with a touch of humor, with which she was "not too popular at the moment" (1975, 243). The speech was given shortly after the cabinet had announced the Banking Companies (Acquisition and Transfer of Undertakings) Ordinance on July 19, 1969, which nationalized fourteen banks and brought 83 percent of the total banking system under state control. Gandhi spoke of the rationale for bank nationalization: "It is not that banks were not functioning well," she explained; rather, "they saw things in a particular light which was a little bit removed from the needs of the country" (ibid.). State control of banks was seen as a way to direct credit to underserved areas that were key to the state's developmental goals, such as agriculture and small businesses. Gandhi then urged the assembled group of bankers to think of new techniques and methods for reorienting credit policies, including mobilizing additional bank deposits to raise capital, expanding branches in the country, and rethinking the "traditional insistence on collateral security or documents of land ownership" (244). The emphasis, explained Gandhi, "must be on the credit-worthiness of purpose" (245). In other words, it would matter less that the *person*, such as a capital-rich industrialist, was creditworthy than that the credit was directed to a worthy *purpose*, such as development.

In 2010, Finance Minister Pranab Mukherjee announced in his annual budget speech the issuance of new banking licenses to the private sector for the first time in almost ten years. In addition to ensuring "that the banking system grows in size and sophistication to meet the needs of a modern economy," he explained that there was "a need to extend the geographic coverage of banks and improve access to banking services." In other words, further liberalization of the banking sector would be premised on expanding financial inclusion. Following this announcement, the central bank governor Duvvuri Subbarao spoke at a bankers' conference in New Delhi in March 2011, almost four decades after Indira Gandhi spoke to bankers about nationalization (*Economic Times* 2011a). He explained that plans for financial inclusion would be a significant factor in the consideration of new licenses. Once more, creditworthiness of purpose had come to the fore in debates over banking policies.

On April 2, 2014, the RBI announced that it had granted approval for two institutions to set up new private banks: IDFC Limited, an infrastructure finance company, and Bandhan Microfinance. Most surprisingly, Bandhan Microfinance, a Kolkata-based MFI, beat out politically connected corporate heavyweights such as Reliance, Birla, and Mahindra for the much-coveted licenses (RBI 2014; *Economic Times* 2012). With a banking license, the approved financial companies could extend credit (as MFIs already do) and also take deposits, enabling them to expand their operations. One of the key determinants for Bandhan's selection was its emphasis on financial inclusion. In fact, in its guidelines for new bank licenses, the RBI (2013) had explicitly stated the need for applicants to demonstrate their efforts for financial inclusion. Bandhan's ascendancy as a fully licensed bank marks the way in which microfinance has been at the heart of the state's policy of financial inclusion, despite the seeming collapse of the sector during the 2010 microfinance crisis.

While the paradigm of social banking shaped earlier policies of finance and economic development, including Indira Gandhi's bank nationalization in the late 1960s, there has been a marked shift to a "financial inclusion" policy since the early 2000s. Financial inclusion was, of course, part of a larger global trend of inclusive growth in development policy. On the one hand, the move from social banking to financial inclusion in India marks a shift from state-led development to liberalization. On the other hand, both social banking and financial inclusion have hinged on the idea of expanding financial services to underserved and unbanked populations. These two paradigms of banking have not only propelled the growth of microfinance; they also reveal the political nature of access to credit.

In this chapter I investigate a set of "technical questions" (Elyachar 2005b, 197) relating to financing and regulation of microfinance.[1] I situate microfinance within a longer history, from colonial banking to postindependence developmental goals, to show how microfinance is shaped by the ongoing politics of credit and the emerging tensions in the financialization of the sector. That is, I interrogate the flows and networks of finance as it connects global capital to the everyday lives of the urban poor in India. Systems of microfinance have to be understood both in the final transaction between the borrower and the MFI and through the "financescape" (Appadurai 1996, 34), the full set of linkages that connect it to the national and global financial economy. Here I unpack and demystify these technical questions about banking policy and regulation. Only by doing this can we see financialization as a process and ideology that constantly unfolds as it enfolds new populations and institutions. I first examine the growth of microfinance under shifting ideas of banking and development: from social banking to financial inclusion. I then turn to an analysis of the 2010 microfinance crisis, which articulated not only the politics of credit in India and regulation but also how it is increasingly entangled in the process of financialization and questions of systemic risk.

THE COLONIAL LEGACY OF
MODERN INDIAN BANKING

In 1947, independent India inherited a formal financial system that had been shaped by nearly two centuries of British colonial rule. Indigenous forms of banking have existed in India for centuries. As networks of kin and caste affines, indigenous bankers provided capital to local and foreign merchants as well as credit to the state (T. Roy 2010). The new forms and institutions of banking introduced under British rule, however, were deeply intertwined with extracting and enabling capital flows out of the colony and into the metropole, as well as with emergent practices of statecraft in and through the economy. Not only was a functioning banking system necessary for extracting and enabling capital flows to Britain; India also served as the "vast social laboratory where juridical and economic changes and reforms could be implemented and observed with minimal political constraints" (Chandavarkar 1983, 762).

The origins of modern commercial banking in India rest in the early nineteenth century with the emergence of private European agency houses, which were primarily trading houses that offered banking services, including accepting deposits and providing loans and mortgages as a side business.[2] The three colonial state-backed "Presidency Banks" of Bengal, Bombay, and Madras were also established during this period. With the Presidency Banks Act of 1876, the government largely withdrew its capital from the banks and its rights of appointing officers while retaining the right to regulate banks. The Imperial Bank of India Act of 1920 amalgamated the Presidency Banks as a joint-stock company (the Imperial Bank), but with the stipulation of opening one hundred branches in five years. In effect, it was an early policy of financial inclusion with the state directing the expansion of access to private banking services. With the establishment of the RBI in 1934, the Imperial Bank stopped being the government's banker, except in places with no branches of the Reserve Bank. The Imperial Bank, however, accounted for more than a third of all commercial deposits in India and had a close relationship with the government and a leading role in setting lending rates (Chandavarkar 1983).

Although there were a number of Indian joint-stock banks, they were often plagued by crises and failures through the early twentieth century. Even as the number and market share of these joint-stock ventures increased, they continued to reproduce lending practices of the Imperial Bank and foreign-exchange banks "instead of filling the gaps in credit structure" (Chandavarkar 1983, 782). Thus, the indigenous formal sector did little to offer alternative sources of credit to the poor and lower middle class in India.

In the absence of formal institutional credit, the informal sector financed the bulk of credit for domestic agriculture, trade, and industry. While there is some religious stigma attached to usury in Hinduism,[3] the moneylender has always occupied a position within the caste system, close to the merchants and traders, and integral to village life (Gregory 1997; Rudner 1994; Sharma and Chamala 2003). Of course, not all moneylenders belong to a specific caste, but they are not outside the existing social world. Historically, indigenous banking flourished during the Mughal period in India, providing credit not only to peasants but also to the state, despite the Islamic prohibition of *riba* (interest) (Schrader 1994). Moreover, indigenous forms of informal rotating credit associations, such as chit funds, which circulate loans to community groups, have long existed in India (Anderson 1966; Sethi 1995).

British colonialism produced the paradoxical consolidation of the negative image of the moneylender along with the strengthening of his power. By the second half of the nineteenth century, lending to peasants expanded with growing exports of grain and cotton to Europe, while industrialization required larger amounts of capital investment (T. Roy 2010, 115). Prior to colonial rule, the power of the moneylender to lay claim to the debtor's property had been constrained because land could not be alienated from the community. However, with the implementation of new laws and a judiciary that gave land titles to individuals, land could then be used as collateral for the debt—a system that empowered the moneylender through the force of law in rural India (Bagchi 1997; Birla 2009; Metcalf 1962).[4] The initial laissez-faire principle of the colonial government toward moneylenders under this new legal framework led to rising rural indebtedness and growing resentment of the newly powerful moneylenders.

Agricultural failure in 1875 led to the violent Deccan Riots, as moneylenders refused to extend credit to peasants (Fukuzawa 1983). Afraid that the large amounts of land moving into the hands of moneylenders would destabilize the colonial government, the state moved to prevent a larger peasant uprising in rural India by introducing new legal measures to restrict moneylending practices. The 1879 Deccan Agriculturalists Relief Act gave power to courts to reduce interest rates and restructure repayments. Created for the Deccan region, the act became a model for the rest of colonial India. While curbing the power of moneylenders over land and addressing indebtedness, the act simultaneously created the problem of restricting available rural credit. The clampdown on the informal sector failed to increase alternative sources of formal credit for the poor, an issue that remained unresolved at independence in 1947.[5]

SOCIALIST DEVELOPMENT TO BANK NATIONALIZATION

While the nineteenth-century laissez-faire market ideologies sought zero state intervention, the twentieth century marked the transformation of the economy into a site of power and governance. National statistics allowed for the management of the economy, while laws pertaining to economic rights, currencies, cross-border flows of capital, and taxation regimes all came to shape the relationship between the state and its citizens.[6] However, the ways in which the state can intervene in the economy have shifted with different economic paradigms.

The Keynesian model of the early twentieth century and sustained through the post–World War II era meant that the state could intervene in the market—for example, through fiscal spending—to increase employment or address social needs. Likewise, the implementation of Nehruvian socialism postindependence brought the financial system under the ambit of the Indian developmental state, which emphasized heavy industry, import substitution, and an extensive public sector (Joshi 2006). By the 1960s, however, the Indian state faced crises in food self-sufficiency following wars with China in 1962 and Pakistan in 1965, as well as harvest failures and droughts in 1965 and 1967.

In 1967, Indira Gandhi's Congress Party faced one of its worst electoral defeats, losing many of its coalition partners and greatly reducing its majority. The debacle convinced Gandhi of the need for her party to take a more leftist turn (Torri 1975). One of these policy measures was social control of banking. Though initially floated by her rival, Moraji Desai, nationalization of Indian banks was ultimately a political maneuver by Gandhi to consolidate left support. This first move toward social control of banking was to address a structural feature of Indian banking: because industrialists owned the banks, credit was not available for agriculture or small businesses.

Between 1967 and 1968, Moraji Desai sought to implement a policy of "effective" social control over banks through the Banking Law (Amendment) Bill and the creation of the National Credit Council. The former was to address the ownership structure of banks by industrialists, while the latter was to assist the credit needs of agriculture and small-scale industry (Torri 1975). Indira Gandhi, however, shifted policy from the social control of banks to the nationalization of banks by 1969 to take a more leftist position. Politically, Gandhi divested Desai of the Finance Portfolio, resulting in his resignation as deputy prime minister. Finally, on July 19, 1969, the cabinet unanimously promulgated the nationalization of fourteen banks. In 1980, a further six banks were nationalized, with public-sector banks controlling 92 percent of the market for banking services.

This new form of "social banking" sought to make financial services part of the planned economy, whereby "banks were not there to cater to the needs of the few, but to enable the realization of the entrepreneurial needs of all, and to generate economic growth with sustainable development" (Joshi 2006, 8–9). This included a growing focus on agricultural credit. Data show financial growth during this period of bank nationalization, with the extension of banking and financial services to a larger segment of the population: Between 1969 and 1990, the number of bank branches increased rapidly, from 8,262 to 59,752, with the average population served per bank declining from 64,000 to 14,000. In particular, rural branches increased from 1,833 to 34,791. Total credit as a percentage of GDP increased from 9.8 percent to 19.7 percent (Arun and Turner 2002, 432).

Critics, meanwhile, argued that banks had become an arm of the government's fiscal policy, financing government spending (Hanson

2003). Financial deepening did not mean that the social banking was highly profitable. Banks were directed to lend to state-mandated priority sectors, including agriculture and small businesses. In the 1980s, banks were required to make 40 percent of their loans to the priority sector. By 1991, however, the banking system had become increasingly unstable with a growing number of nonperforming loans on their books.

LIBERALIZATION TO FINANCIAL INCLUSION

Though there had been a number of moves toward liberalization in India through the 1980s, the Indian government faced a balance of payments crisis in 1991. The crisis was the result of both the state's high level of borrowing to finance state-led development policies and a number of external shocks, including the Gulf War and domestic political unrest leading to capital flight. On the brink of default, the World Bank and International Monetary Fund (IMF) stepped in (Zanini 2001). As they did for other countries in crisis in the global South, both the World Bank and IMF stipulated a structural adjustment program, including liberalization, as a conditionality for the loans. Implemented by Manmohan Singh, then finance minister and later prime minister, liberalization measures began to remove many of the import substitution policies and opened up the Indian economy to foreign products and investment.

Neoliberal economic policies that have emerged since the 1970s mark the massive rollback of the state in the provision of welfare programs and the support of nationalized industries. In contrast to classical free-market ideologies that promote the *absence* of the state in the economic sphere, the neoliberal state proactively facilitates free-market principles by implementing liberalization and privatization measures (Brown 2005, 2015). The expansion of global financial markets in particular has required extensive government intervention, as state actors have been central to liberalizing capital controls on cross-border flows through political and legal mediation (Abedal 2007; Arrighi 2010; Krippner 2011). Liberalization of the banking sector—allowing the global flow of finance capital in and out of India—and its privatization have required the state's very active intervention. Nevertheless, it is important to note that in contrast to the Asian economies hit by the 1997 Asian financial crisis, financial reforms in India were not only relatively gradual but also strengthened regulation and supervision (Hanson 2003), and financial liberalization remains an ongoing process in India.

In 1991, the Narasimham Committee, appointed by Finance Minister Manmohan Singh under the leadership of former RBI governor M. Narasimham to examine India's banking sector, recommended reforms to the financial system (RBI 1991). These included the gradual freeing of interest rates and reducing the burden of directed credit. The government encouraged competition in the financial sector by granting new banking licenses to private and foreign banks. Additionally, firms designated as nonbanking financial companies (NBFCs) were supported as a way to provide further funding to various un- and under-banked sectors. NBFCs can provide various financial services, including loans, but unlike banks, NBFCs cannot accept demand deposits or issue checks. Commercial MFIs are largely regulated as NBFCs.

Despite liberalization, banking and development policies remained deeply entwined. For example, contrary to the Narasimham Committee's recommendations to reduce directed lending to 10 percent, priority-sector lending requirements remained at 40 percent for public-sector and domestic private banks, though lowered to 32 percent for foreign banks. In 1998, the Second Narasimham Committee recommended further reforms to strengthen the banking sector, including correcting the high level of bad debt in directed credit (RBI 2001). The second report included recommendations for improving priority-sector lending by enhancing lending practices, including checking credit-worthiness of small borrowers, a task that became particularly suited to microfinance institutions.

The argument for financial inclusion emerged at this time because despite increasing consumer finance options for the middle classes, a large section of the population remained excluded from access to these services. Financial inclusion is defined as "the process of ensuring access to financial services and timely and adequate credit where needed by vulnerable groups such as weaker sections and low income groups at an affordable cost" (Rangarajan 2008, 1). In India, financial inclusion was first proposed as policy in a 2005 report commissioned by the Reserve Bank on rural credit and microfinance. The Khan Committee report (Khan 2005) noted that despite previous efforts of banking outreach, there remained large gaps in the availability of banking services, particularly in rural areas. In fact, the commercial banks had reached only 18 percent of the rural population in terms of savings and 17 percent in terms of loans.

The report had been commissioned in the wake of a number of high-profile statements on access to finance, including the 2005–2006 budget speech by Finance Minister P. Chidambaram, in which he affirmed the emerging importance of MFIs: "Government intends to promote MFIs in a big way. The way forward, I believe, is to identify MFIs, classify and rate such institutions, and empower them to intermediate between the lending banks and the beneficiaries" (quoted in Khan 2005, 8). In its conclusions, the Khan Committee report suggests that its recommendations are "likely to lead to a financial inclusion oriented growth model that aims at achieving socioeconomic empowerment of the less advantaged sections. This will also provide an ideal platform for the microfinance institutions to grow at a faster pace" (ibid., 60). Microfinance, in other words, had been embedded in the mission of financial inclusion. By 2008, financial inclusion had also been incorporated into the work of the Planning Commission— the development planning agency—in its Eleventh Five Year Plan.[7] Thus, the central bank, the Finance Ministry, and the (now-defunct) Planning Commission—the major bodies determining economic and banking policy in India—all rallied around financial inclusion as a central policy directive, with microfinance at the forefront.

We can then ask how specifically does social banking differ from financial inclusion? While both policies aim to increase access to credit and banking facilities, financial inclusion aims to integrate the poor into a wider network of finance. In its report to the Planning Commission, the Committee of Financial Sector Reforms offers the following: "[The committee] proposes a paradigm shift in the way we see inclusion. Instead of seeing the issue primarily as expanding credit, which puts the cart before the horse, we urge a refocus to seeing it as expanding access to financial services, such as payments services, savings products, insurance products, and inflation-protected pensions" (Planning Commission 2009, 6). While credit remains an integral factor, it is not the only area for consideration in financial inclusion. Financial inclusion aims to integrate the poor into the system of formal finance, not simply as consumers of credit but as a market for an entire range of financial products and services, such as payments, savings, insurance, and pension. Additionally, while recognizing the importance of agricultural credit, the report pushes for greater attention to the urban areas due to increasing migration. Finally, among its recommendations for the financial sector are more reforms in banking, including further liberalization through new licenses for private banks. While social banking sought to make the government and state-owned banks the primary means of providing financial services to the poor, financial inclusion seeks to use the private sector to a greater extent to reach the same goals.

MICROFINANCE MODELS:
SHG BANK LINKAGE AND MFI

Despite the government's promotion of directed credit to the unbanked, commercial banks remained wary of priority-sector lending due to high transaction costs and high risk of default. High transaction costs include labor-intensive operations, multiple transactions of small amounts, and related processing costs. Not only do commercial banks lack the financial methodology and human resources for lending to the poor, but "the institutional mission of banks precludes such forays" (Joshi 2006, 78). That is, the bank is responsible for recovering loans from what is perceived to be a high-risk population and therefore assume the possibility of having a large number of nonperforming assets (NPAs) on their books.

There are a number of models of more formalized community-based credit systems, including cooperative banks such as the Mahila Sewa Cooperative Bank.[8] In general, however, commercial banks have focused on lending to MFIs as a better alternative to meet priority-sector lending requirements while accounting for banks' costs and risks. In extending credit to the unbanked, the government of India has experimented with support for various models of microfinance, including SHGs and MFIs. By lending to MFIs or SHGs, commercial banks can make loans to multiple organizations and diversify their lending risks. Banks are also able to offset the transaction costs of lending to the poor by making fewer, larger loans to microfinance organizations. MFIs and SHGs, meanwhile, take on the risk of lending to the poor while being responsible for repaying the loan to the commercial bank. Although microfinance is often referred to broadly, each of the specific models offers quite different structures and poses different regulatory concerns.

In 1990, the National Bank for Agriculture and Rural Development (NABARD), a public-sector bank, began a bank linkage pilot project with five hundred SHGs. In 1996, financing of SHGs was designated as priority-sector lending. NABARD defines an SHG as "a group of about 20 people from a homogeneous class, who come together for addressing their common problems" (Puhazhendi and Badatya 2002, vii, n2). The groups are encouraged to initially voluntarily pool resources to make small loans to their members and start a savings account at the bank, with the expectation that these practices build financial discipline and credit history for the members. Once the groups show "mature financial behaviour" banks can make loans to the group without collateral and at market interest rates. The initial voluntary savings are described as "warm money," through which "members begin to appreciate that resources are limited and have a cost" (ibid.). This "warm money" comes to structure the "cold money" coming from banks, enforcing credit discipline among borrowers. While formal credit flows occur only when borrowers are deemed sufficiently aware of systems of formal financial transactions, banks also rely on existing social and cultural norms of reciprocity and obligation that are created and strengthened in the groups to maintain high rates of repayment.

As a bank linkage program, the SHG model enables a connection between mainly rural borrowers and commercial banks, primarily through savings accounts and loans. In both cases, the savings account and the loans disbursed from the bank are in the name of the SHG, not any individual group member (NABARD n.d.). Even within the bank linkage program, there are three models: (1) banks directly organize SHGs; (2) SHGs are mediated by agencies other than banks (e.g., NGOs, farmers' clubs, individual rural volunteers); and (3) NGOs and SHG federations act as credit intermediaries, assuming the risk of lending. Between 2002 and 2010, the number of SHGs receiving bank loans increased almost tenfold from around four hundred thousand to four million. Despite this growth, a number of factors have remained problematic for SHGs, including the relatively short lifespan of many SHGs and the poor "quality" of the groups (e.g., poor governance, high dropout rates) (Ghate 2007, 2008). From the borrowers' perspective, the size of loans from SHGs has been relatively small, and the time taken to get a loan is often long.

Since the late 1990s the nonbanking financial company microfinance institution (NBFC-MFI, or MFI) model has grown rapidly.[9] As for-profit commercial ventures, MFIs—the main focus of this book—encourage borrowers to form joint-liability groups (JLGs) but give loans to individual members of the group (Malegam 2011). In other words, loans are made not for the group's project, as envisioned for SHGs, but for individual projects. Individual loans are often, though not necessarily, guaranteed by other group members, and the group meetings principally enable loan recovery. The duration of loans is typically shorter for MFIs (approximately one year) than for SHGs (approximately two years). While many MFIs started out as nonprofit organizations, they converted to MFIs to raise additional capital and expand operations. Other organizations were established from the beginning as MFIs, seeing lending to the poor as a profitable business opportunity. Unlike SHGs, MFIs have attracted large amounts of private equity and investment.

Beyond MFIs and SHGs, the field of microfinance is constantly evolving. The RBI introduced the BC model in 2006 (RBI 2006). Under the BC model, banks, linked with mobile technologies, can conduct business through intermediaries such as cooperative societies, NGOs, MFIs, or individuals authorized by the central bank in exchange for a fee (RBI 2011). The RBI has also extended Small Finance Banks licenses to a number of MFIs (A. Ray 2016). Small Finance Banks are able to offer savings and credit services.

These different and evolving models are also entangled in the ongoing politics of credit. SHGs, often affiliated with particular interest groups or political parties, can become exclusionary to those outside such affiliations. MFIs, capturing potential clients of SHGs, can be seen not as an alternative credit source but as competition to political power. The 2010 microfinance crisis in India brought to light these intersecting politics of credit.

INDIA'S SUBPRIME CRISIS

In the summer of 2009, as the global economy was reeling from the subprime crisis originating in the United States, I was conducting preliminary fieldwork on microfinance in Kolkata. With significant turmoil in the international banking sector, I asked the management at various MFIs whether or not they were affected by the crisis. The answer was almost uniformly no. Senior managers explained that it was not just that the Indian economy was relatively unscathed in the immediate aftermath of the financial meltdown but that poor borrowers and their local economies were simply not integrated at a global scale. This meant that demand for loans remained high, as did the loan recovery rates of the MFIs. It would be another year before the Indian banking sector would encounter its own subprime crisis originating in the microfinance sector.

When I returned a year later to conduct yearlong fieldwork in August 2010, the microfinance sector in India was still booming. DENA's rapid expansion was reflected in its new multistoried office with large gleaming glass windows; it was a significant move from the small makeshift office I had visited just a year earlier. Sitting in the spacious conference room of DENA's brand-new office building, with the just-installed air conditioner blasting cold air, Mr. Guha, one of the regional managers, excitedly recounted the company's recent growth. At the time of our conversation in the summer of 2010, DENA already had 222 operational branches in India and was in the process of adding another 260 functional branch offices by March 31, 2011. While the majority of the branch offices were in West Bengal, they were venturing into other eastern and northeastern states, including Assam, Tripura, Bihar, and Jharkhand.

It was not just DENA that was experiencing growth in the microfinance sector: SKS Microfinance, headquartered in Hyderabad, Andhra Pradesh, had just successfully listed on the BSE, becoming the first Indian MFI to go public. Yet SKS's IPO also served as a catalyst for a crisis that would subsume the Indian microfinance sector. As the crisis unfolded, it revealed the entanglements of commercial banking, banking policy and regulation, and global finance with the Indian microfinance sector and its consequences for poor borrowers.

One of the first signs that all was not well with SKS Microfinance after its successful IPO in July 2010 were rumors that Akula had fallen out with his management—Managing Director and CEO Suresh Gurumani.[10] Reflected in the face-off between Gurumani and Akula were the competing leadership practices of the two men: managerial and charismatic.[11] While Akula, as the charismatic leader, had been the public face of SKS Microfinance, he has been periodically absent in the running of the company he founded in order to finish his PhD, to work at McKinsey, and then to deal with a messy divorce and child custody case based in the United States. As described in an *Economic Times* article, the managerial Gurumani "was SKS' face for investors. . . . Mr Gurumani could speak the language of private equity funds and global investors—return on equity, return on capital, client acquisition—thanks to his two decades of banking with the financial world at Standard Chartered Bank and Barclays" (Udgirkar 2010).

On October 4, newspapers reported that Gurumani had been fired and replaced by M. R. Rao, the deputy CEO at the time, a move that precipitated a 9 percent drop in SKS's share price. Further, Akula had been appointed executive chairman with a greater role in running the company. While there has been speculation over the exact reason of Gurumani's dismissal, including personality and strategic differences with Akula, what the IPO and management scuffle revealed through subsequent debates in the media was the profitability of microfinance.

For example, appointed in 2008, Gurumani was paid Rs 15 million per annum (approximately US$240,000), increased to Rs 20 million in May 2010 (approximately US$300,000) in addition to a performance bonus of Rs 1.5 million (approximately US$24,000) and stock options (*Business Standard* 2010). In comparison, the annual compensation in fiscal year 2009–2010 for the chairman of the State Bank of India, India's largest public-sector bank and a Fortune 500 company, was about Rs 1.5 million (about US$25,000) (*Rediff Business* 2010).[12] In fact, in October 2010, the *Economic Times* (2010) reported that more than sixty employees of SKS had each made more than one million rupees by selling shares following the IPO. They had received these shares through an employee stock purchase scheme (ESPS) in 2007, making a return twenty-nine times their initial investment. Even before the listing, Akula and other senior management, including Gurumani, sold part of their stakes in the company, making significant profits. This very profitability would come to haunt SKS in the crisis, because their stock prices crashed and the profitability hurt the reputation of the company. How, after all, were people making millions off an industry that was purported to be helping the poor?

The revelations in the profitability of microfinance due to the internal skirmishes at SKS emerged at the same time as a report commissioned by the Andhra Pradesh state government. In October 2010, the Society for the Elimination of Poverty (SERP), a service-delivery organization under the Department of Rural Development, Government of Andhra Pradesh, prepared a report on alleged harassment of microfinance borrowers.[13] Of the 123 documented cases of harassment by MFIs, there were fifty-four microfinance-related suicides. In the wake of these revelations, the Andhra government promulgated the Andhra Pradesh Micro Finance Institutions (regulation of moneylending) Ordinance in October 2010—approved by the state assembly in December 2010—implementing state-level regulations of MFIs.

The Andhra Pradesh Ordinance required each MFI operating in the state to register with the district-level authority within thirty days of its introduction, requiring information on purpose, interest rate charged, system of due diligence, recovery practices, and list of individuals authorized for lending and recovering of loans. Without registering, MFIs would be barred from both granting and recovering loans, and the registering authority was granted power to cancel registration at any time, given sufficient reason, including the use of coercive recovery methods. In place of loan officers visiting borrowers, the ordinance designated the offices of the local *gram panchayat* (village council) as the only place for loan recovery. MFIs were barred from recovering loans whose interest exceeded the principal and allowed borrowers to receive a refund of the amount in excess. Along with regulating MFIs, the ordinance also prohibited membership at more than one SHG. Further, the ordinance introduced fast-track courts for settling microfinance-related disputes.

While creating more stringent regulations for MFIs, the Andhra Pradesh state government provided additional relief to SHGs through soft loans from banks, which enabled SHGs to clear MFI loans. In effect, the Andhra Pradesh Ordinance explicitly pitted SHGs against MFIs, accusing private MFIs of exploiting SHGs "through usurious interest rates and coercive means of recovery." Moreover, it argued for the need to protect "the interests of the SHGs" from the "money lending MFIs." By equating MFIs to moneylending, the Andhra government dismissed the developmental claims of MFIs while promoting the work of state-supported SHGs.

MFIs and their supporters in turn critiqued the Andhra Pradesh government for politicizing commercial microfinance while promoting the government-sponsored microfinance initiatives through SHGs (see Mader 2013; Rai 2010). Critics of the Andhra Pradesh government's actions argued that the state government found a scapegoat in the private microfinance sector to promote the more politically strategic SHGs.[14] For example, in an opinion piece in the *Economic Times*, prominent journalist and supporter of microfinance Swaminathan Aiyar (2010) argued that "the government is supposed to be a referee. But in AP [Andhra Pradesh], the referee is also a big player and it wins by disqualifying rivals." Aiyar goes on to argue that despite the need for regulatory regimes in microfinance, "local politicians don't want to empower people through independent access to finance: they prefer patronage networks that can be used as vote banks. Government-driven SHGs can serve that purpose, but not MFIs." From the perspective of MFIs, political involvement can create a "culture of non-repayment" whereby politicians are encouraging borrowers not to pay back loans and thereby disrupting the financial system.[15]

The complicated politics of credit meant that priority-sector lending strategies of the national plan for financial inclusion made commercial microfinance a viable and attractive site for extending credit to the poor. The national agenda, however, came into competition with the state-level politics of credit through the use of SHGs to promote political ends, whether in terms of the state's argument of protecting the poor from usurious MFIs or the MFIs' contention that the state government was politicizing credit.

REGULATING MICROFINANCE

The implementation of the Andhra Pradesh Ordinance, however, had significant consequences for the microfinance sector beyond the state. Andhra Pradesh had, at this time, the highest levels of microfinance penetration in India, including a large number of the major microfinance players headquartered in what was then the state capital, Hyderabad.[16] Because the primary loans are often made from commercial banks to MFI headquarters and then disbursed to regional offices, large firms that operate throughout India, such as SKS, Spandana Sphoorty, and BASIX, found that the Andhra Pradesh regulations created a shortage of capital for loans throughout the country. The impact of the crisis was reflected in SKS's share price, which crashed from a high of Rs 1,396 in September 2010 to Rs 330 by May 2011, falling to its lowest price of Rs 56 in June 2012. Similarly, according to Sa-Dhan, the industry organization, the number of registered MFIs fell from 237 in 2010 to 184 in 2012.[17] Moreover, regulatory uncertainty created by the crisis led to new debates over the regulation of microfinance in India.

In February 2011, I interviewed the manager in charge of microfinance at a public-sector bank in Kolkata. In response to my question about the current situation, he replied, "The RBI has not yet given any clear policy. . . . RBI has not given any additional circulars on regulations since the Malegam Committee report. Unless the RBI gives any further directives, banks don't want to get involved any further. The banks are apprehensive about lending to bad MFIs." The banker's comments reflected the situation in the MFI sector since October 2010 and the crisis originating in Andhra Pradesh. As the least regulated of the formal-sector lending institutions, MFIs suddenly faced higher scrutiny not only by government regulators but also by commercial banks that made bulk loans to the MFIs. The freeze in available funds created a liquidity crunch, and MFIs were increasingly unable to extend new loans to their borrowers. Meanwhile, banks wanted a clearer signal from regulators regarding the future of the sector, something that had long been stymied.

With the rapid growth of microfinance since the late 1990s, the first major regulatory move came in 2007 with the Ministry of Finance unveiling a bill to regulate the microfinance sector to the lower house of Parliament. The Micro Financial Sector (Development and Regulation) Bill was meant to promote and develop the "orderly growth of the micro finance sector." Among its directives, the bill sought to make NABARD the regulator for the microfinance sector. Additionally, it would have restricted lending to a cap of Rs 50,000 for individual loans and to Rs 150,000 for housing projects and would have required registered MFIs to have net owned funds of at least Rs 500,000. The bill, however, lapsed with the end of the Lok Sabha session and was never passed. While there was discussion of reintroducing the bill in 2009, it was not until the 2010 crisis that serious attempts were again made to regulate the sector.

Following the Andhra Pradesh Ordinance there was renewed interest in and pressing need for national regulation of the microfinance sector. The RBI established the Malegam Committee on October 15, 2010, under the leadership of Y. H. Malegam, to report on the microfinance sector and to offer policy recommendations of its regulation. The much-awaited report was released in January 2011 and proposed a number of measures for the RBI to consider.

One of the main recommendations of the Malegam Committee included the designation of the category "NBFC-MFI" to address the specific regulatory needs of the microfinance sector that—unlike other NBFCs—served primarily poor populations.[18] NBFC-MFIs were required to meet a number of new conditions, including having more than 90 percent of its total assets in microfinance. This would mean that financial firms without significant focus on microfinance would not be able to jump on the bandwagon of lending to the poor. The committee stipulated that loans made by MFIs would have to be made to households making under Rs 50,000. These collateral-free loans would not exceed Rs 25,000, and the total indebtedness of a borrower could not exceed Rs 25,000. Thus, an MFI had to be aware of a borrower's outstanding credit from other MFIs so the limit would not be exceeded. The term of the loan would have to be at least twelve months for loans under Rs 15,000 and twenty-four months for larger loans, and borrowers should have the option of repaying by weekly, biweekly, or monthly installments.

Further, based on the financials of nine of the large MFIs (accounting for 70.4 percent of clients and 63.6 percent of the total microfinance loan portfolio), the Malegam Committee found that interest rates ranged from 31.2 percent to 50.3 percent, averaging 36.7 percent. Interest rates at smaller MFIs averaged about 28.7 percent (Malegam 2011, sec. 7.5). Taking into account the overall costs of running an MFI (staff, other overhead, etc.), the Malegam Committee recommended that effective interest rates for individual loans should be capped at 24 percent. The committee also recommended transparency in the fee structure, with no more than three components to the loan: (1) a processing fee not exceeding 1 percent of the gross loan amount; (2) the interest rate charge; and (3) the insurance premium.[19] In addition to restricting borrowers from taking loans from more than two MFIs, the committee recommended the establishment of a credit information bureau. In terms of consumer protection mechanisms, the Malegam Committee suggested that field staff should not be allowed to make recoveries at the residence or workplace of the borrower as a way to mitigate the use of coercive methods. Additionally, it recommended the introduction of a code of conduct for all employees to follow.

Regarding corporate size, the Malegam Committee recommended that NBFC-MFIs should have a minimum net worth of Rs 150 million to reduce transaction costs and improve efficiency with larger MFIs (Malegam 2011, sec. 15.3), an increase from Rs 20 million for MFIs that were registered as just NBFCs. While arguing for the continuance of priority-sector designation for microfinance, the committee noted that such lending should be denied to MFIs that fail to meet regulations. Recognizing the growing practice of securitization as well as the entry of private equity, the committee outlined a number of regulations for these areas. Finally, the committee recommended that the Reserve Bank be the regulator for microfinance and that with the implementation of a single regulatory framework, the Andhra Pradesh Ordinance would no longer be required.

As expected, the Malegam Committee report faced a number of criticisms from MFIs. In a response piece in the *Financial Express*, Vijay Mahajan (2011), chairman of the MFI BASIX and president of the associational body MFIN, proclaimed, "Operation Successful, Patient Dead"; or that while tackling regulatory concerns, the report did not address the issue of nonrepayment in Andhra Pradesh as a result of the ordinance, ultimately resulting in the destruction of the industry. Others wondered if the Malegam Committee was instituting a "slow death" for the microfinance sector.

A number of more specific concerns regarding the regulatory recommendations came up in the aftermath. These concerns were voiced, for example, during the Sa-Dhan organized workshop in Kolkata that I attended at the end of January 2011. First, as one participant argued, in designating the annual income level of microfinance borrowers as no more than Rs 50,000, the Reserve Bank was trying to create a uniform cutoff for poverty. However, people living in urban areas may be making more than Rs 50,000 but would be considered poor by other measures given higher costs of living in the city. Further, he contended that Rs 50,000 meant very different things for a family of three and a family of six. Thus, the Rs 50,000 cutoff was arbitrary for determining poverty levels and neediness of borrowers.

Second, with the introduction of options for monthly, biweekly, or weekly repayments, other MFI representatives at the workshop argued that the committee did not consider the cash flow of households. Offering options for monthly or biweekly repayments did not take into account that it would be difficult for many borrowers who relied on daily incomes to make larger monthly repayments.[20] Moreover, participants at the workshop wondered whether the Malegam Report, in requiring higher levels of capital adequacy, was strengthening the position of investors at the expense of the MFIs, as many small MFIs would not be able to meet these regulations. As an observer at the National Microfinance Conference later in April argued, the Malegam Committee was fostering a system where "big is beautiful" rather than helping smaller organizations.

Despite the hoopla surrounding the Malegam Committee report, little has been done to implement it through a national-level bill, which remains in limbo five years after the crisis. After the draft bill that was proposed in April 2011, the Micro Finance Institutions (Development and Regulation) Bill, 2012 was finally introduced at the Lok Sabha in May 2012. However, last-minute changes raised the credit limit from Rs 50,000 as proposed in the draft bill to Rs 500,000, with provisions to make loans up to Rs 1 million for purposes to be outlined by the Reserve Bank. This is higher than the committee's recommended Rs 25,000, making microfinance a financing option not just for the poor but also for the middle class.[21] Further, the RBI can designate the minimum net worth for an MFI, depending on its size of operations. In February 2014 a parliamentary panel rejected the 2012 Microfinance Bill, and in September 2014, the new BJP government proposed a more diluted version of the 2012 bill. The regulatory landscape of Indian microfinance, therefore, has remained uncertain in the years following the crisis and continues to be subject to the politics of credit.

SYSTEMIC IMPORTANCE

The parallels between the US subprime mortgage crisis and the Indian microfinance crisis, though incommensurable in scale, are striking: the overextension of credit to the poor, investment hype over a new financial product, weak regulatory systems, and the inevitable collapse of a lending bubble.[22] Yet the Indian microfinance crisis was not simply the "micro" or derivative form of a larger, more complicated financial crisis. Rather, the microfinance crisis emerged from its own set of contradictions relating to the politics of credit in India. Indian microfinance and its crisis are products of long-term developments in Indian banking and social policy that intersect with emergent forms of finance. The crisis highlighted not only the bursting of a speculative credit bubble of private capital but also the ways in which state-led social banking policies such as priority-sector lending led to overinvestment in the area of microfinance. The microfinance crisis, as a moment of critical rupture,[23] offers an analytical instance through which to understand these various institutional actors, interests, and histories.

The crisis and the ensuing debates over microfinance reveal its emerging importance and influence in the financial sector. Significantly, one of the ultimate exclusions of the 2012 bill that appeared in the 2011 draft bill was the question of systemic importance. In the draft bill, any microfinance institution that becomes "systemically important" would be required to follow directives issued by the RBI from time to time. The categorization of MFIs that are of systemic importance was to be decided by the central bank. In recognizing MFIs as being of systemic importance, the 2011 bill aimed at highlighting the systemic risk that microfinance posed. In other words, there exists a possibility that problems in the microfinance sector could threaten the financial system as a whole.

On the one hand, it can be argued that the microfinance sector is not yet significant enough in the financial landscape of India to merit identification as systemically important. On the other hand, the continued emphasis on financial inclusion and the impact of the microfinance crisis suggest the more extensive systemic influence of microfinance. For example, as the rupee weakened against the dollar in late 2011, the RBI announced the raising of external borrowing limits for MFIs to US$10 million. Thus, the microfinance sector has been absorbed into the strategies of the central bank to manage the overall financial structure of the economy. Similarly, the awarding of the new bank licenses, including to Bandhan, was also met with caution. The

ratings agency Standard & Poor warned that the entry of new players could undermine the stability of the banking sector if they "relaxed
their underwriting standards or undercut prices to gain market share"
(PTI 2014b). New banks and their customers could threaten the stability of the financial system. The story of inclusion is also one of measur-
ing, assessing, and managing risk.

As Rawi Abedal argues, "Capital regulations and liberalizations
are signals interpreted by financial markets. Market participants, in
this way of thinking, infer meaning from policies" (2007, 17). With increasing financial flows into the microfinance sector, regulatory moves
have become signs for whether or not to invest in microfinance, as reflected in the volatility of SKS's share prices and the liquidity in microfinance. While such structural conditions shape the working environment of microfinance, regulatory measures can miss the everyday
experiences and social interactions of both borrowers and loan officers.
Attempts to replace informal finance through regulation and financial inclusion policies can fail without attention to local-level political and economic dynamics (Tsai 2004). The vagaries of the market as
well as the new trajectories of government policy are often at odds with
the lived realities of borrowers who, in the absence of other options,
have come to rely on microfinance loans to make ends meet. When financial crises stemming from intersecting financial and regulatory interests occur, there is little attention paid to the lives that have been
shaken with sudden changes in monetary flows.

This does not mean that there should be no efforts at regulating
microfinance; rather, it raises the question of what happens when the
poor are directly connected to global finance. While this chapter has
shown the ways in which the state aims to regulate the microfinance
sector, the following chapters examine actual microfinance practices,
including the interactions between borrowers and lenders from an ethnographic perspective. They demonstrate not only the political and
economic dynamics of microfinance but also the influence of local social and cultural values as they are interpreted in everyday practices.

CHAPTER 3

THE RELUCTANT MONEYLENDER

ANAND, A BRANCH MANAGER at DENA, and I took respite from the harsh noon sun in the elusive shade of a scraggly tree. We were waiting for Mithun, the loan officer, to finish his round of house verifications before heading back to the branch office for the afternoon. Standing by the littered stream that had narrowed to a trickle, Anand reflected on his previous experience in loan collections: "Sometimes, you go and there is little you can do. Once, when I was working in the rural area, I went to this person's house because she had not paid back the loan [at the meeting]. Seeing the place, I could not even ask them to pay back the loan; they had nothing. But there was a little boy, and he looked like he had not eaten. When I saw him, I took out my wallet and gave him ten rupees and told him to go eat his *tiffin* [lunch]. It was really the fault of the branch manager who had made the mistake in allowing the loan. They should never have given that loan knowing their situation."

In his recounting of this experience, I was struck by Anand's intertwining concerns for an impoverished family and the possibility of a loan default for the MFI. Poor financial risk analysis had landed Anand in an ethically tenuous position: to have demanded repayment in this situation was impossible. Yet the adherence to this decision meant that the loan would become overdue in the company's books as a nonperforming asset, for which he would be accountable. Anand's story was poignant because it indexed a position of real struggle to reconcile the abstract demands of a creditor assessing financial risk (and profitability) and the ethical position of an individual enmeshed in a particular social relationship. As argued previously, the management at commercially driven MFIs see their role as social enterprises to be providing a social good while pursuing profits, or of "doing well by doing good." Yet instances such as the one Anand described reveal moments when these two aspects are irreconcilable, when the financial enfolding of the poor does not automatically lead to improved social welfare. Here, the relational concerns that loan officers voice in their everyday encounters with borrowers demonstrate the limits of the "ethicalization of market rule" (Ananya Roy 2012, 106) through social enterprise.

This chapter is about the work of finance at the peripheries and the related tensions and ambiguities of expanding financial networks in India. It explores how individuals, acting as creditors, find themselves having to navigate between and make sense of intersecting moral and financial economies.[1] Banking relationships—whether at an MFI or a multinational commercial bank—are always constituted through physical and emotional labor of intermediaries or "proxies" such as loan officers. These proxies do not own the capital they extend as credit and must alienate the debt relationships they produce through their own labor to the financial institution. Financial inclusion of the poor creates new kinds of socialities, obligations, and expectations for both borrowers and lenders. Microfinance loan officers in India who alienate the debts they produce must also negotiate existing social imaginaries such as moneylending and rework the cultural framework for ethical action that makes loan recovery a morally acceptable profession. This chapter examines how microfinance loan officers embody, negotiate, and question the complex intertwining of institutional directives and local relational demands in the process of alienating debts. Moreover, it interrogates the consequences of extending and abstracting the distance between the borrower and lender in the context of financialization and the move toward securitization of loans.

Research on microfinance has tended to focus on its consequences for debtors (e.g., Karim 2011; Moodie 2008; Rahman 1999; Rankin 2001; Sanyal 2009). While providing critical insight into the ways in which borrowers experience these new forms of debt, there is little scholarship on the loan officers, who play a key role in the functioning of microfinance. Moreover, there tends to be little ethnographic analysis of how institutional or formal financial norms and interests have increasingly shaped microfinance practices. Studies that do focus primarily on the global financial networks of microfinance often occlude the ways in which debt is mediated by people and productive of more complicated outcomes than the smooth dissemination of capital and, importantly, the possibilities for change in these gaps (e.g., Mader 2015; Ananya Roy 2010; H. Weber 2004). This chapter focuses on loan officers as necessary intermediaries in doing the everyday work of enfolding the poor into networks of global finance.

FINANCIAL LABOR AT THE PERIPHERY

In his classic work *The Devil and Commodity Fetishism in South America*, Michael Taussig observes that financial pages make mention of "the 'sagging dollar,' of 'earning booming ahead,' of 'cash flows,' of treasury bills 'backing up'" (1980, 30–31). Without actors, Taussig notes that "capital appears to have an innate property of self-expansion" (ibid., 31). Against this naturalized representation of financial markets still common in the financial papers of today, there is a growing body of scholarship in the social studies of finance exploring the social construction of financial markets through actors and networks and mediated by financial technologies.[2] Anthropologists have also begun to ethnographically document the work of investment bankers, traders, lawyers, and regulators in producing financial markets (Fisher 2012; Ho 2009; Miyazaki 2013; Riles 2011; Zaloom 2006). These works show that markets do not operate—almost magically—on their own but are produced and sustained by various actors in different places and different times.

Nevertheless, Annelise Riles (2010) has rightly critiqued much of the scholarship in social studies of finance for focusing primarily on elites (e.g., traders) rather than those who work at the peripheries of financial assemblages (e.g., back-office workers). Even these peripheries of finance often remain in the metropolitan centers of the global North, while finance is seen as irrelevant to the lives of the poor, particularly in the global South, except indirectly. Yet the work of financialization extends beyond Wall Street or the BSE to the everyday lives of people at the margins (see Elyachar 2005a). While they are subject to the forces of global capital, there is little examination of how people at the peripheries themselves produce and participate in financial markets.

Financialization at the peripheries and the incorporation of the poor into financial networks is part of what David Harvey terms "speculative raiding" (2003, 147). It is by inclusion into financial networks that the poor are constituted as new consumers of commercial credit and an additional source of capital for banks. Nevertheless, this process very much involves people, creating contexts in which individuals encounter, debate, and negotiate the complex web and multiple demands of economic life. Financial inclusion requires the use of and innovation in abstract financial technologies (corporate debt, equity, etc.). Nonetheless, financial capitalism "is not all smoke and mirrors. There has to be something there to begin with" (Leyshon and Thrift 2007, 109). For microfinance, that "something" is the debt relationship constituted between the loan officer and the borrower. In addition to the tools of abstraction, financializing the peripheries depends on labor of loan officers to actively produce and sustain these debt relationships.

THE WORK OF THE CREDITOR

At DENA, the work of loan officers is both mundane and eventful. A typical workday begins early: The first group meeting of the day starts at eight in the morning. Many of the MFIs require their staff to live dormitory-style in the branch offices for six days a week. This is in part because of the early-morning meetings but also because loan officers cannot belong to the neighborhoods where they work. On busy days, loan officers cover four to five group meetings by noon: one hour for a meeting and any related work, such as house verifications or loan applications, leaving just enough time to get to the next meeting. They navigate Kolkata's unpaved alleys and the potholed roads teeming with the morning rush-hour traffic to get to the group meetings held in the homes of the borrowers. Bicycles are the only allowed means of transportation, although there are rumors that some firms have given their staff motorbikes. During the summer months when the sun beats a deadly heat, or during the monsoon season when staying dry is a challenge as Kolkata streets become waterlogged, the journey is tiring and even dangerous. Loan collections happen even during Kolkata's notorious *bandhs* (strikes), when most other businesses in the city shut down for the day.

There are a number of institutionally codified practices for the meetings: The group leader, cashier, and secretary make sure that all the women have assembled by the time the loan officer arrives and have collected all the passbooks and money. The loan officer refers to all the women borrowers, regardless of age, as *Didi*, while the women refer to the officer as "Madam" or "Sir."[3] There is supposed to be a group floor mat for the meeting, but in many one-room homes in the urban slum settlements, there is barely room to sit. In such cases, the loan officer and the group cashier sit on the bed, which may still be occupied by a sleeping or ill family member, while the other borrowers huddle on the floor or stand outside. At the meeting the loan officer has to write the amounts received in the women's passbooks and in her own collection ledger, quickly count the money, follow up on any loan applications, and then head out to the next meeting. On most days someone is late, and on occasion a borrower does not turn up at all. On such days, staff must convince the other borrowers to remain until they have solved the problem by pooling the missing amount from among the members present. There are also house verifications to be conducted for loan applicants, which must be squeezed in within the hour for the group meeting. Branch managers are also required to go out to the field every morning and conduct house verifications and monitor group meetings.

Back at the branch office around noon, the loan officers have to double-check the collected amounts before lunch. In recent years, MFI staff have become targets of robbery, since they are known to travel with large amounts of cash. There is also fear that any missing cash will be taken out of their salary. Once the cash is accounted for, there is time for a short break before the afternoon's work of loan disbursements, when borrowers with new loans come collect them at the branch office. Finally, the staff has to complete the various forms of accounting (daily, weekly, monthly). The day's work ends around four or five in the evening. Sometimes, there is an outstanding loan that requires visitations later in the day, though MFI staff are technically not allowed to visit borrowers' homes at night. The loan officers have Saturday nights and Sundays off to go home but have to be back by Sunday night for the Monday-morning shift. There is, perhaps unsurprisingly, a high turnover rate in the staff at MFIs. The work is exhausting, and the pay is not adequate compensation.

Consider the employment trajectory of Samit, who had joined DENA just two months before we met. He was from a small town near the India-Bangladesh border and had recently graduated from college, majoring in literature. He learned about this job in microfinance through a friend who was applying. While his friend failed the interview, Samit landed the job. Even while feeling bad for his friend, he had accepted the position at the insistence of his elder brother, who thought he would learn new things. Samit expressed dismay at what he termed the "money situation." Pay at the office was low, at about Rs 5,000 a month, and after deductions for living costs at the branch office (e.g., meals), he was left with just about Rs 3,000 in hand.[4] When he had started, a regional manager had praised Samit, saying he was sure to be promoted quickly. But Samit found that this kind of lifestyle was not sustainable in the long term: "One of the women [loan officers] is married and has a child. But she has to leave her child with her parents and stay here. Men will also be expected to spend more time at home once they are married." Even his brother told him: "*Bhai* [brother], you have to find a job that pays better. You won't be able to get by on that salary." Samit's experience highlights the difficulties of working in microfinance in terms of hours and pay. Yet he, like other MFI staff, was tasked with enfolding the poor into financial networks.

PRODUCING DEBT

Interest-bearing credit can be considered "capital as a commodity," where the lender alienates the use value of the money so that it can be put to use by the borrower as capital and returned with interest (Marx 1991, 462). Marx's original analysis of credit limited capital as a commodity to exchange between capitalists.[5] However, credit to workers (noncapitalists) is no longer a traditional form of usury and distinct from the capitalist mode of production, but it is central to the smooth flows of capital (Harris 1976, 158). Thus, even though poor borrowers do not convert borrowed capital into commodities (as would industrial capitalists), the growth of credit markets and the related development of new financial products and their circulation have meant that the range of capital as commodity has expanded. For example, under contemporary financial regimes, debt instruments circulate as commodities without ever being converted into productive use value, and surplus value is created not just through labor but also through circulation and speculation (Lee and LiPuma 2002; K. Sunder Rajan 2005). Interrogating these new forms of capital as commodity then requires tracing the social life of credit from production to exchange (Appadurai 1988).

With investment firms seeing credit markets of the poor as an "opportunity rather than obligation" (Sinha and Subramanian 2007, 6), microfinance loans have become new sources of capital for financial products, such as securitized debt. These financial instruments fuel the process of "accumulation by dispossession" (Harvey 2003, 147) by enfolding the poor into the wider financial networks. However, as noted earlier, this is not a process that happens easily or without ambivalence and fissures, because the transformation of capital into capital as commodity requires the labor of microfinance employees. It is only once the loan is established between the borrower and the lender—the cash handed over to the former and entered into the books of the latter as an asset that will be realized in the near future with interest—that the loan is taken to be part of the MFI's net worth and can enter capital circulation. Thus, both commercial banks and MFIs use what I call a "proxy-creditor" to mediate the creditor-debtor relationship. In other words, loan officers exist in microfinance debt relationships as people who produce the debt relationships (i.e., the loan product) but are not themselves the owners of capital.

While scholars have examined the shift toward flexible labor and disciplinary regimes of labor under contemporary capitalism (e.g., Freeman 2000; Ong 2006), in identifying the work of loan officers as labor here, I primarily aim to defetishize the financial product as a pure abstraction and to show how financialization at the peripheries depends on the labor of MFI staff. Of course, this is not just the case in the peripheries of finance: Gillian Tett's (2009) account of the development of collateralized debt obligations in the 2008 subprime crisis traces how these products were conceptualized, developed, and put into circulation by particular individuals and networks at investment banks. Like other commodities, debt instruments do not magically enter the lives of poor borrowers in India or homeowners in the United States, and capital does not appear in the books without the work of intermediaries. However, once fetishized, the loan is no longer seen as a product of labor tied to relations of production but as a mysterious, powerful, and almost natural thing that circulates freely.[6] In its commodity form, the debt can be alienated from its producer and finally moved to the balance sheets of the company.

Yet loan products are unique commodities precisely because they are debts. Unlike other commodities, credit returns to the lender with interest and with the use value of the lent capital intact (Harris 1976). While economic debt entails this particular financial arrangement, the monetary aspect is only part of what constitutes the debt relation. Even with its increasing abstraction through processes of financialization, debt remains inherently relational. From Marcel Mauss's (2000) theorization of the gift as a form of debt, to Pierre Bourdieu's (1977) analysis of credit and debt in maintaining hierarchical dominance, anthropological work has long identified the social productivity of debt in creating networks of obligation. Others have destabilized the economic hegemony of credit by demonstrating the intrinsically cosmological meaning of financial relationships (e.g., Chu 2010; Langford 2009; Maurer 2002). Fundamentally relational, debt is not just the financial transaction of owing and being owed money but ties together the creditor and debtor in extensive relationships and obligations of exchange over time and space (Graeber 2011a; Munn 1992). Microfinance provides critical insight because it relies on close and informal interactions between loan officers and borrowers while transforming the loans into financial products.

IN THE SHADOWS OF
THE MONEYLENDER AND THE BANK

The Indian government has promoted microfinance as a formal-sector alternative to informal moneylending. Yet speaking to the *Economic Times*, Y. V. Reddy, former RBI governor, critiqued MFIs: "If it is profit and if there is lending, aggressively, then it's just moneylending" (quoted in Nayak 2010). It was an ironic description of a sector that had purported to be the formal alternative to the moneylender who offers loans at exorbitant rates of interest. There has been the persistent negative stereotype of the moneylender as essentially exploitative in the Indian cultural imagination: "coldly preying upon their cultivator clients, luring them further and further into debt, and finally sucking them dry of surplus, savings, property and liberty" (Rudner 1994, 36). For example, a classic representation of this stereotype is Sukhilala, the merciless moneylender in Mehboob Khan's epic film *Mother India* (1957), who exploits the peasant debtors in newly independent India.[7] It is this image of the moneylender that continues to shadow the microfinance loan officer.

The invocation of the moneylender by government regulators in reference to MFIs indexes a complicated history of banking, credit, and development. With the growth of the formal financial sector, the figure of the moneylender came to mark the "backward" informal sector, while banking came to represent integration into modernity. As the formal financial sector remains out of the reach of most Indians, many still rely on the moneylender for access to credit.

Despite tendencies to collapse all moneylenders into one category, there are both formal (licensed) and informal (unlicensed) moneylenders. Most states, including West Bengal where I conducted fieldwork, have laws curbing moneylending and require moneylenders to be licensed. According to a survey by the RBI (2007), many people continue to rely on the informal moneylenders due to limited outreach from the formal sector, confidentiality, and the provision of "door-step service," ready lending for consumption purposes, and the speed of getting the loan. For most of my urban poor informants who lacked landholdings, low-interest loans from commercial banks were deemed impossible without adequate collateral and documentation, while interest on loans from moneylenders was exponentially higher. Though attempts at bridging these inadequacies have been made, for example, through the introduction of cooperative banks and financial inclusion drives by public-sector banks, MFIs in recent years have filled this gap between the local moneylender and the inaccessible commercial bank.

Posited to exist between those of the moneylender and the commercial banks, the lending methods of the MFIs also rest somewhere in the middle: They have fixed, scheduled collections, but with a modified door-step service (i.e., loan officers visit groups, rather than borrowers having to come to the office); they offer interest rates that are higher than those of commercial banks but lower than those of moneylenders; and they use formal loan application procedures but rely on regularized social interactions to monitor and assess risk. Borrowers also distinguished MFIs from informal moneylenders by referring to borrowing from the latter as taking "money on interest" (*sūdhe taka newa*), even though MFIs also charge interest on their loans. Borrowers tended to refer to the MFI as a "bank," while commercial banks would be referred to by their proper names (e.g., State Bank or Axis Bank). As arbiters of both formal finance and socially embedded relationships in the communities where they work, MFI staff are emblematic of the experiences of mediators in various contexts. Yet such an existence between the formal commercial banks and the informal moneylender creates complicated creditor-debtor positions, particularly for the loan officers who administer the microfinance loans.

Samit, for example, was extremely uncomfortable with the coercive elements of working at the MFI. "I don't like going to people's houses and sitting around and waiting for the other women to come up with the money [for repayment]," he said, indicating his dislike of a crucial part of the job. His discomfort stemmed from the fact that the loan collections took him into the borrowers' homes, where he felt intrusive. This feeling was amplified when his role shifted from passive to active loan collector, whose job was "making people pay" (Rock 1973). Shortly after, Samit told me he was leaving the job; he was going back to school to get a teaching certificate. Loan officers like Samit may express class distinction in their dislike of doorstep loan collections, especially in comparison to office work.[8] However, there was something particularly unsettling for the MFI staff in the very act of collecting loans. These anxieties were sharpened when debtors became defaulters and loan officers had to become debt collectors—a shift that brought loan officers into uncomfortable proximity to the negatively marked moneylender.

Challenging the popularly circulating critiques of MFIs as moneylenders, Anand offered an alternative perspective of microfinance, contrasting it to the central bank. We were at a meeting held in a small bamboo hut built on stilts atop a polluted pond in the city's eastern periphery. Anand explained that it was a BPL, using the state's categorization of extreme poverty. There were few furnishings, except for a bed and a television balanced on a makeshift shelf. While the MFI staff, including myself, sat on the bed, most of the borrowers clustered at the door and sat on what little space there was on the floor.

The meeting started normally, with borrowers handing over their passbooks and weekly installments. However, as borrowers demanded to know when they would get new loans, Anand sought to calm the angry protestations. With the ongoing liquidity crunch in the microfinance sector, there were not enough funds to go around. "It's the Reserve Bank's decision," Anand tried to explain, only to be met with grumbling from the group that he could sanction more loans if he wanted. Anand's explanation was only partially correct, as the RBI had not directly stopped MFIs from making loans. More important, however, he could not explain to the borrowers what the Indian central bank had to do with their microfinance loans. After all, the RBI was an institution that most borrowers had little idea existed, let alone encountered in their daily lives.

Anand tried to clarify: "You want to borrow, and *we*," he emphasized, "want to give you more [loans]. But we can't because of the RBI."

The two big losers in this whole crisis, he explained, were the borrowers and the MFIs: the former who wanted to borrow and the latter who wanted to lend but could not. "Don't you think we want to give loans? You would be better off with larger loans, and we would profit too. My hands are tied. But who knows better what you need?" he demanded. "Tell me, who is next to [stand with] the poor: us or the RBI?" This contrast between MFIs and the Indian central bank points to real presences and absences in the everyday lives of the urban poor. In describing both Anand's misunderstanding and the borrowers' lack of knowledge about the central bank, I do not imply that they were incapable of comprehending it. Rather, at margins of the state where most people exist in the informal economy, the regulatory body of the central bank simply did not figure into everyday economic practices (see Das and Poole 2004; Roitman 2005). Yet, as part of the formal financial sector, MFIs are under greater regulatory scrutiny by the RBI and the Finance Ministry than informal lenders. At the same time, it was their very proximity to the borrowers that subjected MFIs to the association with moneylending. Against the general "financial dualism" (Schrader 1994, 186) of formal and informal lenders, microfinance chafes at both.

NONVIOLENT CLAIMS

The loan officer's social position is tenuous because of the ambiguity in her role as creditor caught between formal and informal lending practices. Ethnographic work has consistently documented the conception of the powerful position of the creditor and the weakness of the debtor (Peebles 2010). The position of the creditor in a dyadic relationship is one of power over the debtor. However, as proxy-creditors, staff at MFIs must enter these unequal creditor-debtor relationships without actually owning the capital. Loan officers attempted to clarify their own position within the existing norms of power in debt relations. This was illuminated during one group meeting in January. The early-morning cold seeped through cracks in the walls and the thin mat on the concrete floor, as the women huddled together. The women wanted to know why they could not get new loans, and Anand, as branch manager, had come along to explain. In his retelling of the crisis, Anand attempted to distance microfinance from accusations of wrongdoing in recovery practices.

Anand began by telling the women of the problem in the state of Andhra Pradesh where a number of people had committed suicide, partly it was said, due to overindebtedness to MFIs. However, he noted that this had happened at a time of elections, and politicians who needed to get votes blamed the MFIs for their failures. He continued:

> But what is *really* happening? MFIs aren't forcing people to take loans; borrowers want loans, and that's why they take loans. You often say that you want larger loans. Do we give that to you? No, we give less. And what are the other options people have to borrow? There are the banks that offer loans through cooperatives or the local *mahajan* [moneylender] who takes high interest rates. If you don't return these loans, then the banks can bring in the police and the moneylenders can bring in local *mastans* [thugs]. But MFIs don't use any such means to recover loans; they don't call in the police or hire other people to make you return the loans. They can only rely on your goodwill to continue to repay the debt.

In his positioning between the moneylender and the bank, Anand purposefully distances MFIs from the ability to inflict violence on the body of the borrower. Unlike banks that have established a legal right to property in the form of collateral or to call on state violence, and the moneylender who assumes informal authority to compensate for delayed payment through physical intimidation, Anand deems MFIs to be passive. This does not mean that there are no other forms of violence inflicted on the borrowers by MFI staff (e.g., social and mental pressure); rather, I am interested in the ways that loan officers narrate their relationship as creditor to the debtors.

"We have to be Gandhian in our work," said Amit. We were sitting in the branch office one afternoon as he finished his day's accounting. "You know what Gandhi said—that if someone strikes you on one cheek, you should give the other? That's what we have to do; no matter what they [borrowers] say, we just have to listen and wait. I heard this story from my friend who works at a different bank [MFI]. He and the branch manager had gone to this woman's house, and she dumped water on them, and they could not do anything. They just had to sit there until she paid," he added with dramatic flourish. It was a strange reworking of the constitution of violence in the debt relationship, for in this narration, it was the proxy-creditor who was under threat of verbal and physical abuse. Amit was not alone in describing his position of vulnerability; throughout my conversations with MFI staff, I often heard stories of such encounters. In another case, an officer had been locked in a borrower's house because the MFI had not sanctioned a new loan. He had called his office from his mobile and had to be rescued by colleagues. Anand had also explained that they "worked with lowered heads," suggesting a position of deference rather than authority toward the borrowers. These claims to the reversal of the power relations in the loan officer's narration signify a more complicated relationship with their borrowers than is typically described both in popular and academic writing about coercive microfinance recovery practices.

Against the growing criticism of microfinance institutions in India, particularly the coercive tactics used to recover outstanding loans, Amit's invocation of Gandhi articulated a much deeper ethical struggle working in for-profit microfinance. Of course, Gandhian nonviolence should be read as an active political strategy in which actors assume the position of moral agents rather than passive victims (Devji 2011). Similarly, MFI staff would aim to ultimately accomplish loan recovery through claims to moral authority. Moreover, the system of borrower groups has enabled MFIs to turn over certain forms of violence related to the recovery of outstanding loans to the other group members, such as locking borrowers out of their home. Thus, direct violence on the part of loan officers is no longer required, as extreme levels of community and peer pressure come to substitute for the threats of police or thugs. In practice then, borrowers have little power to challenge the MFI when defaulting on a loan.

CIRCULATION OF ALIENATED DEBTS

Mithun had been working in microfinance for a few years when we spoke. He had put himself through college, studying hardware networking. He had decided that there was no future in this area, because technologies were changing so fast that nobody would pay for repairing equipment that had broken down. Mithun entered microfinance when an uncle, who ran a rural SHG, offered him a job after he had finished college. He had started working at DENA a few months before we spoke. Asked if he liked working in microfinance, he replied with a laugh that of course he did not like it at first, "but then nobody likes work." But as he worked, he had to start "thinking of it [the money] as my own." Against the rote work of collecting weekly installments, Mithun found ways to perform his duties with greater attention and skill. For example, he explained that he would come up with ways to make sure the loans were recovered. When they had switched groups earlier, he had taken on four overdue (OD) loans. "But I recently just managed to recover one OD," he said proudly, demonstrating his skill at his job and in managing a difficult debt recovery. For Mithun, loan collections were not inherently enjoyable as work, but thinking of the loans as his own made it at the very least more interesting. As stated earlier, while the labor of the debt is primarily that of the loan officer, the capital belongs to the company. Thus, loan officers had to alienate the product of their labor—the debts—to the MFI. However, by imagining a kind of ownership of capital, Mithun attempted to reappropriate his personal investment in the debt.

Mithun's attempt to recover the debt on his own terms marked the limits to the alienation of the debt in its commodity form and undermined the MFI's efforts at signaling the difference between microfinance and moneylending. Attention to the debt relationships between borrowers and loan officers reveals the constant possibilities of the commodity form of the loan to rupture and expose something more than just the financial transaction. Although the alienated microfinance loan circulates over time as a commodity, the weekly meetings ensure that relationships embedded in the debt are constantly worked on beyond its point of origin by both the staff and the borrower.

The senior management of DENA contends with this possible reappropriation of the debt relationship by loan officers as a danger. There is always the chance that the relationship between the loan officer and the borrowers will devolve into a patron-client relationship. This concern became explicit in the wake of the microfinance crisis as MFIs sought to manage their reputation as extractive moneylenders. These measures included setting up a complaint box at the headquarters and telephone hotline to address borrower grievances if their loans were not handled sufficiently by the branch office staff. Yet concerns about the relationship between the loan officer and borrowers were quite often not about complaints from customers. The head office was committed to managing relationships between loan officers and borrowers because of the social productivity of debt (Roitman 2005). The everyday interactions did not create only grievances on the part of the borrowers but also relationships that had to be monitored by the head office for reasons I now explore.

I had frequently heard the MFI staff refer to their jobs as "transfer jobs," while borrowers complained that the "Sir" or "Madam" changed too often. During an interview, I asked the deputy general manager of DENA, Mr. Guha, about the loan officer (LO) transfer system:

> Mr. Guha: We have a policy that loan officers have to be transferred after one year. This is because we may be satisfied with an LO, but he or she might not fit well with the area or with other people at the branch office. Then he or she can be transferred. . . .
>
> SK: So the LO stays in the same branch office but goes to a different field?
>
> Mr. Guha: Yes, exactly. Also, if there are problems, the LO could hide it if he or she thought they were going to be there for a long time. But if officers change, then the problems are exposed.
>
> SK: Sometimes the borrowers in the field would say the loan officer changes too often. . . .
>
> Mr. Guha: Borrowers are told when they join that a new person will come after one year, so the borrowers know this when they join that this is a rule. The borrowers are comfortable. Normally, they take it sportingly.

With the transfer system, loan officers are never in charge of a given group for more than three to six months. While MFI staff members are occasionally transferred to a completely different branch office, usually they are circulated within different groups at the same branch office. Transfers mean that the new loan officer will uncover any unofficial transactions of the previous officer. As stated earlier, in establishing the formalized loan agreement, the loan officer is alienated from the product of her wage labor and the debt becomes a commodity. Without ownership of capital, the loan is supposed to be free of all ties with the person who established the loan, while the transfer system is meant to reinforce this abstraction by systematically cutting ties between the loan officers and the borrowers. However, despite the attempts by the head office to control ties between loan officers and borrowers, these relationships often extended beyond financial exchanges.

THE EMOTIONAL LABOR OF DEBT RECOVERY

Microfinance practices wed together more tightly the futures of both loan officers and borrowers as both sought to know and call on personal commitments. Women would often ask a new loan officer about previous staff and, in particular, explain that the previous "Madam" had made particular promises (e.g., larger loans). For borrowers, this was a strategy to ensure future loans. Similarly, loan officers paid attention to the intimate details of borrowers' everyday life to ensure a smooth loan recovery. Despite the alienation of capital, for both loan officers and borrowers, these concerns were persistent reminders of the original debt relationship.

Loan officers, in particular, relied on the relationality of debt to ensure loan recovery. MFI staff used powerful affective ties created through everyday interactions to pressure women into payment by calling on the obligations of the debt relationship. In one case, the loan officer and branch manager both attended the group meeting to convince an overdue borrower to repay her loan. As we arrived at the group meeting, most of the members were already present. Once we sat down, some of the women whispered to the branch manager. The borrower in question, Ruma, an older woman, sat mutely in a corner, the end of her faded sari draped over her bowed head. She avoided looking at anyone, staring at the floor. She had stopped repaying her loan the previous week, explaining that her husband had just retired and only one of her sons worked, making barely Rs 500 a week for the family of four.

In trying to convince her to repay the loan, Mukul, the branch manager, told her that Tania, the loan officer, had paid the amount due the week before on her behalf to make up the difference (although she had not done so in reality). "But," he said, "now that Madam [Tania] had paid that amount on her [Ruma's] behalf, what would she [Tania] tell her husband when she went home without her full income?" Here, the branch manager draws on existing gender and marital norms and calls on the borrower to empathize with the loan officer's situation. Ironically, this kind of logic contradicts how MFIs position themselves in terms of women's rights and empowerment by reinforcing patriarchal gender norms. Tania further pushed the borrower to consider her [Tania's] position: "I can't lose my job because of this. I've been up for promotion, and I don't want to be held back because of this situation." Following these exchanges, the woman eventually agreed to start repaying, though with a smaller weekly installment than the original contract. Tania's concern that she may be held back from a promotion is a real one, as the MFI management does look at the number of OD loans under a given loan officer in considering promotions. Tania also invokes a form of loyalty from the borrowers to redress this situation, as well as empathy with a woman whose domestic life is represented as under stress. Such affective pressure on the borrowers obliges them to recognize their personal responsibility to the loan officer rather than an impersonal legal obligation to the MFI.

In their study of doorstep moneylending in England, Andrew Leyshon and his colleagues have found that "friendship" is often used as "a technique to retain the most profitable customers" (2006, 181). However, I suggest that this kind of care work can be identified as emotional labor: "to induce or suppress feeling in order to sustain the outward countenance that produces the proper state of mind in others" (Hochschild 1983, 7). Through marks of deference and caring, the loan officers produce feelings of obligation in the borrowers. As Anne Allison (1994) demonstrates in her ethnography of "hostess clubs" in Japan, while women's affective labor creates a pleasant environment for men, it also helps male white-collar workers feel a strong attachment to their work. The hostesses' emotional labor extends beyond the interpersonal relationship with the customer to help structure social life more broadly. By being attuned to the everyday needs and concerns of the women borrowers, the MFI staff assemble knowledge not only about the emotional worlds of borrowers but also about their riskiness.

To mobilize affective pressure during recovery, loan officers had to maintain emotional bonds with borrowers throughout the loan period by demonstrating care in their everyday encounters. Officers would remember details about the women's lives and attempt to address the particularities of their situations through expressions of care and concern. Amit, for instance, needed to check all the passbooks for any errors, a task done every month or two. Usually, this would be done during the hour-long meeting and the women would have to wait until the work was complete. At the end of this meeting—only twenty minutes into the allotted one hour—Amit said that he would take all the books back to the office with him to check and bring them back later. Afterward, Amit explained that he had left because the group met in the room that also served as the kitchen. Until everyone departed, the borrower who lived in the house where the meeting was held would not be able to cook for the day. So, he explained, he tried not to take too long with the meetings.

Such practices are not just utilitarian in their ends; rather, such expressions of care become central to the ways in which loan officers understand and value their own social role or position. For instance, loan officers navigated the negative association with the moneylender by emphasizing their care work. Further, emotional labor can counter the alienating effects of wage labor itself. Against the objectification of workers, Elizabeth Dunn demonstrates how women in a Polish baby food factory "[revalue] themselves and their labor by bringing ideologies of motherhood" (2004, 143), such as care for children's safety. This practice of resisting commodification simultaneously contributes to workers' disciplining of themselves and reinforces gendered norms of mothering. MFI staff repeatedly expressed to me their desire for respect (*samman*) as a fundamental part of their work. For loan officers, respect meant having borrowers respond politely without arguing, and trusting and attending to the advice given by loan officers. To lose respect was a dangerous possibility, not because it undermined the formal code of conduct but because it affected the loan officer's valuation of her work and sense of self.

For instance, Putul had joined DENA only a year ago, though she had been working in microfinance for four years when we spoke. Asked whether there were any differences in all the various neighborhoods where she had worked, Putul replied, "When you give advice to people in the rural areas, they listen to you and analyze that information. In the urban areas, people don't have respect for us. They will call the head office or regional manager directly to say that they're not getting a loan or they want more. Of course, there is more need in the city, but they don't analyze or think about what we say; they just want more." The foregrounding of respect marked the ways in which Putul wanted to be seen as more than an intermediary for getting loans. She valued her own knowledge and expertise in helping the poor. Like other loan officers who mentioned respect in response to my question of what they enjoyed most about working in microfinance, Putul felt there was more to her role than sanctioning and distributing loans. The perceived differences of respect, however, were not without their own repercussions for borrowers. MFI staff could respond to what they felt was a lack of respect from a potential borrower by designating that person as "high risk" and hence deny the loan.

In an effort to address criticisms, MFIs formalized rules for loan recovery practices. At DENA, Mithun showed me the newly mounted "Code of Conduct" on the wall of the branch office. It was a list based on suggestions from Sa-Dhan, MFIN (two Indian MFI associations), and CGAP, the World Bank–based microfinance think tank. Mithun started listing items on the code of conduct as they remembered it—integrity, quality of service, fair practice, and social work—as if reciting answers to an examination. "Since the Code of Conduct is laminated and posted on the wall now, if we don't follow the rules, then human resources can fire us at any time," Mithun added, almost as an afterthought.

Given the negative side of loan recovery practices, there is certainly a need for regulatory oversight. However, with the budding cottage industry of consultancies and ratings agencies that offer evaluation services to MFIs, workers' care work has become subject to new forms of scrutiny. These consulting firms conduct evaluations and ratings, including whether and to what extent MFIs adhere to their mission statements. Branch offices can now be evaluated in terms of how well they are adhering to the Code of Conduct, and loan officers are made to adhere to company standards of emotional labor. Emotional labor, once an unregulated part of the job, is undergoing increasing standardization and formalization. This further reflects what Arlie Hochschild terms the "commercialization of feelings" as companies increasingly initiate, direct, and monitor workers' emotional life through their work (1983, 136). Mithun's observation that one could now be fired for not adhering to the Code of Conduct marks a heightened monitoring of workers and the precarious position of loan officers.

CARE IN BANKING

Ambivalences about the alienability of debt remain unresolved in more formal financial relationships as well. In a television commercial for ICICI, a private Indian bank, an elderly woman comes in to deposit a check. As the bank officer processes the check, she proceeds to talk about her son, who is now in America. The bank officer continues to work throughout the conversation, processing files. Soon the lights are being turned off in the office, and the officer indicates to leave a light on and encourages the woman to continue her story. When she apologizes for delaying him, he responds, "No problem, Ma'am, please," allowing her to continue. The commercial ends with a narration that "there is nothing too small." The commercial is part of a series showing interactions between bank officers and customers. IDBI, a public-sector bank, also has a well-received campaign depicting the relationship between a young boy and a baby elephant. The commercial ends with the statement that "some relationships grow deeper over time." Despite emerging technologies in Internet and mobile banking that decrease the number of actual interactions between banks and customers, the message in these advertisements is the same: the relationship between the banker and customer is more than the financial transaction.

In analyzing these commercials, I do not mean to take at face value what is being represented: an equal relationship between bank and customer. The commercials mark the emergence of "emotional capitalism" where the "economic sphere, far from being devoid of emotions, has been on the contrary saturated with affect" (Illouz 2007, 23). Yet these representations do suggest a particular ambivalence or vulnerability even in formal finance toward debt relationships. What is especially tenuous in the banking relationship is its appearance as a starkly financial one. As Jonathan Parry, challenging the distinction between gift exchange as good and commodity exchange as bad, has argued, commercial exchange can also become the focus of "symbolic elaboration" (1989, 65–66). Like the loan officers working at MFIs, there is a desire for the relationship to be "something more" than the mere financial transaction; however, that something more demands emotional labor from the proxy-creditor, whether an MFI staff member or a commercial bank employee. Such work is meant to extend the peripheries of finance by enfolding new populations into global financial networks. However, corporations that actually own the capital must constantly monitor this relationship between its staff and customers for what it sees as an "excess" of sociality that is embedded in the debt. These forms of excess can be both negative and coercive but also forms of friendship and care that complicate the alienability of the loan. As in the case of microfinance, the everyday enmeshment of loan officers' and borrowers' lives means that there is more to the debt relationship than the basic transactional necessity. Loan products, constructed through debt relationships of the borrower and the proxy-creditor, have elements of inalienability or "something" that remains in exchange relationships (Weiner 1985). Even while the capital in the debt relationship is technically handed over to the MFI, traces of the original debt relationship remain with the proxy-creditor, which cannot be retrieved by the financial institution.

SECURITIZATION AND
THE SOCIAL DISTANCE OF DEBT

As the microfinance crisis unfolded, commercial banks became increasingly unwilling to lend to MFIs, unsure of the regulatory environment and the future of the industry. Faced with a liquidity crunch, MFIs sought new funding opportunities to raise capital. One such avenue was the securitization of loans. While MFIs had begun securitization even before the crisis as a source of capital and also as a way to reduce debt on the MFI's books, the lack of ready loans from commercial banks made them turn increasingly toward securitization as a way of infusing cash to sustain lending. For instance, in April 2011, the Kolkata-based Bandhan Microfinance had inked deals to securitize Rs 4 billion (approximately US$80 million), while Hyderabad-based SKS Microfinance had Rs 6 billion (approximately $120 million) in securitized deals.

As a form of structured finance, securitization of microfinance means that the MFI pools together loans into a special-purpose vehicle (SPV) (K. Fernandes 2011). The SPV then issues securities that are backed by the cash flows from the pooled loans (i.e., the interest and principal of the loan as it is paid back). The securities are often sold in tranches according to the riskiness of that particular portion. A "senior tranche," with a high credit rating but lower yield, is paid off first, followed by the lower ones with lower credit ratings (i.e., higher risks) but higher yields. Speaking to the *Economic Times*, Sucharita Mukherjee, CEO of IFMR Capital, a Chennai-based firm specializing in microfinance securitization, explains that investors are willing to buy securitized loans because they can get better returns from microfinance than from top-rated nonconvertible debentures (corporate bonds) and securitized auto loans (Menon 2010).

Before the crisis, MFIs already boasted of loan recovery rates above 90 percent, making them relatively low risk. Bundling loans further reduced the overall risk of the debt products because it is statistically unlikely that a significant number of individual loans from such varied branches will all default, whereas there may be knock-on effects of defaults within a given branch. For example, IFMR Capital arranged the securitization of loans from the Chennai-based MFI Equitas (K. Fernandes 2011). In this case, it pooled 55,993 individual loans (transactions valuing Rs 514 million) in an SPV. A private bank and a mutual fund bought the senior tranches, while IMFR Capital and another private bank bought the lower-rated tranches. The collection efficiency (recovery rate) for the securitized transaction in this case was 99.64 percent.

Ironically, securitization of home mortgages fueled the US subprime crisis, while it took the microfinance crisis to further promote securitization in India. That is, without loans from commercial banks, MFIs turned to securitization as another means of raising capital. In response to the sudden securitization spree, the RBI released regulatory guidelines in September 2011 for the securitization of microfinance loans, including requiring MFIs to hold loans for a longer period of time—six months compared to the earlier three months—before creating structured financial products. As securitization practices gain popularity, it leaves open questions about the alienability of debt and its repercussions. With securitization, a debt that is established between the poor borrower and the MFI can now be owned by a distant financial institution with little interest in the identity of the borrower.

As microfinance scales up, it has turned to increasingly financialized instruments to raise capital. Further, these new financial products expose the poor to the systemic risk of finance, while the ties between the borrowers and the owners of the debts are increasingly obscured. As Parker Shipton argues, borrowers and lenders "tailor the terms of their loans and repayments according to interpersonal relationships" (2010, 7). Financialization extends this "social distance" (ibid.) between borrowers and creditors, making debt relationships more formal, less lenient, and ultimately more abstract. Securitization is now central to the circulation of capital: MFIs raise capital to lend to the poor through securitization deals, while banks and other investors seek out the high rates of return on capital through securitized loans.

Yet in my conversations with loan officers, they repeatedly remarked on the responsibility of working with "poor people's money" (*garib loker taka*). As Mithun explained one day, "If a rich person loses one hundred rupees, it doesn't mean anything, but it's a lot for a poor person, so we have to be careful with it." Here, it was not the amount of money that mattered but how it was valued by the person. By socially marking the loan money as special, loan officers differentiated the money they worked with from other kinds of money (see Zelizer 1989).[9] In other words, loan officers add social meaning to "poor people's money," making it distinct from the abstract and utilitarian notions of money. If "micro"-finance tends to emphasize smallness, loan officers attached meaning to this very smallness of the loan by imbuing it with additional value. Moreover, if financialization works to produce undifferentiated capital from loans made to poor women, loan officers continuously attempted to mark the money that they worked with as distinct from circulating capital.

REASONS AND RELATIONAL ENDS

The labor of financialization at the peripheries is not primarily that of abstraction and knowledge production, as often discussed in the social studies of finance. As I have described, it is the emotional and physical labor of loan officers who enfold the poor into the expanding networks of finance. This work demands that loan officers produce debt relationships and alienate them as formalized loan products. However, even as the capital of microfinance *is* alienated and increasingly financialized, practices of care continue to enmesh the lives and livelihoods of borrowers and loan officers. Care work not only serves as a utilitarian end of debt collection but also becomes the way by which loan officers attempt to attend to the ethical dimensions of debt recovery practices as they are shaped by local social imaginaries. From narrating the vulnerability of their position as proxy-creditor to explaining the desire for respect in their work, and differentiating "poor people's money," MFI staff try to distinguish the blurring of their role with that of moneylenders, whom they have supposedly replaced for the better.

On our return to the branch office, Anand and Mithun were discussing the accusations they faced earlier. Turning to Anand, Mithun said, "It was a good thing you were there. If I were there alone, they would have stopped taking loans from us, because, really, I have no reason to give [concerning why they could not get new loans]. Other times I can find a reason, but they do return their loans on time and without problems." The microfinance crisis highlighted the increasing financialization of the lives of urban poor borrowers, where consideration of systemic risk compels commercial banks and the central bank to curb microfinance lending. The logic of these financial maneuvers is never fully communicated in the interactions between loan officers and borrowers. Both of these parties remain at a loss to explain and understand why their lives are being reshaped by banks and bankers they never encounter. The alienated debt circulates as capital; yet it also haunts the proxy-creditors and the debtors, for whom the original inalienable debt relationship remains. These moments reveal the ethical consequences for MFI staff who create and alienate debt relationships as loan products: the impossibility of giving a reason for why credit cannot be offered to someone who has so faithfully maintained the debt relationship. The next chapter explores the other side of the debt relationship, tracing the experiences of microfinance borrowers.

CHAPTER 4

THE DOMESTICATION OF MICROFINANCE

THE ROOM where the microfinance group meeting was usually held was under construction, so we sat outside in the open. It was early March, the start of the summer, and hot even at eight in the morning. Mithun, the loan officer I was accompanying, and I had arrived early. As the group members gathered, one of the borrowers, Bharti, sat chatting with me. In a faded "maxi" dress, her hair pulled into a tight bun, she looked older than her forty or so years. Deep lines framed the edges of her eyes, and her mouth was reddened by years of chewing *supari* (areca nut).

"Sir," she said, turning to Mithun, "I have to leave a little early today. I have to go to court for a *dolil* [land deed]. I'm going by myself. My husband usually doesn't let me go anywhere. He always says, 'No, I'll take you.' He thinks I'll get lost or something!" she said with a wry laugh. "Your husband still doesn't trust you?" quipped Mithun, amused. "Oh, he beats me if I say anything," she responded. "Everyone at home is scared of him. If my sons want anything, they come to me; they never ask their father; they're scared of him, and when I say something, he hits me. My middle son tries to stand up for me. He's the only one. He's away studying now, but he'll be back. When my husband hits me, my [middle] son tries to stop him. 'Where is Ma going to get the money?' he'll ask. But the other two, they're a little thick-headed—my eldest and youngest sons. They don't really do anything," she continued, expressing dismay at her sons who seemed to lack an understanding of her situation.

As the meeting progressed, Bharti elaborated on her experience with microfinance. She had taken the loan for a hired car that she leased out. "I have an old car now," she explained. "I get about one thousand rupees per week from it now. But I want to buy a newer car, so maybe I'll get two thousand rupees per week instead. I'll get part of the loan from the bank. I have two properties—one here, and one on Bypass [road]." "Has it [microfinance] helped?" I asked. "I always ask the other women, why should you get beaten by your husband?" Don't waste [*pete pore khete noi*; literally, don't stomach/eat] the money; use it to stand on your own feet; start your own business!" she responded, evading the question. Asked what her husband did, Bharti responded, "*I* take care of my husband. I bought a pipe for the car with the last loan. I use the money to take care of him. I came here in my parents' arms from Bangladesh when they fled.[1] We had land in Bangladesh. But my parents died when I was still young. My husband is non-Bengali; but he is what god gave me. There is neither love nor affection [between us]." Entwined in the discourse of microfinance were concerns of kinship, care, and domestic life. The loans sustain Bharti's ability to care for her family, yet they do not, as suggested by the popular discourse on microfinance, empower her to escape abuse. She asserted her agency in being the one—subverting gender norms—who was taking care of the family; though she also marked the places where these relationships fall apart.

The contradictions in Bharti's narrative highlight the complicated role of microfinance loans in the lives of poor women. On the one hand, Bharti found ways to utilize the loans, not only to support her family but also to acquire land in her own name. On the other hand, she remains subject to domestic violence; she uses her income to support her abusive husband and unemployed sons. Ironically, it is her marital status—including the need of her husband as guarantor—that enables her to access the loans. Ultimately Bharti is resigned to her condition of abuse from her husband and neglect from her sons.

Nevertheless, Bharti remains hopeful that other women will escape the same fate by accessing loans. She noted, however, that it was important to be diligent about who joined: "There's always discussion among the women [about MFIs]," Bharti explained. "When someone learns about a new place, they'll share it, and so we find out. But we have to get good people to take loans, people with their own homes. I scold the people who are bad and exclude them." The global success of microfinance, particularly within development policy, has been attributed, first, to its creation and use of social capital between group members as collateral in the absence of material collateral. This social capital, in addition to economic benefits of running a micro-enterprise, is expected to lead to women's empowerment. Yet women like Bharti carefully manage entry to these groups, making microfinance exclusionary as well, and requiring women to manage their relationships with neighbors. Before the meeting ended, Bharti asked and was allowed to leave early to attend to her errands, reflecting the multiple demands on women's time.

Critics of microfinance have emphasized the negative effects of social capital in terms of the production of new kinds of obligations and discipline such as new forms of patron-client relationships and neoliberal discipline (e.g., Ito 2003; Karim 2011; Rahman 1999). In this chapter, however, I consider the domestication of microfinance as it is incorporated into the everyday domestic lives of urban poor women and the ways in which microfinance is absorbed into existing forms of gendered relationality.

Domestication, as argued by Suzanne Brenner, has a double meaning: it is both to bring "something under control as well as [to turn] it into something of value to the family" (1998, 17). In domesticating microfinance, women access valuable financial resources necessary to the household economy. Simultaneously, however, through emphasis on domestic spaces and their intersection with domestic work, microfinance becomes enfolded into women's existing schedules of domestic labor, limiting its impact on women's empowerment.

I first trace how the theoretical concepts of social capital and empowerment were absorbed into development policy. I then demonstrate that social capital does not simply exist in situ; most borrowers labor to produce these relations, while also balancing borrower meetings with other demands on their time, including domestic and wage labor, collecting documentation and proof of housing and identity from local politicians, and working to maintain neighborly relations with other borrowers. Finally, I argue that this domestication has to be understood within the context of local class ideologies, resulting in the reinforcement of class difference rather than social change.

SOCIAL CAPITAL AND EMPOWERMENT IN DEVELOPMENT

In his autobiography, Muhammad Yunus, founder of the Grameen Bank, recounts meeting with a commercial banker to try to get loans for poor women. Asked why the bank cannot make such loans, the branch manager responds: "They simply don't have any collateral. . . . That is our guarantee." When Yunus persists in asking why the bank needs collateral when it should be primarily interested in getting its money back, the banker retorts: "You are an idealist, Professor. You live with books and theories" (2003, 54). The lack of material collateral has been described as one of the primary reasons the poor do not get access to credit. Yunus's solution to this problem of collateral is to form what is known as a joint-liability group. Developed as one way to counter the lack of collateral, JLGs utilize social networks as a means of ensuring recovery. Yunus describes how group membership both creates support and protection and also "smoothes out the erratic behavior patterns of individual members, making each borrower more reliable in the process. Subtle and at times not-so-subtle peer pressure keeps each group member in line with the broader objectives of the credit program" (ibid., 62). Many MFIs, including DENA, have in fact moved away from the classic Grameen JLG structure. They have, however, retained the group meetings and the effects of social capital as an efficient way of recovering individual loans (see Armendáriz and Morduch 2000; De Quidt, Fetzer, and Ghatak 2016).

While the use of groups in microfinance emerged somewhat independently from the theoretical configuration of social capital in the 1970s and 1980s, the popularization of the latter bolstered the enthusiastic reception of microfinance within the field of development.[2] Social capital is "the ability of actors to secure benefits by virtue of membership in social networks or other social structures" (Portes 1998, 6). Earlier development paradigms (e.g., modernization theory) tended to see social relations as "singularly burdensome, exploitative, liberating, or irrelevant" (Woolcock and Narayan 2000, 228). Social capital theory, however, reinstated social networks as both positive and central to effectuating development. By the 1990s, social capital had entered mainstream development policy, including that of the World Bank, appealing politically both to the free marketers on the right, who were skeptical of the role of the state, and on the left, with its emphasis on grassroots-level participation.[3]

Yet as Julia Elyachar has argued, while social practices and embedded relationships had been seen earlier as an obstacle to economic development, they were now conceived of as a resource for expanding global markets and achieving economic growth. The popularization of social capital theory enabled the "conceptual transformation of social networks among the poor into an economic resource for capital" (Elyachar 2005b, 10; see also Fine 1999; Molyneux 2002). The problems of poverty could, in other words, be sidestepped by assuming that social capital would substitute for other forms of state intervention.

The popularization of social capital theory dovetailed with the shift in development policy away from the singular focus on economic growth and top-down policies to human capabilities and empowerment, with a particular focus on women (Amartya Sen 1999). While early development models had generally ignored the role of women, second-wave feminism in the 1960s and 1970s began to impact development theory as well.[4] Influenced by economist Esther Boserup's work on women in agriculture in Africa, the women in development (WID) paradigm made women a central focus of development by the 1980s.[5] Income-generating schemes such as microcredit were introduced under WID as a way to incorporate women more fully into the market economy. While bringing women back into mainstream development, this shift to WID did not fundamentally challenge the premise of modernization theory, leaving in place Western ethnocentric assumptions about gender (e.g., the role of women in the domestic and public spheres) and the value of market efficiency (Sharma 2008). In particular, the "bureaucratic resistance to gender redistributive policies" (Razavi and Miller 1995, 7) necessitated WID advocates to continue to produce efficiency-based arguments in relation to gender.

Critiques of WID led to an eventual shift to the gender and development (GAD) paradigm. Solidified at the 1995 United Nations Fourth World Conference on Women, also known as the Beijing Platform,[6] GAD emphasized the social construction and reinforcement of gender roles (Razavi and Miller 1995). In its implementation as policy, GAD advocates emphasized empowerment as a way to challenge existing inequalities.[7] Yet empowerment discourses also made the individual's ability to make strategic life—and market—choices a key focus, again sidestepping questions of structural inequality (Sharma 2008; see also Fraser 2013). GAD became a way to dispose "of both 'women' and 'equity,' two issues presumably most likely to meet a wall of resistance from policymakers primarily interested in 'talking economics'" (Razavi and Miller 1995, 15). In other words, with its incorporation into the empowerment policy framework, the more radical elements of gender analysis became neutralized.

Microfinance programs emerged at this intersection of social capital theory and programs for women's empowerment in development (Guérin, D'Espallier, and Mersland 2013; Sanyal 2009, 2014). The Grameen model of group lending became a "prime example of the effective mobilisation of social capital for poverty reduction where both the market and the state have failed" (Ito 2003, 323). The Grameen model was not created with direct reference to social capital theory but was absorbed in development practice by proponents of the theory as an exemplary case. The JLGs were designed not only to collateralize the loans but also to develop social capital that would empower women (see Schuster 2014, 2015). On the one hand, frequent social interaction between group members pools risk among borrowers who come to know each other better and improves economic outcomes (Feigenberg, Field, and Pande 2013). On the other, participation in microfinance groups is meant to yield "not only an economic payoff in increased access to financial services, but also an empowerment payoff in new forms of bridging and linking social capital" (Rankin 2002, 12).

In India, the SHG model of microfinance adopted social capital arguments in making women's groups the central units of lending. Commercial microfinance, however, has proliferated more rapidly with the "financial inclusion" directive. Consequently, inclusion has focused more on providing women access to formal-sector credit and integration into the market economy and less on the developmental ends of building social capital or solidarity, though it continues to draw on the same discourse.

IN DOMESTIC SPACES

"Come in and sit," loan officers would often tell the women during meetings. But with meetings held in one-room homes, this simple suggestion was often physically impossible in the slums of Kolkata. With barely enough space for the loan officer and the group's cashier to sit and do their accounting, the remaining members of the group often stood outside or at the door. Moreover, meetings taking place in the homes of borrowers often coincided with daily household work. The aroma of spices would pervade meetings, with lunch simmering on the stove in the same room. Children would navigate the room, hopping over women to get ready for school, while ill family members would be asleep on the bed in many single-room houses. The microfinance meetings were both absorbed into and disrupted the domestic everyday.

From early works in feminist anthropology, the domestic/public dichotomy has been a dominant mode of gender analysis.[8] While the feminine domestic sphere constitutes women's worlds, the public sphere is considered to be masculine. Numerous cross-disciplinary studies have shown that microfinance programs directed at women can change domestic relations in addition to income or economic gains, though interpretations have been mixed about whether these changes are primarily negative or positive. In some cases, microfinance gives women an improved position in household decision making by being the source of access to credit (Holvoet 2005; Kelkar, Nathan, and

Jahan 2004). Others have been more cautious about the overall impact of microfinance in changing women's domestic power, suggesting that credit overwhelmingly remains within male control and can even increase violence toward women (Goetz and Sen Gupta 1996) or reinforce and intensify existing gendered codes of shame and honor (Karim 2011; Rahman 1999). While these works show how domestic relationships are managed through the loans themselves, the everyday practices of microfinance such as meetings also shape domestic life.

Microfinance group meetings are meant to serve as spaces for discussion of issues affecting women, including women's rights. The meetings, however, take place not in public spaces such as community halls but in the domestic spaces of borrowers' homes. In her feminist critique of the public sphere, Nancy Fraser argues against a strict division between the public and private (domestic) spheres, noting that there are linkages between the private and public spheres and there are "no naturally given, a priori boundaries" (1992, 129) of what constitutes a public or private concern.[9] Michael Warner similarly argues that despite the ideological and architectural distinctions between private and public spaces, the two often intermingle. Thus, "a private conversation can take place in a public forum; a kitchen can become a public gathering place" (Warner 2005, 23). The very differentiation of gendered private spaces "turns the home and its adjunct spaces into a functional public for women—spaces that can be filled with talk and with the formation of a shared world" (ibid., 37). Microfinance group meetings can be considered to be such spaces in which the public and private comingle: women can associate in largely domestic spaces, but discussions at the meetings are supposed to incorporate public issues and allow for counterhegemonic discourses of gender.

A number of studies have examined how the meetings create spaces in the women's lives to discuss and address issues such as domestic violence. For example, Paromita Sanyal's (2009) work on microfinance in rural West Bengal shows that while it has a limited economic impact, the group structure enables new forms of collective action. The group structure lets women borrowers meet other women outside their homes and organize against domestic violence. Megan Moodie (2008) similarly argues in her study of microcredit in rural Rajasthan that despite limited financial benefits, women wanted to get loans to discuss issues ranging from caste relations to burdens of raising daughters. These works show the porous boundaries of the private and public and the ways in which meetings can reshape the experience of domestic life in various ways, offering an analytical shift away from the singular emphasis on economic outcomes. However, group meetings also intersected with women's everyday domestic work and lives that bubbled to the forefront of meetings. Borrowers frequently pressed the loan officer to let them leave early to finish up their everyday chores, including shopping, cooking, or picking up children from school.

In part, differences in space shape the ways in which these meetings function and limit opportunities for public discussion during group meetings. Compared to rural microfinance, urban microfinance operates in very different physical spaces. For instance, Figure 4.1 shows women standing in the doorway and outside the room during my own fieldwork. This was a typical scene during the course of my research, where meetings often took place in slum settlements with little extra associational space. In contrast to the quintessential image of women sitting around in circles to discuss issues beyond loans, urban microfinance is marked by its lack of space. It was a situation that was commented on by loan officers who had worked in both rural and urban areas. In response to my question about meeting space, Anand, a branch manager, explained: "Space is a problem in the city. In rural areas, there are always houses with verandas, or everyone can sit in front of the house. Sometimes it was a problem when it rained and it was muddy or waterlogged. But in the city it was really hard to find places for the meeting."

With space at such a premium, loan officers were always on the lookout for potential meeting places, including during home verifications to sanction loans. On numerous occasions, as I accompanied MFI staff during house verifications, they would comment on the space available for meetings in a potential borrower's home. Having

FIGURE 4.1 *Women at group meeting in Kolkata slum settlement*

space can then become one way of accessing credit: women with larger houses can receive loans not only because they have larger incomes but also because they can provide the space to obtain loans.

As microfinance spreads through the neighborhoods of Kolkata, borrowers and non-borrowers can be enterprising by renting out their homes for group meetings. In one case, a meeting was held in what seemed to be the front room of a relatively spacious house. There was a chalkboard on the wall, and one of the women explained that the woman who lived in this house taught poor children for free. However, the homeowner was not herself a borrower; rather, she was charging Rs 10 per person per month to meet there. Most of the women seemed to agree to it, saying, "It isn't that much. Nobody will mind." However, Krishna, one of the borrowers, responded that her husband would not agree to pay an extra Rs 10 per month for a meeting fee, which could be spent on other things. The microfinance staff did not want the women to be paying a fee either. They spent considerable amount of time during the meeting trying to decide on another place to meet within the neighborhood, but everyone had the same answer: they had no space. Finally, one of the three women from another neighborhood said that the meeting could be held in one of their houses, though it would be a little farther away than the desired radius for a group meeting. With the proliferation of microfinance, domestic space comes to attain a new economic value both as both borrowers and MFI staff seek out locations for group meetings.

Yet the transformation of domestic spaces into "centers" (the house where group meetings are held) also puts multiple demands on domestic spaces. Women were often hesitant to offer their homes for meetings because family members would be getting ready for work and school in morning. Another popular reason women gave for declining to host meetings was that they had children who were studying for the notoriously competitive school and university exams in India.

One such moment of conflicting claims to space emerged when I was revisiting one of the groups, but the meeting had shifted to a different home. It was now held in a small flat in government quarters. Similar to the rotation of loan officers, MFIs regularly move meeting spaces—usually once a year—in order not to burden one borrower but also to ensure relations do not get entrenched in one place. I later learned from the branch manager Putul that this had been a sudden rather than planned move. The group had previously met in the house of Laxmi, who was recently widowed. Laxmi had just received a larger business loan from DENA for her clothing store, but she had been willing to keep the weekly meetings in her house. The business loan is a larger loan, between Rs 30,000 and 50,000, generally given for people who have more established businesses and have formal documentation such as business licenses and tax files, but with monthly repayment at a higher interest rate.[10] Putul explained that this business loan had been perfectly justified as Laxmi had all of her documentation in order and had been running the business for many years. But some of the other women in the group gossiped behind her back that "she had changed" after her husband's death and that she really should not have gotten the business loan. "It hurts their ego," explained Putul. "They think, 'why should *she* get more than *me*?' and they try to prick [*khuchiye*] her." She added that Laxmi lived with her son and daughter-in-law who just had a baby. "You see how loud everyone is in this group? You know how they say she's changed after husband's death? Well, what happened was that her grandchild had been ill and had just come back from the hospital. She got upset and said if everyone was going to be loud and bicker, then they couldn't have the meeting there anymore. That's why they moved the meeting."

When domestic spaces are transformed into MFI centers, private life is also affected. This does not mean that these private spaces were never accessible to the neighbors who now enter these spaces for group meetings. Unlike rural areas where distance can play a role in the relative isolation of women in their own homes, and meetings can serve to build social capital, people are constantly present in the lives of their neighbors in the urban slums. However, the form of this presence is now different: women are no longer just neighbors, but they are also responsible to for each other's creditworthiness by providing both space and time to attend the meetings.

TEMPORAL DEMANDS

Initial access to microfinance loans requires potential borrowers to establish relationships with other women in the neighborhood. When asked how they first learned of microfinance, most borrowers told me that they had learned of it through word of mouth. In fact, after setting up the branch office and initial drive to establish groups, MFIs do very little publicity or promotional work in the neighborhoods where they work. Rather, they rely on women in the neighborhood to learn of the MFI from existing borrowers. After learning of the particular MFI, the potential borrower must establish ties with the existing group members or, in some cases, establish a new group altogether with at least ten other women. In joining a group, most of the other existing group members must approve of the new member. Thus, women with poor neighborly relations cannot easily get access to loans.

As mentioned earlier, one of the operational practices of MFIs is that the group meetings take place in the home of one of the members. At DENA, group members in the urban context are required to live within five minutes' walking distance from the meeting place. This system ensures higher loan recovery rates than the typical commercial bank practice of having customers come to a branch office to repay. Two primary reasons are, first, borrowers not only monitor each other more closely, but loan officers can more easily find borrowers for various monitoring and verification purposes around the meeting time. Second, there is a lower cost in terms of time and expense on the part of borrowers to return the loan. If a woman has to go to the branch office, she would have to take time, and possibly pay for transportation to get there, making the cost of repayment too high. As highlighted in the following vignette, however, these operational practices are not outside women's work; rather, they have become part of the rhythm of everyday life.

It was the fourth meeting of the day, and I was accompanying Mukul, the branch manager. Mukul was substituting for Radha, the loan officer, who had been ill with the flu. The collected and counted money lay in neat piles according to denomination under the weight of a book, so it would not be blown away by the fan spinning overhead. Shanti fidgeted anxiously, clutching her purse. "I have to go shopping. By the time I get there now, all the fish will be gone," she sighed. "I was going to go shopping too," chimed in Bina. "There will be nothing left by the time we get there." The meeting had started at 10 a.m., it was nearing 11:00, well past the time collections were usually finished, but two of the group members had not repaid and the women present would have to wait until the two women came up with the money.

The meeting had started normally enough, but twenty minutes into the meeting, there remained three loans outstanding. One of the three borrowers was ill, but the others said that she usually sent her money. Eventually, her young son turned up with the money in hand. However, there were still two unpaid loans. As it turned out, the two women had not been paying on time for the last two weeks. Radha had not reported this to the office, preferring not to create problems for the group's creditworthiness, as she always eventually managed to recover the money. Impatient with having to wait, Mukul went to their houses to look for the absent borrowers but came back saying that neither was at home.

The two women had come by the meeting briefly at around 10:30 to say that they did not have the money now, but they could get it by the next day. Under heavy protestation from the remaining women in the group who were worried about the creditability of their own group and the added burden of having to pay off the women's loan for the week, the two women said they would get it by 11:30 a.m. that day. As the minutes crept by, some of the women stealthily slipped out of the room against Mukul's instructions. The few who remained in the room—just six of around twenty—had been unable to escape the branch manager's gaze. Arati, a slight young woman in her early twenties, wondered about her two boys, a toddler and a baby a few months old. "I left my sons at home. My sister-in-law is going to give me an earful [*kotha sonabe*]. I told her I would be home quickly." With so much work left to do throughout the day, the women in the group were itching to leave; yet they had to ensure repayment for the two outstanding loans before they could be dismissed.

As the clock ticked, the women got increasingly annoyed and agitated; but no one was willing to take on the burden of paying the outstanding amount. The borrowers present explained that the two women's husbands were in a failing business venture together. Between the two, the outstanding repayment for the week added up to a substantial amount of Rs 750. Most of the women paid anywhere between Rs 150 and 400 per week. As Rima, the woman in whose house the meeting was being held, observed, "Nobody has that kind of money just lying around," especially to be given to women they did not fully trust. Shanti clutched Rs 100 in her hand said, "This is all I have, and I have to go shopping. I can't spend it on them—and I don't know when I'll get it back if I do." Conversation revealed that Arati had been sick a few weeks earlier and had sent her weekly payment with one of the now absent women. But the money had never been received in the group, and everyone assumed that the woman had circulated Arati's money as her own. But there were other concerns too: "They don't think about anyone else," said Bina. "We're meeting in this house, and there are expenses [for electricity] with the fan running and the lights turned on. We used to meet at one of their [the absent women] houses before, and she would always say, 'We have to be done in fifteen minutes' and see, now you see, they keep us waiting." At around 12:30, Mukul finally convinced the women to pool together the outstanding amount of Rs 750. In return, he would send a loan officer later in the day to collect the amount from the two absent women in order to assuage the group's concern that they would not pay it back.

The meeting demonstrates some limits to the idealized narrative of social capital as collateral in microfinance. The women required formal intervention from the MFI and the promise to send a loan officer to recuperate the amount collected from the group in the absence of the two borrowers. More significantly, the example highlights the experience of anxious waiting as the group meeting intersected with the multiple demands on the women's time within the domestic sphere: Shanti and Bina had to find time to shop for groceries; Arati was caught with child-care and the relational demands of her sister-in-law. Similarly, the constant pleas at meetings to "let us go early" reflect the ways in which poor people's time is ascribed (Auyero 2012). It becomes necessary to understand the intensity through which women experience time when microfinance is absorbed into everyday routines.

DOING CREDIT-WORK

As the routine of microfinance group meetings is absorbed into women's everyday domestic duties, it comes into conflict with existing ones, such as collecting water. One morning, a loan officer and I entered a nearly empty room. One of the women informed us: "Everyone left because they have to go get water and oil [kerosene]." "Does water only come once a day?" I asked. "Twice: once around eleven a.m. and once in the evening. At the tap in our area, we get it regularly; in other places, it sometimes only comes once a day." "We just get a trickle at home [from the tap]," said another woman, meaning she had to get water from public sources as well, even if she technically had running water in the house. At other meetings, women would often come late because of water collection or would suddenly have to find sources of water when a local pump stopped working. One of the borrowers explained, "Our biggest problem is water in the morning. We have to go and collect the water, and it takes time and sometimes people are late or have to leave to get water." Asked if there were any problems, one woman added that people were sometimes late in getting to the meeting. There was water to be fetched in the morning, and "there was always women's work" (*mēder kaaj to achei*).

The absence and intermittent presence of water were very much a part of the textures of everyday life of Kolkata, particularly in informal slum settlements.[11] Yet getting water, like microfinance, had become marked as and absorbed into women's work (O'Reilly 2006). Their intersection is a powerful reminder of hidden labor of domestic work: they both emerge as distinctly gendered work when women have to decide between collecting water and attending a microfinance meeting. Against the expectation that credit would liberate women, it added another task to the already long list of women's domestic work.

In writing of the work that women do to maintain kinship relationships, Micaela Di Leonardo identifies three forms of women's labor: housework and child care, work in the labor market, and the work of kinship, or "kin work" (1978, 442). Similarly, while intersecting with domestic labor, gaining and maintaining access to microfinance require a different kind of work, or what I term "credit-work." Credit-work is the everyday set of practices that women engage in to access, maintain, and repay loans. It highlights the multiplying demands on women's time, while—as with much of women's unpaid work—goes unrecognized as labor.

While there is a long and cross-cultural history of women as arbiters of household credit (e.g., Jordan 1993; Lemire, Pearson, and Campbell 2001; Tebbutt 1983), microfinance demands a particular configuration of women's work. The networks on which social capital is based do not simply exist, but there is a constant expenditure of time and labor to create and maintain them. As argued by Pierre Bourdieu, the production and maintenance of social capital requires an "unceasing effort of sociability, a continuous series of exchanges in which recognition is affirmed and reaffirmed." Building social capital is "work, which implies expenditure of time and energy and so, directly or indirectly, of economic capital." Rather than assume that women tap into social capital that readily exists, credit-work means that women have to actively turn the "contingent relations" of the neighborhood into an institutionalized network of a microfinance group (Bourdieu 1986, 249). It is only through this continuous effort and labor that borrowers are able to access to economic capital in the form of loans.

Once a woman has established a loan, she must attend the weekly meetings both to repay and to maintain her creditworthiness. Attendance is taken at every meeting, and a woman who has missed too many meetings may become ineligible for a subsequent loan even though she has paid back her loan on time (e.g., by sending the money through another borrower or family member). The MFIs insist on attendance as a way to keep track of their borrowers and ensure that their loans do not become overdue. Since most women I spoke to had two to four microfinance loans from different institutions, many mornings are occupied with group meetings.

Credit-work intersects with various other forms of labor that women are expected to complete, including domestic, wage, and other income-generating forms of labor. These seemingly invisible tasks become evident in the moments at which women who perform multiple forms of labor have to choose between or prioritize them. For some women engaged in waged labor (formal and informal), the meeting times can coincide with working hours. For example, one woman who worked at a hospital had to keep pressing the loan officer to let her leave the meeting early. "We don't even have time to eat," she explained, "but we still come to the meeting on time. I come home from work [at the hospital] just to pay off the loan, but now it means that I won't be back in time to get *tiffin* [lunch]." For this borrower, maintaining creditworthiness through attendance at the meeting had to be balanced not only with the hours she worked but also with access to the meal that was provided as part of her job. Other women who ran small food stands found that attending meetings could mean loss in business. Again, access to credit had to be managed and coordinated with other income-generating activities that cannot be abandoned. Thus, women are constantly juggling their time and schedules to both attend meetings and keep up with other obligations.

One of the most common problems women faced by attending meetings was finding child care. Group meeting times often coincided with time for school to start or end, so women were typically in a rush to drop off or pick up children from school.[12] Borrowers like Arati had to find people to provide child care while they attended the meetings, creating networks of obligations with neighbors and kin. Still others with sick or elderly parents also had to provide elder care alongside attending the meetings. Thus, women were constantly negotiating credit-work with other forms of gendered labor to ensure that they could fulfill obligations in various areas of family life from income generation to child care. Credit was absorbed into the existing demands on women's time, becoming another necessary form of women's work.

But credit-work can also fail to produce or sustain the requisite amount of social capital. For example, during one DENA meeting an enraged woman confronted the group's cashier about her inability to get a loan from a different MFI. "She's stopped me from taking loans there!" the woman exclaimed. "Just because they've made her a group leader [for the different MFI group], she thinks she can do what she wants. She wouldn't give me a signature for a loan! I sent the money, I gave it to my son to take to her, and she scolded him. Why should she talk to a little boy like that? I sent the money! I gave it to my son to take to her [the cashier], and she scolded him." While the other women tried to defuse the situation, telling her to come later to talk, not in front of the loan officer and myself. The loan officer asked if it was to do with the DENA group, and when she replied that it was for a different MFI, he told her to discuss it later since it was not related to this meeting. Even as the woman moved outside, she continued to shout accusations at the women. The woman in whose house we were meeting wondered out loud: "What will the neighbors think with all this racket?" Such disputes in domestic spaces spilled over, as the woman worried about what her neighbors would think.

As the meeting ended and the room cleared out, the woman who had accused the cashier came back in. Finding none of the borrowers at the meeting willing to listen to her story, she turned to me, tears now streaming down her face: "I needed a loan, and she wouldn't give me a signature," she said. "It was before [Durga] Puja, and I really needed the money, and I was running around everywhere. I had to take a loan from a moneylender in the end just so I could buy my children new clothes [for the festival]." This borrower had failed to make the right connections and to find and enter the right networks, so she was now unable to get a loan. Such moments of accusation, mistrust, and rejection were not uncommon during the course of my research, as group members would publicly doubt another's difficulties—including family illness or unemployment—in repaying. Rather, these moments were a reminder not only of the power exerted by dominant members of the group and neighborhood who can advise loan officers but also of the ways in which private and domestic life becomes subject to public scrutiny (Kar 2017c). While neighborly relations become entangled with access to credit, documentary requirements ask women to manage other kinds of relationships, including those with landlords, local councilors, and bureaucrats.

COLLECTING DOCUMENTS

Access also requires having the right set of documents, the right income profile, and the right answers to questions from the MFI staff. Typically, the set of documents necessary for a loan are (1) age proof (e.g., permanent account number [PAN] card, voter identity card, or ration card); (2) photo proof (PAN card or voter ID); (3) address proof (PAN card, voter ID, or ration card); and (4) a joint photo with the guarantor (see Table 4.1).[13]

Borrowers most commonly had ration cards, which are issued by the state government and enable cardholders to get subsidized essential commodities (e.g., rice, lentils, kerosene) through the public distribution system. However, ration cards in West Bengal do not include a photograph. The PAN card, which is issued by the Income Tax Department and is required for filing taxes, fulfills the age and photo proof but does not include the address. However, most urban poor borrowers (especially women) do not file income tax papers so do not have a card. The most complete form of identification was a voter ID. The address on the card, however, often would not match the current address, especially for migrants or recently married women. A borrower often had only a voter ID but with her natal rather than marital address; or she had a ration card without a photo proof. In such cases, she had to go to the local councilor and get a signed letter with photo confirming her identity. When a borrower lived in a rented house or apartment, she had to get a letter from her landlord vouching for her as a tenant. Gathering all of these documents required considerable time, work, and expense.

A photo identity with address proof must also be provided for a male guarantor, typically the husband of the borrower, but in cases where she has been widowed, it can be a son, a son-in-law, or even a father-in-law. When I asked the management at DENA about this requirement of a male guarantor, it was explained that, first, men were more likely to be the primary earners in the household, so they had to verify that income stream. Second, the MFI was preempting the possibility that a man would prevent the female borrower from repay-

TABLE 4.1 *Forms of ID needed for loan application*

Type of proof	PAN card	Ration card	Voter ID
Age	✓	✓	✓
Photo	✓	✗	✓
Residence	✗	✓	✓

ing her loan by claiming that he was not aware that she had taken out a loan. Numerous scholars have observed the ironic tendency of microfinance to enforce or even strengthen prevailing gender hierarchies (Karim 2011; Rankin 2002). Similarly, the practice of requiring male guarantors produces new relations of guarantee, which require borrowers to constantly provide signs of their kinship relations to MFIs to assess their creditworthiness (Kar 2017c). In this process, patriarchal norms that assume men as heads of households are enfolded into lending practices as a way to mitigate the risk of lending to poor women, even in cases where there are no income-earning men in the household.

Consider, for instance, Moonmoon, a woman in her forties who had applied for a loan from DENA. When asked about her guarantor during the initial house verification, a part of the loan application process, Moonmoon explained that her unemployed eighteen-year-old son, not her husband, would be the guarantor. While her husband lived and worked at a hospital outside the city, Moonmoon lived with her son in their flat in Kolkata. Her son, however, lacked the necessary documents to prove that he was over eighteen because his newly applied-for voter ID was still being processed. When Joy, the loan officer, asked if he had taken the West Bengal class 10 exams, which would indicate his birth date, Moonmoon said no. Finally, Joy asked her to get a letter from the local councilor verifying his birthday. At this request, Moonmoon became agitated. "Everyone knows everyone," she said, hesitatingly. "I don't want to ask him for something like this." "You don't have to tell him what it's for," pressed Joy. "Just ask him to verify your son's age; that's all we need." Though still hesitant, she agreed.

Even as we walked out of the apartment, she continued to repeat that she did not want to go and ask him for these things.

Although Moonmoon claimed to have a sari business, Joy confided on our way back that he did not believe she actually ran it. The loan, he guessed, was probably for her son, whom we briefly met during the verification when he woke up and stuck his head into the room where we were talking. I asked about whether having seen all this—the absent husband, an unemployed son without sufficient identification, a seemingly absent business—she would still get a loan. "Of course, why wouldn't she?" asked Joy. She had requested Rs 10,000, but Joy anticipated that she would get about Rs 8,000 sanctioned by the MFI. Given the continued emphasis on guarantors, I asked whether it was a problem that she should have her son as a guarantor when her husband was still alive. "Well, her husband's in a different town, so it makes it easier to have the son," Joy replied, noting her husband's absence as perhaps more complicated. "Also, we often prefer to have the son rather than a father, since they are younger. It's because the son still has the capacity [*khomota*], not because we think they'll live longer," he added quickly. But after thinking, he observed, "Sons ask their mothers, and she can't say no." Even as Joy suggested it was the unemployed son's "capacity" they were assessing, he ultimately turned to the maternal obligation as the real source of security.

Though the requirement for a male guarantor is typically explained as the ready income stream to repay the loan, Joy turns the logic of the guarantee on Moonmoon's expected maternal obligations. While male guarantors may be considered the material collateral for these seemingly unbacked loans, it is also the relational force between mother and son that comes to the fore. Kinship ties, in other words, come to back the loans. Women, it is expected, will do whatever is necessary for their children. What made Moonmoon creditworthy in Joy's eyes, despite her seeming lack of employment and her absent husband, was the productiveness of the mother-son relationship, to which she could not say no. In other words, it was not the assumption of a static kin relationship that made her son viable as a guarantor but that this relationship would produce certain obligations, including the obligation to be creditworthy to access loans for her son.

Most often, sons would serve as guarantors for widowed mothers, or, as Joy mentioned, in cases where the husband was elderly. The cut-off for women to get loans was fifty, and for men to serve as guarantors was sixty. Thus, the absence in her everyday domestic life of a working-age husband marked significant relational unraveling in Moonmoon's life. Specific life events in women's lives—marriage, childbirth, and widowhood—transform familial relationships (Lamb 1997; Pinto 2011). The need for guarantors can disclose times when key relationships in women's lives fall apart, as they search for alternative guarantors. In the absence of immediate male kin, women sometimes seek out fictive kin, asking neighbors or friends to sign as a brother; or, men will seek out particular female kin (usually sisters) to take out loans on their behalf (Kar 2017c).

While women who are widowed are eligible for loans, women younger than thirty-five years who have never been married are not able to access credit, even if they were to get a brother or father to serve as guarantor. Coded in the language of risk, MFI staff explained this practice in terms of the fact that young Bengali women will likely leave the neighborhood after getting married, making them higher "flight" risk. A widowed woman, however, was considered safer, because it was assumed she would not remarry and would either remain in her marital home or with her children or return and stay in her natal home (see Fruzzetti 1982, 103–107). Occasionally, unmarried women over the age of thirty-five would be given a loan. The age cutoff is made in the expectation that unmarried women over the age of thirty-five will likely never marry. Such expectations mark the ways in which women's life choices are conscribed by marriage.

On the one hand, the fluidity of everyday kinship relationships is nothing new, as people live in constantly changing arrangements with family, friends, and neighbors. On the other hand, in requiring these relationships to be formalized as financial relationships, microfinance recodes their nature, asking people to affirm particular relationships to gain access to credit. While women used these familial relationships to access loans, they were also the basis for which women sought loans, including the provision of a "better life" for their families.

BEING MIDDLE CLASS

Dressed in her usual "maxi" nightgown with a towel thrown over her shoulders as a *dupatta* (scarf), Sheuli was explaining her experience with microfinance. She had organized the group she was in, and the meeting was held in her apartment. She lived with her sixteen-year-old son on the third floor of the unfinished concrete building. It was her natal home, and she had moved back when her husband had died some years earlier. She had taken a loan to help pay for her son's education and was trying to get an additional loan through her mother for the same purpose.

When asked about microfinance, Sheuli responded that it helped because "women can do something for themselves from home." She continued:

> Most people do things like [food] home delivery or sell sari/clothes [*kapor*]. At least women are able to get money from somewhere. Most of the time [women's] husbands' incomes are enough to keep households going [*sansar chalano*]. But it's the extra income that these loans bring in. After all, belonging to the "middle class" [using the term in English] means that we need the extra money to send our children to better schools, to try to get them a better life in the future. People want to provide their children a better education because they want the next generation to do better than they had. Our parents didn't really think that education for their girls was that important. A little bit of schooling would be enough. Then it was time to get them married. Now people want their girls to succeed.

As in many other contexts, the term "middle class" or "working class" masks internal fractures and the ways in which class is lived (Dickey 2016). Sheuli's use of the English term "middle class" demonstrates how urban poor women seek to perform and maintain middle-class identities through debt.

Linguistically, the urban working class, often rural migrants to the city, is already marked as inferior by the urban middle class. Consider, for example, the derogatory Bengali terminology for lower classes, which also imply lower castes: *chotolok* (lowly people). This term was never self-ascribed by my urban poor informants; more often, they would describe themselves as *garib* (poor) or, as Sheuli did, used the English "middle class." Although *madhyabitta* is another Bengali term for middle class, its connotation is often of economic rather than cultural capital. However, I suggest that the borrowers' preference for the Bengali *garib* or the English term "middle class" was an attempt to bridge the exclusions created by the *bhadralok* class, marked particularly by cultural capital.

Bhadralok translates literally as "respectable folk" and is a Bengali Hindu class category that emerged under British colonial rule and marked the new urban middle class of Calcutta. The *bhadralok* emerged out of the economic transformations, including land reform and trade policies, of colonial rule: "It was an internally differentiated, heterogeneous in its caste composition (though kayasths, vaidyas, and Brahmins predominated) as well as in the routes through which individual members achieved and/or consolidated their economic status" (Mani 1998, 43). The *bhadralok* are also defined as a middle-income group distinct from the rich *baralok* (big people) (Sarkar 1992). While there is some correlation between upper caste and *bhadralok*, the two are not coterminous; *bhadralok* has greater caste flexibility, making it primarily a class category.

West Bengal has had a long history of class politics through three decades of Communist Party rule. The 2011 electoral defeat of the Communist Party, however, marked the failure of the party to politically address class inequality over the course of three decades. The Communist Party, led primarily by *bhadralok* intellectuals, was inflected by elite, not working-class radicalism.[14] As Parimal Ghosh notes, "To achieve that [class-based equality] a price had to be paid, and how far the bhadralok was willing to foot that bill is open to serious doubt" (2004, 251). Or, as an obituary in 2010 of the late and long-serving Communist leader and West Bengal chief minister Jyoti Basu noted, "All his life Basu was a gentleman and never the perfect Communist" (in Majumdar 2010). If the *bhadralok* class emerged under co-lonial rule as the promulgators of a liberal ideology, elite radicalism was necessarily limited by unequal power structures. The ascription to greater social and political equality would require the *bhadralok* class to accede power, which they did not.

Meanwhile, after decades of stalled economic growth, liberaliza-tion of the Indian economy in 1991 led to the rise of the "new" In-dian middle class.[15] The rise of the aspirational new middle class has produced an aspirational urban working class that—often through loans—engages in middle-class consumption practices (see James 2015). Sheuli was herself seeking loans to pay for her son's private ed-ucation rather than to expand her business. Thus, by using loans for middle-class consumption purposes (rather than the stated purpose of growing a business) and identifying as middle class, women like Sheuli sought to participate in a new class identity that challenged the exclu-sionary force of the *bhadralok*.

WOMEN, CLASS, AND PATRIARCHY

Meanwhile, empowerment discourses in development are often framed in terms of gender, but they can overlook the ways in which class and gender identities intersect for working-class women. Even as women like Sheuli sought to aspire to the "middle class," the *bhadralok* ideolo-gies of middle-class womanhood shaped her view of gender. Hearing that I was visiting from the United States, Sheuli said that there was a young woman in the neighborhood who was studying in Barcelona. She spoke with pride that a girl from the neighborhood was studying abroad. The other women in the group also knew of this young woman and praised her for being intelligent. Although the woman in Barce-lona was married, her younger sister, who worked for an outsourcing company, was not. Some of the women snickered while speaking of the sister as being successful professionally but unable to get married. Jux-taposed to the earlier conversation of wanting a better life for women, the comment pointed to the easy slippage between ideas of a good life: between the desire for success in the workplace and that in the domes-tic sphere. Even as Sheuli identified as middle class against the exclusionary force of the *bhadralok*, what the women's conversations index is a specific Bengali *bhadralok* ideal of womanhood. The endorsement of such a gendered ideal emerges as a limiting factor to the discourses of women's empowerment in relation to microfinance.

From anticolonial struggles to the present, the *bhadralok* identity, particularly of women, has been carefully managed as both modern and distinctly Indian. Under colonialism and anticolonial struggles, Partha Chatterjee has argued, the *bhadramahila* (gentlewoman) "was to be modern, but she would also have to display signs of national tradition and therefore would be essentially different from the 'Western' woman" (1993, 8). Similarly, postliberalization, the "modern" Indian woman must be aware of the global public world but is nevertheless most active in the domestic sphere as a responsible mother and wife (Oza 2006). In her ethnography of middle-class women in Kolkata, Henrike Donner (2008) argues for the need to understand how the domestic sphere constitutes the reproduction of the Bengali *bhadralok* middle class. The role of women in the middle-class domestic sphere now is not to protect it from the influx of outside (i.e., global) influences (as in the nationalist discourse) but to reproduce class privilege and hierarchy, which may include learning to adopt more cosmopolitan practices.

What then are the implications of this ideology for those who fall outside the expectations of modern Indian middle-class womanhood? Minna Saavala, for example, finds that upwardly mobile lower-middle-class women in Hyderabad "feel caught between the ideologies of women's work in the public domain and the value placed on remaining in the domestic sphere" (2010, 37). Smitha Radhakrishnan writes of "respectable femininity" in India whereby "women must navigate between the pressure to work—the promise of independence—and the pressure to work less or not at all, equated with the norm of staying home" (2011, 83). Indian middle-class morality demands that women remain within the domestic sphere as a sign of class distinction. This is not to say that middle-class or elite women do not work outside the home, as is increasingly the case (see Kar 2018). Rather, the public visibility and laboring conditions of working-class women comes into contrast with that of middle-class and elite women. Or, as Donner suggests, "a lack of respectability and of commitment to domestic roles were attributed to the working class because of their 'public' lives" (2009, 3).

One example of this experience of conflicting gender and class ideals came not from a borrower but from a loan officer. Like many of the other loan officers, Nilima, working at DENA, identified herself as middle class (again, using the English term). Her father had been active in the Communist Party and had encouraged her to work from an early age. Before coming to DENA, she had spent time volunteering to teach at a prison in the city. Although she was married, she lived apart from her husband at the branch office, as required by the MFI. One day as we were going around to her group meetings, she expressed her frustrations as a female staff member:

> There are some things that you experience as a "lady" [English], and I can say this to you as another lady. It's difficult sometimes to be a woman going alone to some of the neighborhoods. But what is worse is how you are perceived by middle management at the office. It's hard to get a promotion. People just assume that if you are a woman and you have to work, then you must be from a bad background. It's different if you're very rich [*baralok*] or very poor [*garib*]. Then you can work and nobody will say or think anything.

Although Nilima self-identified as middle class, her very presence in the public sphere disrupted existing gender and class norms. Nilima struggled with the conservatism of the management in the very sector that is supposed to be providing women's empowerment. Yet it was not simply her presence in the public sphere that brought on such critiques but her choice to be absent from the domestic sphere. She was, in fact, in the process of studying for a teaching certificate so she could leave the microfinance sector. Saswati, another female loan officer at a different MFI, faced opposition from her in-laws in her continuing to work after marriage. Her in-laws insisted that she wear a sari rather than a *salwar kameez* as a sign of modesty. This meant she could not use a bicycle to go to meetings and had to walk quite far distances between meetings.

In an ironic reworking of the public/domestic dichotomy, the intersection of class and gender imaginaries reformulates the very presence of working-class women in the public sphere as untoward and negative. Bengali *bhadralok* ideology marks the laboring body of the working-class woman who is present outside her own domestic sphere not as an ideal of a "modern" working woman but as inferior to the ideals of middle-class domesticity.[16] If elite or middle-class and upper-caste women come to embody the ground on which modernity and tradition are inscribed, working-class women come to signify an unruly and degenerate other.

Microfinance enabled women not necessarily to work outside the domestic sphere but to consume and claim a certain kind of middle-class respectability that is otherwise foreclosed to them.[17] Several of my informants wanted loans to pay for increasingly expensive "English-medium" private school education for their children.[18] For example, one woman needed to pay an Rs 10,000 fee every year for her son's high school education.[19] If we take seriously the multiple values that people give to debt, its ultimate use, and circulation, the entrepreneurship and empowerment discourses fail to capture the multiple reasons why poor women access loans, including how local categories of class difference are constructed.

In their work on domestic workers in Calcutta, Raka Ray and Seemin Qayum observe the ideological hegemony of what they term "*bhadralok* patriarchy" (2009, 122). Modeled after the ideal middle-class family, *bhadralok* patriarchy expects that men occupy the "outer domains" and women, the "inner." Yet, as Ray and Qayum note, working-class men who labor within households as domestic workers and working-class women who work outside their own homes, are reconstituted under this framework as "responsible women and incapable men" (ibid., 127).

Microfinance, too, relies on this narrative of the failures of working-class men. As occurs in the *bhadralok* patriarchy, microfinance staff often reproduce stereotypes of working-class men as unreliable, drunk, and likely to waste money, while working-class women are expected to manage the household and be responsible debtors (Kar 2017c). Moreover, women who work outside their own home and men who do not earn enough alone to support their families not only represent a "failed patriarchy" in the eyes of the middle class but force working-class men and women to "compensate for the painful gap between their lived experience and the expectations of a dominant ideology that demands that women tend to their homes, husbands, and children. Many seek to create a home life of their own under circumstances that militate against it" (Ray and Qayum 2009, 129). In other words, the domestic sphere is not simply reconstituted as a gendered space but also tethered to expectations of middle-class respectability that locates the presence of men and absence of women in the domestic sphere as failure rather than a positive sign of empowerment. The notion of "failed patriarchy" signifies the power of an ideology that hierarchizes both gender and class relations within the domestic sphere. In effect, it raises the question of what exactly women's empowerment entails, when its "success" (i.e., the presence of women in the public sphere) can be recoded as a socially sanctioned failure.

The popular representations and discourses of women borrowers being liberated from oppressiveness of local traditions—this time through empowerment and entrepreneurship—parallels what Third World feminists have critiqued as universalizing women's lives and experiences in vastly different social conditions (Mohanty 1991). If microfinance has sought to empower borrowers through entrepreneurship, women domesticated these loans as a way to address class inequalities.

"ALL WILL BE AS IT WAS BEFORE"
Eight-year-old Rimi sat perched on the edge of the bed. Her mother had a loan, and the group meeting was being held in her house. With short hair and a serious countenance she clutched her mother's passbook and observed the meeting. Seeing her, the women borrowers joked whether she too had her money ready to return or if she was going to ask "Sir" for a loan. Teasing young girls about their future wifely duties is a relatively common practice in India. Along with rituals, such everyday language expresses gender ideologies and conveys

the expected role of women as wives and mothers (Dube 1988; Fruzzetti 1982). Just as they might have teased Rimi about cooking for a husband, getting a loan was now constructed as another job for a married woman to do.

Differences between the intended purpose (e.g., investment in business) and use (e.g., consumption) of credit has marked a point of departure in my analysis from a number of existing critiques of microfinance that focus primarily on neoliberal discipline and governmentality (e.g., Karim 2011; Ananya Roy 2010; H. Weber 2004). I have shown how the "cultural articulations" (Rankin 2001, 29) in the gendered domestic sphere and within indigenous class ideologies condition urban poor women's experiences of microfinance. The competing ideologies of what women should get out of the microfinance ironically often produce conservative rather than transformative outcomes for borrowers, a process in which microfinance is domesticated. Yet the ways in which women act in the domestic sphere and within constraints of *bhadralok* patriarchy reflect the agentive capacity in the "ways in which one *inhabits* norms" (Mahmood 2005, 15).[20] Thus, working-class women who self-ascribe as "middle class" over indigenous terms, while performing middle-class gendered identity, challenge the very exclusions and discriminations of elite and upper-class Bengali society. Attending to the meaning that women themselves give to the loans reveals both the actual use of the loans and the limitations to microfinance as a tool of social change.

"We used to be dependent on our husbands," explained a borrower, Mintu. "But after the loans, we are able to compromise on many things. The loans have spread everywhere. We use them to buy things for ourselves or schooling our children, so now it will be a real problem if we can't get loans. Our biggest problem would be if they stopped getting loans, not interest rates or anything. The end of loans would be bad. . . . What would happen? [*Ki aar hobe?*] All will be as it was before [*ja chilo phirejabo*]," she concluded. In domesticating microfinance, borrowers like Mintu have brought something into the household of value. Simultaneously, however, her observation that "all will be as it was before" in its absence marks the ways in which the project of empowerment through microfinance has been tamed. Mintu's experience of microfinance and her prediction for the future demonstrate the ambiguities of a system that offers the possibility but does not actualize social transformation.

CHAPTER 5

FINANCIAL RISK AND
THE MORAL ECONOMY OF CREDIT

IT WAS A routine house verification by a branch manager at a borrower's single room in her joint family's compound. The borrower, Arati, wanted the loan for her husband's construction business. The young family of three lived in the room furnished with only a bed, a small bench for sitting, and an *almirah* (cabinet). The baby, a few months old, was asleep on the bed when we visited. "How much do you want?" asked Anand, referring to the loan amount. "Ten thousand rupees," Arati replied. After some routine questions on what she wanted the loan for, Anand announced that she would get Rs 9,000, briskly packing up his papers. After we left, Anand explained his decision on the loan amount. "You know why I gave them less? They have money; they could have gotten a larger loan and it wouldn't have been a problem. They have money, but they still don't have 'class' [English], don't you think?" he asked, and continued without waiting for my response. "Everything was dirty and not in order [*gochano noi*]. That's why they won't get a larger loan. If everything is in order in the house, you know that their money is in order too."

While there are standard loan application forms, the seemingly idiosyncratic decisions of MFI staff about whether a borrower would get Rs 10,000 or Rs 9,000 are based not on the strictly financial measure of the borrower's income and expenditure (required on the loan application) but on the much more culturally informed aspects of these house verifications, as reflected in Anand's comments. Some of these aspects of risk analysis were shaped by loan officers' and branch managers' own interpretations of social acceptability, while others, such as the system of male guarantors discussed in the previous chapter, were institutionally reinforced.

Popular images of and writing on microfinance tend to reproduce an almost universal representation of entrepreneurial poor women, whether African, Asian, or Latin American (Ananya Roy 2010). Despite differences among borrowers, not just across continents but also within the same branch office, the poor tend to be represented as a homogeneous category. The "aesthetics of poverty" (Shah 2010, 70) often project uniformity between all poor people. The similarities in the appearance of poverty can mask the multiple social, political, and economic factors that distinguish *between* people marked as poor. The point of noting the aesthetics of poverty is not to reproduce categories of deserving and undeserving poor. Rather, it is to destabilize the representations of homogeneous poverty and to understand why microfinance often produces such socially conservative—risk-averse—outcomes despite its claims otherwise. Contrary to the paradigm of inclusion, categories of risk and creditworthiness mark points of social exclusion as loan officers determine who ought to get loans and how much.

This chapter discusses the entanglements of moral and material economies, highlighting the ways in which social and cultural valuations underpin financial decisions. Microfinance loan officers conduct credit risk analysis by evaluating and interpreting the lives of women borrowers. I demonstrate here that in contrast to the statistically calculated financial risk through formal measures of income and expenditure, existing social and cultural categories, including class, linguistic, and religious differences, inform loan officers' lending decisions. I argue that despite discourses of empowerment and inclusiveness, the increasing integration of microfinance into the formal financial sector requires "low-risk" borrowers, ironically reinforcing socioeconomic inequalities.

MANAGING RISK

In June 2009, I attended the annual meeting of a Kolkata-based microfinance institution. The audience consisted of branch managers and loan officers from branch offices of the MFI from across the states in which it operated. One of the speakers, a senior banker from a public commercial bank, was explaining risk management to the audience. He stated that everything has risks, even crossing the road: "You might get hit by a car and run over. So, you take the necessary precautions by looking both ways." He clarified that similarly, in banking there are three kinds of risk to manage: market, operational, and credit. Most of the audience did not have to deal with market risk, he continued. Market risk, such as market fluctuations, was something that the MFI management and the commercial banks that fund the organization have to deal with. Operational risks, like equipment failure or branch office security, could be dealt with through the implementation of insurance. Credit risk, he noted, has to be managed through a close relationship with the borrower. In a subsequent interview, anticipating the 2010 microfinance crisis, the same banker raised concerns about risks relating to the lack of regulation in the microfinance sector despite its rapid growth. Just as MFIs had to worry about the "quality" of their borrowers, he observed that commercial banks needed to distinguish between good and bad MFIs through credit ratings systems. Both these concerns highlighted the underlying threat of systemic risk that microfinance posed. Risk and its management thread throughout the network of financial flows of microfinance, from the borrower to the banking institutions and regulators.

Microfinance was popularized through the discovery that despite risks posed by low and fluctuating incomes, the poor could also be profitable; that is, "the poor always pay back" (Dowla and Barua 2006). This transformation of the poor into a "bankable" population through microfinance begs significant questions about conceptualizations of risk and poverty. MFIs rely on social capital among women and the relational monitoring of borrowers by branch office staff to hedge against poor borrowers' lack of capital and collateral and to ensure high recovery rates. Further, the creditworthiness (and hence riskiness) of borrowers has to be mediated in a two-step process by loan officers and branch managers who fill out the loan applications and conduct house verifications to determine who gets what amount. These practices of risk assessment are often taken for granted, leaving unanswered what it is that is being judged and why these particular aspects become central points of valuation and indeed of risk.

Social scientific analysis of risk has centered on the sociological concept of risk society. As a constant process of anticipation, contemporary risk society is preoccupied with preventing disastrous events in an unknown but possibly predictable future (Beck 2006). This includes areas such as disaster management and biosecurity (Collier, Lakoff, and Rabinow 2004; Petryna 2002). These concepts of risk have also transformed the economic sphere. Since the nineteenth century, the economy and economic risk have emerged as areas that the state could isolate and manage through analysis of statistics and calculability (Foucault 1991; Mitchell 2002).

Beyond the state's management of macroeconomic risk, its measurement, analysis, and circulation have become central to the contemporary financial regimes that capitalize on risk itself. Developments in information technologies have enabled faster expansion of global equity markets.[1] These technologies further enable constant monitoring and management of calculated risk. Under these conditions, as Benjamin Lee and Edward LiPuma argue, the "leading edge of capitalism is no longer the mediation of production by labor, but rather the expansion of finance capital. Capitalist social relations are no longer only mediated by labor, but also by risk" (2002, 208). In other words, there is an increasing gap between the material aspects of the economy and the driving forces of speculative finance capital. Similarly, Kausik Sunder Rajan (2005) posits that surplus value is created not so much, as Marx theorized, from the difference between labor and wage but in relation to risk.[2]

While credit risk analysis in some form has always existed, whether as an understanding of the debtor's character or her income, contemporary systems of credit are intimately linked to newer practices of risk management. The shift of speculative practices from being a "pariah practice" (Comaroff and Comaroff 2001, 5) to becoming central to the global economy has required a change in its valence from gambling to calculability. Since the 1980s, the financial sector has grown "based on the idea that the behaviour of financial markets can be interpreted and outsmarted by mathematical models" (Shirreff 2004, 2). For instance, writing of the use of mathematical modeling in complex derivatives, Bethany McLean and Joe Nocera argue that traders on Wall Street "came to believe the formulas were not approximation of reality but reality itself" (2011, 280; MacKenzie 2007). Investment decisions must be seen and understood as based on rational, calculative logic and assessment of acceptable risk, not random or arbitrary choices.

As traders embraced new information technologies that modeled risk through complex mathematical models, risk management became a practice that valued, parceled out, and created new financial products. Securities and collateralized debt obligations (CDOs) enabled financial institutions to expunge risk from their books while simultaneously creating a market for trading risk itself. The consequences of these practices have been well documented by numerous authors concerning the 2008 US subprime crisis (e.g., McLean and Nocera 2011; Mian and Sufi 2015; Rajan 2010; Tett 2009). Despite their central role in the disastrous financial crisis in 2008, in 2009 major financial institutions were producing CDOs for MFIs.[3]

MICROFINANCE AND
THE DIVERSIFICATION OF RISK

The popularization of microfinance as a commercial venture is linked to this changing value of risk. Earlier, commercial banks had largely been unwilling to lend to the poor because of their lack of capital and collateral. The risk of default in lending to the poor was simply too high to be desirable for banks. Until recently, lending to such un- or underbanked segments of the population was promoted through government initiatives such as priority lending because of the lack of interest on the part of commercial banks. Why, then, have commercial banks increasingly and willingly lent to the poor through microfinance? Despite the existing challenges, the segment of the unbanked remains a potential pool of banking customers. As intermediaries between the banks and the poor, MFIs have become the means by which banks can both cut costs and manage some of its risk in lending to the poor while still profiting from the sector. Microfinance institutions have been central to reconstituting the risk of lending to the poor. The Boston Consulting Group report on financial inclusion observes that because the "grass-roots connections give them [MFIs] a clearer view of individuals' credit histories" (Sinha and Subramanian 2007, 26), they enable greater risk management. By lending to MFIs and not directly to the poor, banks can both capitalize on this bottom of the pyramid and manage credit risk more effectively.

In addition to commercial banks, microfinance investment vehicles (MIVs) or specialized entities mediate between private investors and MFIs.[4] One of the consequences of the Indian microfinance crisis has been that it has further encouraged MFIs to look for capital from foreign private investors as funds from domestic commercial banks have dried up. In December 2011, the RBI changed regulations to allow cash-starved microfinance institutions to borrow up to US$10 million (up from $5 million) from overseas.[5] Beyond the aspect of "doing good" (i.e., that supporting microfinance supports social businesses), why would investors consider microfinance an appealing option to also "do well"?

Studies in finance suggest that a number of factors make microfinance an opportunity for global investors looking to diversify risk in their investment portfolios (Bystrom 2008; Dieckmann 2007; Galema, Lensink, and Spierdijk 2011; Krauss and Walter 2009). First, government subsidies to the sector create the impression that MFIs are like banks that are "too big too fail" and that the state will dilute market risks (Krauss and Walter 2009, 94). Second, MFIs are seen as relatively less sensitive to global market fluctuations since they are more detached from international capital, making it an option for diversifying investment risk (ibid.,101). Finally, within emerging market economies, MFIs are considered to be less affected by domestic macroeconomic shocks than commercial banks (100). One reason for such differences is that the poor are less integrated into the larger formal economy. This kind of analysis considers how the particular risks of microfinance can be used to hedge against other kinds of risk in the global and domestic economies. In other words, MFIs—and the related lending to the poor—are perceived not as an additional risk but as a way to lessen or diversify the risk of an investment portfolio. Of course, as MFIs expand and increase their customer base from the poorest borrowers, the poor become increasingly exposed to the effects of systemic risk (e.g., global or domestic crises) through the process of inclusion.

RISKS OF MICROFINANCE

Faced with multiple crises, risk management has become a central practice in microfinance (see Table 5.1). In February 2011, I attended a workshop conducted by Sa-Dhan, the microfinance industry association, titled "Governance and Systems against Reputation Risk." The workshop had been organized to address the ongoing microfinance crisis, in particular, how to deal with various forms of risk. The workshop also introduced a burgeoning industry of microfinance consultancies, all of which offered various forms of risk management strategies to MFIs. At the heart of these services was the notion that there was an increasingly complex risk landscape faced by MFIs, which could be analyzed, calculated, and managed through the right set of tools.

For instance, M2i Consulting advised MFIs on management and investment. In particular, its representatives described the mixed qualitative and quantitative method M2i had developed for assessing borrower risks.[6] Meanwhile, Grameen Capital, set up as a joint venture between the Grameen Foundation, Citi, and IFMR Trust, offered investment-banking services to companies with a "social mandate," including MFIs.[7] Grameen Capital provided equity and debt solutions, including credit guarantees, to MFIs to enable them to get access to loans from local commercial banks and address liquidity risks.[8] Another consulting firm, EDA Rural Systems, focused on the management of reputational risk, which, the speaker suggested, was shaping

TABLE 5.1 *Risks in microfinance lending*

Type of risk	Risk to MFIs
Credit risk	Possibility that borrower will default on contractual obligations (e.g., fail to repay the principal and interest); reasons include lack of income, absconding borrower
Market risk	Possibility that fluctuations in the financial market will affect operations (e.g., interest rates will change, currency fluctuations will affect foreign private equity)
Operational risk	Possibility that internal processes will fail or that operations will be affected by external factors (e.g., political and regulatory environment)
Reputational risk	Possibility of negative social performance (e.g., mission drift, unsympathetic civil society, and media)

and being shaped by numerous other risk factors: external, operational, financial management, and mission drift. EDA offered services to help mitigate these risks.

Yet the greatest risk exposure faced by MFIs remained credit risk, or the risk of the borrower failing to repay the principal and interest on the loan. Credit risk has to be mediated by the loan officers and branch managers at MFIs through analysis of each potential borrower's capacity to repay the loan. At DENA, credit risk analysis is done in a two-step process: first by the loan officer and second by the branch manager. When a borrower asks for a new loan or newly joins a group to get a first loan, the loan officer makes preliminary inquiries with the existing group members concerning whether or not to make a loan to the applicant. Often, particularly for members who are getting subsequent loans, this is a very cursory and open process at the end of the meeting. If the loan officer has had or suspects there to be any problems with a borrower, she may corner one or two of her more trusted members to decide whether to go forward with the loan application. The decision to sanction a loan, however, is decided by the loan officer and branch manager, not other group members.

Once the loan officer deems it possible to go ahead with the application, she will go the borrower's residence to fill out the loan application. During this review, the loan officer double-checks that what the borrower is saying can be corroborated (though not necessarily with concrete documentation). For instance, if a borrower has a sari business, the loan officer can ask to see her stock. The loan officer also asks how much the borrower is requesting and will write down that amount. Once the form has been filled out, the branch manager has to visit the house of the borrower and again verify the details on the form and decide, often in consultation with the loan officer, the amount of the loan to be sanctioned. While the process is simple enough, the decisions are mediated by social and cultural norms of risky borrowers.

In his formulation of risk society, Ulrich Beck contends that risk is *"particularly open to social definition and construction"* (1992, 23; emphasis in original). Similarly, Mary Douglas observes that while risk analysis tries to "exclude moral ideas and politics from its calculations," there is always the political question of "acceptable risk" (1992, 44). Regardless of its technical and apolitical appearance, risk is not simply a calculation of statistical probabilities but something that requires a fuller understanding of the social, cultural, and political dimensions that constitute perceptions of riskiness. I turn now to these practices of due diligence as an intersection between perceived abstract calculability and sociocultural construction of risk.

FITTING THE FORM: THE MICROFINANCE APPLICATION PROCESS

Standing in the small, dark front room of a borrower's house, Mukul, the branch manager, unfolded the creased paper and began to ask his questions for a standard house verification. Printed on the cheap A4 paper was the application form for a loan from DENA. "Loan purpose?" asked Mukul. The borrower, Rekha, said that she needed the loan for her taxi-driver husband. "Do you own the taxi?" asked Mukul. "No," replied Rekha. They had leased the taxi, paying the owner Rs 400 every day that he took it out on the streets. The taxi would be theirs when or if they ever paid up the Rs 3 *lakhs* (about US$5,000) for it. "But why do you need a loan if you don't own it?" demanded Mukul. "We have to do the repairs. If something goes wrong, we have to fix it." Rekha explained. Thus, even as they continued to pay down the lease on the taxi, the expenses for its maintenance continued to add up.

DENA also needed Rekha's husband's signature on the form as guarantor, so Rekha slipped into the other room to call him. Her husband entered wearing gray trousers—part of his taxi driver's uniform—and a white undershirt. "You're not going out today [with the taxi]?" asked Mukul, seemingly oblivious to the uniform, but also implying that Rekha's husband was not doing his job. "I go out [to work] every day," her husband replied curtly, indicating his commitment to work and to earning money. Rekha's husband signed the form and, without saying much more, turned to go back to the other room. At the end of these interactions, however, documented on the form for loan purpose was just "taxi."

These moments of inscription and verification of these loan documents—moments that do not appear in paper documents but occur because of them—demonstrate the ways in which the moral economy of credit operates. Although all that will appear in the loan application form will be "taxi," the process of filling out the form and verifying it is the point when lenders establish the creditworthiness of borrowers. The exchanges at the moment of filling out the form index both the precariousness of the borrower's household income and of her ability to pay back the loan. Thus, even though "taxi" seems a stable enough category for loan purposes, it masks the reality of driving a leased taxi, including the constant expenses of paying the daily fee and of repairs. Similarly, whether or not Rekha's husband is a reliable income earner is ascertained not by the fact that he is a taxi driver, as documented, but whether or not he is a disciplined worker, fully engaged in the employment every day as judged by the branch manager. The paper form, to be filed away as documentary evidence for possible financial audits in the future, will bear no traces of these exchanges. In ethnographically revisiting these moments during which the form is filled in, I argue that borrowers' creditworthiness is produced not so much because of the financial and biographical information documented in and accounted for in the forms themselves but in their social interactions with MFI staff.

The house verification is a significant part of the loan application process for microfinance borrowers. Given that the majority of microfinance borrowers work in the informal economy, most do not have formal financial documents such as tax returns that would confirm their stated incomes on the application form. Instead, loan officers rely on qualitative analysis of borrowers in determining creditworthiness. DENA's institutional policy required that application forms be filled in at the home of the borrower. In comparison to the more institutionalized space of the branch office, or even the more neutral meeting space in a different borrower's house, requiring the form be completed in the home of the borrower reflected the importance of the actual encounter. In other words, the time and space of filling out the form have meaning beyond what is actually inscribed on paper.

For example, I asked Putul, a branch manager, whether there were cases where she had not given a loan. "Yes," she responded. "Just yesterday we had to say no to someone. She just pointed out a house and said that is mine. But when we went there, she sort of sat in a corner and seemed uncomfortable with the place. I asked for a glass of water, but she seemed sort of hesitant. If it really was your own house, you wouldn't hesitate to get a glass of water. You could tell it wasn't her house. It turned out she was a schoolteacher in the neighborhood. All her documents—her voter ID, ration card, et cetera—were for another place. But she knew someone here, who said she should join, but everything else was for somewhere else." Putul's observations required placing women in the attendant spaces (e.g., the house) and the kinds of interactions that these should readily produce.

Writing of legal documentation practices, Annelise Riles notes that users hardly look at the printed portion of forms. Rather, they "jump to the blanks and complete them, most likely in the order they appear." For Riles, forms are tools for engaging in technical routines, but they are also "normatively and socially thin" (2011, 54). Riles suggests what is important in these forms is the aesthetic criteria that users abide by. Yet the aesthetic criteria of forms are also productive of social relations when forms are filled in jointly. While filling in the blanks is part of the task, the process of documentation also requires a certain social engagement between the loan officer and borrower. Completing the loan application is not simply routine practice; it also implicates the users of the forms in certain modes of sociality. While the final product—the completed form—is indeed "socially thin," we have to look more closely at the moments in which these documents are produced to fully understand their value.

There is also the question of which blanks in the form are left unfilled. At the bottom of the form, there was a line to note if borrowers belonged to any officially recognized "Scheduled Caste, Scheduled Tribe, or Other Backward Classes" (SC/ST/OBC) to encourage lending to groups historically discriminated against. Loan officers I spoke to almost never asked borrowers about this formally recognized status. Joy, a loan officer, explained that this was unnecessary as he "already knew" if a borrower should be designated as such, but did not fill it in. Against the aesthetic and indeed technocratic need to fill in this blank, loan officers like Joy often avoided asking about borrowers' backgrounds, even though this is often obvious, where names can signify a borrower's ethnic, caste, or religious background. The avoidance marked the awkwardness that these questions posed for the social interaction at the time of filling in the form. This knowledge was also always already enfolded into the morally inflected assessment of a borrower's "capacity," and sometimes to the detriment of the borrower.

REASONABLE NUMBERS

Continuing their assessment of Rekha's loan application form, Tania, the loan officer who was also present, was trying to ascertain the family's income and expenses. "How much do you earn a month?" she asked. "I don't know . . ." hesitated Rekha, "maybe eight thousand rupees . . . ," she trailed off, as Tania wrote down the amount under the column for income. "How about expenses? Do you pay for school?" "Yes, I have two children, so there is school and also tuition [after-school coaching]." "How much is that?" persisted Tania. "I'm not sure . . . maybe four hundred rupees?" Going down a list of possible expenses—housing, education, food—Tania continued to ask Rekha what her expenses were, as Rekha either claimed not to know or gave figures off the top of her head. In this seemingly haphazard way, Tania filled in the loan form to create a table of the family's income and expenditures to assess creditworthiness.

Given the ambiguity of what was being documented in this process, one can ask, what is the value of the form? To what extent did the numbers documented in the form represent the real financial situation of the borrower? Raising these questions is not to suggest that the information that the borrower was giving was false or to argue for a need to corroborate the stated income or expenses against receipts or other formal ways of accounting. Rather, the very process of eliciting information as enabled by the form produced a different kind of knowledge. Analyzing the practice of due diligence in offshore banking regulations, Bill Maurer points to "the way ethics interfaces with social knowledge." Maurer notes "a new form of managing financial risk offshore that relies not on calculation but on judgment and ethical self-fashioning" (2005a, 476). The practice of due diligence calls forth what Maurer calls the "reasonable man" over the "economic man" through its invocation of "whether or not 'reasonable care' has been taken to ascertain the identities of offshore entities" (ibid., 483). Following Maurer, the documentation of borrowers' incomes and expenditures by the loan officers reflects this goal to conduct due diligence with *reasonable* care. Loan officers sought not so much quantitative confirmation but a qualitatively reasonable understanding of borrowers' creditworthiness.

On our way back from Rekha's house verification, Mukul and Tania discussed the neighborhood: "They have good income," explained Mukul. "They get maybe ten thousand rupees a month or so. Driving a taxi every day, what, you'd get at least one thousand rupees [a day]? They have the capacity here—and there aren't many other MFIs here, so we can give [loans]," explained Mukul. "People have good income," said Tania. "Sometimes they say less [income], because they think that if they say less they're more likely to get a loan," she added, noting the irony of promoting microfinance as a service to the poor. MFI staff like Mukul and Tania realized and accepted that the numbers they were getting from borrowers did not fully reflect their real incomes. In recognizing this, they did not fault borrowers as falsifying information.

Rather, they were interested in figuring out ways to determine creditworthiness through other forms of due diligence and to designate a reasonable expectation of a borrower's income. The stream of questions on income and expenditure is less to arrive at a singular number than to give loan officers enough information to make a reasonable judgment on creditworthiness.

Once the loan was sanctioned, there was no follow-up on the part of the MFI whether the loan was used for the stated purpose. The loan purpose and its verification by loan officers often served as a kind of legal fiction. With a legal fiction, one "creates a placeholder in order to overlook it. In other words, it is a technique for working with and in the meantime" (Riles 2011, 173). The "loan purpose" is something that is inserted in the form, without either party holding it as fundamentally true. The device, however, enables the transactions to take place, while both parties recognize its seeming falsity, as long as other forms of due diligence have been met during the process, including observation of the household's capacity to repay.

When seeking a second loan, loan officers would occasionally note discrepancies between what a borrower stated as a loan purpose for a previous loan and the new one. However, this in itself did not warrant exclusion if the borrower repaid on a regular basis. I observed no prosecution for what could be deemed a fraudulent claim (i.e., the loan being used for other than stated purposes). Loans can seem to be "special monies" (Zelizer 1989) that people will only use only toward the stated end. However, within the context of informal economies with limited accounting and poor households, debt money is often more fungible as it is put to use for various socially acceptable and culturally valuable ends (Cattelino 2008). For loan officers, repayment records were more valuable than tracking the use of the loan.

Upon its completion, the form is filed away and stored for audits. Yet in microfinance the form is most "alive" in its moment of being filled in and verified. In particular, because the borrower does not herself fill out the form, it becomes a tool of communication, a reference point, but the information collected in filling out the form is never fully documented. Indeed, the excess of information and sociality that emerges in the moments of filling out the form is something that produces the creditworthiness of borrowers but cannot be recovered from the material form. Assessing creditworthiness in microfinance then is not an abstract or objective measure of a borrower's ability to pay back a loan based on hard numbers; rather, it emerges as much from the social and moral world of the MFI staff as from the economic capacity of the borrower herself. To determine creditworthiness, MFI staff members rely on countless codes of social difference among the poor, including class, gender, and religion, or a moral economy of credit.

THE MORAL ECONOMY OF CREDIT

In referring to the moral economy of credit, I am interested in the ways in which creditworthiness depends on local social and cultural conceptions of who "ought" to get loans through appeals to traditional arrangements of distribution (Thompson 1971), not simply about crunching the numbers on a family's financials. The moral economy, as E. P. Thompson (1991) argues, uses existing cultural and social forces to form a basis of economic distribution in place of market forces, such as supply and demand. The moral economy of credit traces the distributional logics of credit along the multiple social and cultural axes— visible at times of interaction between debtors and creditors—not just the economic one. Credit risk is the organizing concept by which various forms of judgment come together to mark particular people as worthy, not only of monetary credit but also of greater social recognition than others. Of course, such traditional arrangements of distribution in the moral economy are not necessarily radically egalitarian (Scott 1976) and are "political constructions and outcomes of social struggles" (Edelman 2005, 332; see also Roitman 2005).

Loan officers' deliberation on the moral economy of credit is best captured in their use of the term "capacity" in English or *khomota* in Bengali, which they often used interchangeably. *Khomota*, meaning "power," also loosely translates to "capacity" or "ability." When referring to capacity, MFI staff implied something beyond the simple financial accounting of expenses and income; rather, they called on the moral economy of who ought to get loans. The requirement that the application forms be completed in the house of the borrower, for instance, gave loan officers the opportunity to assess this nonquantifiable information to ascertain a borrower's capacity. As in Arati's case, capacity of a borrower could be arrived at through the condition of the borrower's house—including neatness—or what was being cooked for dinner as a way to understand a borrower's frugality. Capacity was invoked as an ethical judgment of a borrower's ability to repay a loan and was understood not through a seemingly objective analysis of financial data but through the repeated exchanges with the borrowers during the verification process. Significantly, the moral economy of credit was also the basis of exclusions, from religious minorities to migrants.

CATEGORIES OF EXCLUSION: RELIGION

On a different morning, Mukul, Tania, and I were heading to a group meeting in an old neighborhood in North Kolkata. On the sides of the road that stretched along the river were piles of plastic bottles. Many people in the area collected such recyclables—mostly plastics such as PET bottles—or had small businesses processing them. An acrid smell of burning plastic pervaded the area. To get to the meeting, we had to cross a small bridge, and as we neared it, Mukul warned me that there would be a bad smell. Already struck by the chemical smell, I wondered if it would be an intensification of the same. Turning to Tania, she already had the end of her *dupatta* (scarf) covering her nose and mouth in anticipation. As we crossed, I braced for this new smell, but nothing changed. As we passed by a row of butchers, Mukul turned to me and said apologetically, "Lots of beef here." We were in a Muslim neighborhood, and both Mukul and Tania, as Hindus who did not eat beef, were visibly disgusted by the rows of hanging meat. While these kinds of open butchers are common enough throughout the city, most sell goat meat and do not elicit the same response as those selling beef.[9]

On a different occasion, a borrower was asking how I liked Kolkata and whether I found the neighborhood we were in dirty. Mukul interjected that "this was nothing," since we had already passed through the Muslim neighborhood. "There's 'meat' [beef] hanging on either side of the road. It makes me feel sick, and I can't eat on days we come back from there—I feel nauseated [*ga guloi*]." Compared to other staff that went to the same neighborhood, Mukul was particularly vocal about the presence of beef, though others expressed their consciousness of this difference more subtly. These reactions exemplified the ways in which dominant groups evaluate religious minorities through everyday practices.[10]

In his discussion of taste or "manifested preferences," Bourdieu argues that tastes are "perhaps first and foremost distastes, disgust provoked by horror or visceral intolerance ('sick-making') of the tastes of others" (1984, 56).[11] As habitus, taste leads to "rejecting others as unnatural and therefore vicious" (ibid., 173). What then are the consequences of such embodied understanding of social difference for assessing creditworthiness? When determining creditworthiness of borrowers, essentially a practice of judgment, the MFI staff brings into play their own taste and distaste; that is, they find people who are similar to them as being less risky than those who offend their sense of taste. A study on loans made by Western donors through the Kiva website found that "more attractive," thinner, and lighter-skinned borrowers were more likely to be funded (Jenq, Pan, and Theseira 2015). Similarly, Mukul's physical repulsion to Muslim neighborhoods, as exemplified by his beef-induced nausea, trickles into his perspective of Muslim borrowers, whom he simultaneously discriminates against as less reliable.

The microfinance crisis served to intensify forms of discrimination as funds became more limited. On one occasion, as I accompanied Anand and Sandeep on their rounds, they joked that they should just stop the loans in the Muslim neighborhood because there were so many overdue there. Anand said that if they stopped operating there, their work would be much easier. When I asked why, Sandeep explained: "They [Muslim borrowers] all have big families, and they live in these crowded places. Someone will show a room somewhere as belonging to her, and the person living there will agree to that for a while. Then, they [the borrower] will run away after getting the loan." Sandeep's description of the Muslim borrowers and area reproduced many of the existing stereotypes of the religious minority, including lack of reliability, a family size too large, and social backwardness, and are popular tropes of Hindu nationalists (e.g., Bacchetta 2004; Hansen 1999; Atreyee Sen 2007).

While Sandeep suggested their decision was premised on higher rates of default by Muslim borrowers, this was not held to be true by other loan officers. For instance, there had been a problem at the meeting when two of the borrowers—sisters—were having trouble repaying. "They're very good groups. There's just been this problem," said Tania, the loan officer. "The two sisters?" I asked. "Yes," she replied with a slight laugh. "It's really just one of them. But what can you do, if it's your sister. . . . These groups—they're mostly non-Bengali and Muslim, but they're very good. Everyone is very open, and they'll sit and talk to you very openly. But if there is a problem with one person then everyone . . . ," she trailed off. Tania was not the only one to make this observation. In an earlier conversation I had asked another loan officer, Amit, about non-Bengali members. "With non-Bengali and Muslims," he answered, adding Muslim to the question, "you don't know that much about them. But, you know, probably ninety percent are good. Like in other [Bengali Hindu] cases, probably ten percent have problems, and they give a bad reputation for everyone else." Both Tania's and Amit's comments highlight that problems of one or two group members have significantly different consequences when they are minorities. Although I saw problems with borrowers in many of the groups I visited, when these borrowers were Muslim or non-Bengali, their delinquency came to represent the community as a whole.

By identifying migrant Muslim borrowers as high risk, MFI staff could attribute blame for failures in microfinance practices and larger social inequalities to the borrowers themselves. In other words, the default rates among migrant Muslim borrowers may be higher. However, as occurs in the larger development discourse in India regarding the Muslim minority, rather than recognize the structural inequalities by which this group is marginalized as being part of the problem, the MFI staff ascribes these failures to something inherent in Muslim borrowers.[12]

The Hindu MFI staff's response to Muslim borrowers is informed by the history of Hindu-Muslim relations in India. Religion is one of the primary markers of social identity and difference in India. South Asian modernity has been marked by the presence of religious movements in the public sphere rather than its absence (Van der Veer 2002, 180). Thus, religion is central not just to the private sphere but to the region's public life more broadly, including at times of identification for everything from housing to credit. Ashis Nandy describes this as "religion as ideology" rather than "religion as faith" or religion as a way of life. Religion as ideology refers to "religion as a sub-national, national or cross-national identifier of populations contesting for or protecting non-religious, usually political or socio-economic interests" (Nandy 1990, 70). Religion as ideology does not mean that religion as faith is necessarily absent or lost, but it signifies the multiple ways that individuals and communities in India position themselves, or are positioned, within political discourse with regard to religious identity.

Religious identity in public life has also marked continued questioning of Muslim Indians as hyphenated citizens, particularly given the history of partition (Pandey 1999).[13] The unmarked citizen, even in a secular state, is now the Hindu, while the Muslim minority— more than any other religious minority—must be constantly tested and monitored. Such suspicions seep into everyday life and the assessment of Muslim borrowers and considerations of their creditworthiness. Among the loan officers, there were no overt or political expressions of antagonism against Muslim borrowers (e.g., identification with the Hindu nationalist BJP). However, more mundane forms of discrimination against Muslim borrowers, such as disgust at beef eating or perceptions of high fertility, were often present.

CATEGORIES OF EXCLUSION: CASTE AND CLASS

The Hindu MFI staff's reaction to Muslim borrowers existed in marked contrast to that of other religious or caste groups.[14] Unlike the heterogeneous caste makeup of borrower groups and the inclusion of Christian and Sikh borrowers in predominantly Hindu groups, groups with Muslim borrowers were most often "one hundred percent Muslim," as one loan officer described them. In part, this reflects the segregation of Kolkata's Muslim population in particular neighborhoods. Most predominantly Hindu borrower groups I encountered were mixed caste, reflecting caste relations in West Bengal. Compared to the more contentious caste politics of other Indian states, particularly in North India, caste relations have been deemphasized in social and political terms in West Bengal, particularly under the Communist government (Basu 1992; Kohli 1989). The Communists also historically deemphasized caste because of their ideological focus on class, which at times could itself obscure the problems of caste.[15] Moreover, urban Indian slums in general tend to be less segregated by caste than rural areas (Atreyee Sen 2007).

This does not mean that caste does not exist in urban West Bengal, but it does so in a particular convergence with class (L. Fernandes 1997). The local category of *bhadralok* indexes a complex set of interweaving caste and class relations. Examination of social inclusion/exclusion in West Bengal has had to contend less with Brahmanical caste ideology or lower-caste political mobilization and more with the *bhadralok* ideological hegemony. These distinctions are marked, as shown in Anand's earlier comment that the borrower had "no class." Similarly, on the way to a different group meeting, a loan officer told me: "It's so dirty here. The people here are a little low class; I feel disgusted [*ghenna korche*]. They don't keep things clean." The MFI staff repeatedly designated particular areas as less desirable than other neighborhoods for doing work because of physical repulsion to conditions that were often outside the inhabitants' ability to control, such as sewage infrastructure.

As in the opening vignette, perceptions of class difference are drawn out through loan officers' observations of women's domestic habits. Just as the microfinance spills into women's domestic lives, domestic life enters the assessment of creditworthiness (Kar 2017c). For example, on the way back from a loan meeting, Anand discussed how he judged borrowers' ability to repay loans based on their ability to be economical, which he assessed through their cooking habits: "You know, here," he said, waving his arm to indicate the area we were in, "people are very good and they pay back the loans. But their capacity is less, so we give them smaller loans. With better education, people spend money more wisely. Here, they get money and they'll spend it all on one thing. We," he continued, pointing to himself, "are not even middle class, we're poor, but we know how to spend money. We'll make sure there is enough for what we need. But I was in a village where people didn't have money, but I saw they were cooking lots of fish in a big *karai* [pan] with eggplant. *We* would have had just one small piece of fish and made a second dish with the eggplant. But they don't really know that."

Knowledge of how to spend money correctly was important for Anand in his conceptualization of poverty. While self-identifying as poor but educated, he distinguished it from the practices of people he considered frivolous in their use of money. Yet the example of cooking two dishes with fish and eggplant instead of one suggested concern with both having enough to eat (an economic decision) and eating well according to local food customs by having multiple dishes with rice during a meal (a cultural value). Knowing how to spend money can make one more creditable, but such knowledge of food is classed and culturally coded (Utsa Ray 2010). Anand's explanation demonstrates how his own conceptions of proper household economy are privileged in his understanding and analysis of deserving microfinance borrowers.

CATEGORIES OF EXCLUSION: LANGUAGE

Many of the Muslim neighborhoods in Kolkata are doubly marked as other, being both Muslim and non-Bengali—largely migrants from the Hindi heartland, particularly Uttar Pradesh and Bihar. Most migrants from other states do not speak the linguistic norm of standard Bengali.[16] Language differences often made communication between borrowers and the loan officers difficult, resulting in misunderstandings. On numerous occasions, one borrower who was more fluent in Bengali would translate for other borrowers, or the loan officer would use her basic knowledge of Hindi to converse with borrowers. Despite these efforts on the part of both borrowers and lenders, there remained gaps in communication.

The case of pamphlets handed out by DENA exemplified such gaps in communication. In early February, DENA printed pamphlets with details about interest rates and regulations for all borrowers. It was actually the first time that the borrowers were given these details in printed form. The pamphlets were all in Bengali. We were at a group meeting in a Muslim neighborhood, and the DENA staff handed out the pamphlets. When Anand asked if anyone could read Bengali, most of the women shook their heads. One woman mentioned that her children could read it. Anand finally decided that he would read the pamphlet out loud and try to explain it in Hindi. He read over the first two pages and interpreted it into cursory Hindi. The final two pages consisted of short poems and a fictionalized letter from a borrower to her mother, intended to convey information about the problems of over-indebtedness and syndicate borrowing.[17]

Getting to these last pages, Anand said he was not going to read them because the borrowers would not really understand them. When some of the borrowers asked if there were any Hindi pamphlets, Anand explained that DENA had published the pamphlets in the language that the majority of borrowers understood. He said that since about 70 percent of DENA's borrowers in the area were Bengali speakers, they had published only in the one language. Thus, linguistic difference becomes another category of difference by which migrant, particularly Muslim, populations are marked as higher risk based on assumptions that they will fail to understand regulations in a language that is chosen without regard to its exclusion of them, as well as the more cultural meanings implied in the narrative section of the pamphlet.

THE WILY CITY

While loan officers generally legitimized exclusions based on their own perceptions of risk, there was one case in which the moral economy of credit countered the actual practices of credit distribution: urban borrowers. The loans to this category could not, of course, be excluded since these were urban microfinance branch offices. Nevertheless, loan officers and branch managers repeatedly expressed disdain for urban borrowers, particularly when they compared them to rural borrowers. "It is totally different work," explained Anand on his differing experiences:

> In the rural areas, people are very poor; they fish or farm. In the village, some people make *tant* [traditional Bengali woven cotton] saris. But in the city, people mostly have small businesses such as groceries, selling fish and other goods. The urban recovery rates are better because many people have these small businesses. In agriculture and fisheries, the "feedback" [using the English word to mean repayment] is not good. For example, people will buy fish to harvest, but then the fish die and they can no longer pay back the loan. So it is a benefit in the urban areas in terms of [loan] recovery.

In other words, rural incomes were more precarious and subject to fluctuations based on weather and harvests, leading to lower rates of loan recovery than for urban borrowers. From the institutional perspective of the MFI, income streams in the urban areas were considered to be more consistent than rural ones.

Despite the positive rates of loan recovery, however, Anand expressed concern about urban borrowers: "There is the rental problem in urban areas, as there is the danger of people absconding. In the urban and semiurban areas, people are more *chalak* [clever/cunning]. So there is a greater occurrence of syndicate loans and overlapping loans—the two biggest problems. This happens more in urban areas than in rural areas where people are more afraid." Other loan officers and branch officers repeatedly categorized rural borrowers as "nicer" and more satisfied with the loans than urban borrowers. I was often told that in order to see "real" poverty, I would have to go to the rural areas. City dwellers, in comparison, were marked as *chalak*, disrespectful, greedy, and demanding of larger loans.

Most of the loan officers and branch mangers that I encountered were not themselves from Kolkata but had made the journey to the city from small towns or villages in neighboring districts. In part this reflected the MFIs' desire to not have loan officers from the vicinity in which they worked. For many of the loan officers, their encounters with urban borrowers were marked by their own expectations about and experiences of city life, often speaking nostalgically about their own rural or small-town homes. Thus, *despite* the higher recovery loans in urban areas, loan officers found it more difficult to trust urban borrowers.

With rapid urbanization in much of the global South, the city, particularly the slums, has been conceived of by both loan officers and policy makers and academics (e.g., Mike Davis's *Planet of Slums* [2006]) as dystopic spaces of social breakdown (see Prakash 2010). Such imaginings of the dark city were framed in relation to the more docile and more guileless country. Writing of the relation between the imagined city and the village in India, Ashis Nandy notes that "the village symbolizes control over self; the city reeks of self-indulgence and the absence of self-restraint" (2001, 13). The utopian imagination of the rural village is contrasted to the corrupt city. Yet the city also offers spaces of freedom from "caste-specific vocations, ascribed status, and crosscutting obligations of the *jajmani system*" (Nandy 2001, 12). More entrenched forms of hierarchy in rural areas can make borrowers more deferential to loan officers, producing patron-client relationships.[18] For loan officers, rural borrowers appreciation' of microfinance and greater degrees of deference to MFI staff counter what is seen as the lack of gratitude on the part of urban borrowers.

Yet the urban context produced its own particular set of problems relating to credit risk, particularly flight risk. Problems such as absconding borrowers were more common in urban areas because many were migrants, who had greater anonymity and therefore the ability to escape undetected. As a precautionary measure, DENA required the address of a borrower's natal home when making a loan. In case a borrower fled without repaying the loan, the MFI would first go to the woman's parents, as this was the most common destination. If it were far from the branch office, they would send the relevant information to the branch office closest the woman's natal home. Someone from that branch office would then make inquiries to locate the missing family to recover the loan. Thus, the MFI kept track of borrower's social networks to enable closer monitoring of their clients and track down absconding borrowers.

The requirement of "address proof" discussed earlier also marked concerns particular to the urban context and the related risk of tenancy. Around 30 percent of Kolkata's population lives in slums, with around six thousand *bustees* (Sengupta 2010). *Bustee* is the indigenous term for "slum" but also designates legal urban entities with a three-tiered tenancy system: (1) the landowner; (2) the hut owner (*thika*); and (3) the *bustee* dweller or tenant (*bharatia*). The 1949 Calcutta Thika Tenancy Act and subsequent revisions have transferred greater rights to the *bharatias* against eviction and provisions against the alienation of land (i.e., land can be inherited but not sold) (Banerjee 2002). For many of the borrowers who were *bharatias*, their eligibility for loans required signatures from their landlords.

Although the increasing popularization of microfinance in India has, to some extent, lessened the stigma of debt, borrowers nevertheless expressed a sense of embarrassment or shame in having outsiders know of their indebtedness. One woman, who had finished paying off her loan, told the loan officer she did not want another one. Inquiring why she chose to stop taking loans, the woman replied that her family had moved to a new house. She found it shameful (*lajja kore*) to ask the landlord for a signature, particularly since it was a new place and they did not really know him very well. To get another loan, there would be house verification, and she repeatedly expressed embarrassment at having to ask the landlord for this. "Not all landlords are the same," she continued. "Some people have no problems, but others don't want to sign. What are you to do then? It hurts your prestige to have to ask. I don't have any problems with things like going to the councilor [for a signature], but I really don't like going to the landlord." Thus, along with the actual labor or credit-work of acquiring this documentation, having to ask landlords for signatures was repeatedly expressed by women as being embarrassing or shameful by making public the private state of one's financial affairs.

The risks of lending to the urban poor without landholdings became apparent with the microfinance crisis. MFIs such as DENA became increasingly reluctant to lend to borrowers who rented homes rather than owned them. Putul, the branch manager, suggested that this was only for relatively new tenants and that people who had resided at the same address for a long period of time would not be subject to the same rules. Nevertheless, it placed added pressure on women who were seeking loans and continued to add to the burden of creditwork. Even though microfinance claims to operate without collateral, in the urban context, home ownership provided a kind of guarantee that was unavailable to renters who became marked as flight risks.

KNOWING YOUR CUSTOMER

When attending to credit risk analysis of borrowers, loan officers engage in practices of due diligence. Head office staff explained to me that like retail banks, DENA follows KYC (know your customer) norms to ensure the reliability of potential borrowers. Mandated by the RBI (2004), KYC norms are primarily meant to prevent money laundering. As a practice of due diligence that ensures banks know the risks of their customers, these regulations are also part of the risk management system of the financial institution.[19] As NBFCs, MFIs in India are also required to implement KYC norms through practices of due diligence.

For the MFI staff, due diligence in the form of credit risk analysis is colored by everyday social norms and knowledge. Yet, as Bill Maurer argues, this kind of knowledge "does not seek coherence but care" (2005a, 491). Due diligence and "reasonableness" are a form of art rather than a scientific concept. Reasonableness is "a continuous effort" (ibid.) in the constitution of the self as an ethical subject, one that "always begs more words" (493). What is reasonable can seem like an endless process of description. Beyond the documentary practices as required and regulated by the central bank, however, is what happens when this form of knowledge is formalized. While loan officers and branch officers make judgments on the creditability of borrowers, we have to simultaneously ask what happens to borrowers who are judged.

In response to the microfinance crisis, Microfinance Institutions Network (MFIN), the self-regulatory organization consisting of forty-six of the largest MFIs in India (excluding SHGs), launched a credit bureau in partnership with High Mark Credit Information Services Ltd. High Mark, a Mumbai-based credit information company, set up a dedicated microfinance credit bureau with the data of around thirty million loan accounts. The credit bureau would provide, among other things, client data to inform MFIs of a borrower's repayment behavior and outstanding loans to avoid overindebtedness, as well as credit histories that borrowers can use leverage larger loans or lower interest payments (*Business Standard* 2011).

The introduction of the credit bureau meant that DENA would now have access to the repayment history of a potential borrower and would know how many and with which other MFIs a borrower had existing loans. Based on this information and the directives in the Malegam Committee report, DENA would now lend only to borrowers whose total indebtedness (including the loan from DENA) was either no more than Rs 25,000 or whose loans were from no more than three different MFIs.[20] For example, if a borrower had an existing loan of Rs 10,000 from one MFI, then she could get a maximum of Rs 15,000 loan from DENA; or if she already had loans from three other MFIs, even if the total amounted to less than Rs 25,000, she would no longer be eligible for a loan from DENA. Prior to the introduction of the credit bureau, loan officers would simply ask the borrower about her outstanding loans. Most often, the MFI staff told me, they assumed women would tell the truth, though on occasion the real figures would come out only with repeated questioning or some sleuthing through neighbors.

Keeping in mind that the new credit bureau can account only for the large MFIs belonging to MFIN (i.e., borrowers can still access loans from smaller organizations that are outside the regulatory ambit of the RBI), it nevertheless reshapes the credit market for the poor. The introduction of the credit bureau is meant to protect borrowers by regulating the level of possible indebtedness. Credit reporting is seen as a way of providing "reputation collateral" for poor borrowers without physical collateral. Credit data also serve the purpose of "improving the efficiency of financial institutions by reducing loan processing costs as well as the time required to process loan applications" (M. Miller 2003, 2). While regulations to protect consumers of credit are certainly necessary, the standard credit histories mark the increasing formalization and integration of microfinance in the financial markets.

The credit bureau can provide seemingly objective measures of borrowers' credit histories to financial institutions. Yet Brett Williams, writing of the United States, where the documentation of credit histories has been normalized since the 1970s, observes that "bad credit appears such a marker of citizenship that poor people even find it hard to rent an apartment in many cities" (2004, 99). There is not the same history in collecting consumer credit data in India as in the United States. In fact, CIBIL, India's first consumer and commercial credit bureau, was established only in 2000. Like CIBIL, the microfinance credit bureau provides a new marker of good citizenship: creditworthiness. As creditworthiness comes to mark social identity, one may well ask what effects such constant measurement by lending institutions have on borrowers who interpellate themselves by these assessments of worth.[21] As Mary Douglas has argued, risk "is a socially constructed phenomenon, in which some people have a greater capacity to define risks than others" (1992, 333). Powerful and preexisting social codes and forms of prejudice inform the designation of creditworthiness.

The assessment of creditworthiness absorbs existing forms of social exclusion. In contrast to the discourse of inclusiveness, the size of a loan—or whether one gets one at all—is determined by a borrower's financial viability to repay; but it is also determined by whether the borrower is *understood* by loan officers to be in a particular risk category. These decisions include long-standing prejudices against minority communities or migrants. The decision makers also perceive women as more responsible, but only insofar as they do not challenge existing forms of gendered inequalities. What the credit bureau normalizes is not an objective measure of creditability—the simple accounting of one's financial position—but the social markings of more or less deserving borrowers. It is the distributive logics of the moral economy of credit as much as market forces that determine who gets credit and who does not. I have shown the ways in which practices determining creditworthiness are inherently risk averse. In Chapter 6, I examine how new financial technologies such as micro–life insurance comes to further the risk aversion of microfinance and its consequences for the lives of urban poor borrowers.

CHAPTER 6

INSURED DEATH, PRECARIOUS LIFE

IT WAS A cool, rainy Kolkata afternoon in early December at the on-set of winter. I was observing the afternoon tasks at the branch office. While mornings were spent "in the field," collecting repayments and conducting house verifications, afternoons at the branch office were for completing accounting tasks and making loan disbursals. Unlike re-payments, loans were given out at the branch office, so borrowers had to come by to pick up their loans. While the loan officers—bundled in sweaters and shawls—recorded the day's collections in the accounting ledgers, Putul, the branch manager, prepared the disbursals. On a slow day, there would only be one or two people coming in for loans.

As Putul counted out the notes for the new loans, I asked to con-firm some of the fees that were attached to the loan. Putul explained that there was 5 percent margin money that would be returned at the end. These fees would not be subtracted from the loan but would be taken from the borrower at the time of disbursal. "This way, people feel like they are getting the full lump sum," explained Putul. Another 1 percent would be taken for the insurance. "The borrower doesn't get this back," continued Putul. "But if the person taking the loan or her guarantor dies, then the loan is closed for the full amount. This could be the case even if it were the week after [getting the loan]."

I asked if there were many cases where life insurance was claimed.

"We have the files," she said, pulling out a thick black folder from her drawer, with a stack of claim forms that dropped with a thud on the table. "In most cases, it's the husband [who dies]," she explained. "You told me about a woman who committed suicide; are there any others?" I asked. "You mean Shilpa-*Didi*?" replied Putul. "Yes, we've cleared two people so far for suicide. But one person's family didn't want to claim the insurance. They didn't want to provide the documents for it. I think someone worked in government service. They said they would continue to pay off the loan. I think they wanted to hide the issue. In the other case, it was the husband who committed suicide." At this moment, one of the borrowers came in and work commenced on handing out the new loan.

In recent years, MFIs have increasingly bundled mandatory life insurance with loans as a way to recover outstanding debts in case of the borrower's or her guarantor's death. As is the case for credit risk management strategies discussed earlier, life insurance is another mechanism by which to account for the riskiness of lending to the poor. Yet the introduction of life insurance into microfinance loans also highlights the linkages between life, death, and debt. Putul's thick folder of documents on insurance claims is evidence of the way that death, including suicide, shadows these debts. The resistance on the part of some families to claim insurance, meanwhile, marks the ways in which the normalization of life insurance requires more than financial rationality, such as reworking ideas of a good life and death (Zelizer 1978).

This chapter examines how insurance has been absorbed into the operating practices of MFIs as a risk management strategy to account for higher mortality rates among poor borrowers. Though operating without material collateral, life insurance has come to collateralize life itself in microfinance operations. The practice of financial risk management, however, falls short of addressing the uncertainty of life for many urban poor borrowers, who are burdened with spiraling levels of debt and mounting everyday expenses for everything from food and education to health care. While MFIs sought to overcome risk through the introduction of insurance, they simultaneously indexed the precarity of everyday life for poor borrowers.

Microfinance-related suicides are often read alongside the crisis of farmer suicides relating to indebtedness that have received widespread media and political attention in India. In both cases, however, the emphasis on death often occludes uncertainties of life at the margins. The chapter concludes by arguing that while suicidal death becomes the primary means of talking about the problems of indebtedness in both policy and popular discourse, the conditions that lead to initial indebtedness, from illness to social obligations, remain underemphasized.

INSURING POOR MORTALITY

As argued previously, the development of microfinance has had to contend with the riskiness of lending to poor borrowers, including through new practices of credit risk management. While assessment of creditworthiness can attend to some aspects of risk in lending to the poor, there is one risk that cannot be assessed away: mortality. A study on mortality rates and socioeconomic measures in India has found— perhaps unsurprisingly—that those in the bottom quintile of household incomes had 76 percent higher odds of mortality than those at the top; similarly, those in the bottom quintile of household had odds of mortality that were almost three times that at the top (Po and Subramanian 2011). One way for MFIs to manage this additional risk of mortality is through the implementation of mandatory life insurance for borrowers.

At the time of taking a loan, borrowers are often required to pay an additional fee for life insurance (*bima* in Bengali). These insurance policies cover the repayment of the loan in case of the borrower or her guarantor's death, and some provide additional benefits for the policyholder's family. "The insurance is a two-way protection," explained Mr. Ray, the regional head of an MFI:

> Insurance covers risk both for the individual as well as for the bank [MFI]. The death rate is very high for the people who take these loans. When we started, in one month, six people who had loans died. At first we thought that they were cheating the system, that this many people [borrowers] could not have died in one month. However, we realized that there are reasons

for such high death rates among our borrowers. There is the case of suicide, where the husband is a drunkard or is having an affair. Basically, there is a lack of peace or a lack of food, and women commit suicide by setting themselves on fire, or something. There is also malnutrition, which leads to death. Insurance provides a security.

For Mr. Ray, working with poorer populations reveals not only higher mortality rates based on health and malnutrition but also cases of suicide. Insurance, Mr. Ray suggests, provides security for a price, but for whom? While identifying high rates of mortality among microfinance borrowers, Mr. Ray does not address the role of debt itself in producing unbearable living conditions for borrowers.

MFIs have various structures of life insurance. In one method the MFI buys a group life insurance policy from insurance companies such as the Life Insurance Corporation of India (LIC), Bajaj Allianz, or ICICI Prudential. In the second, less common method, as was the case with DENA when I conducted research, the insurance policy is in-house. DENA, however, was also in the process of switching to buying insurance from an outside life insurance company. Some microinsurance providers offer livestock or health insurance, but most only offer life insurance (Ghate 2007).

At the time of getting a loan, borrowers are required to purchase life insurance. Although borrowers essentially buy a separate life insurance policy for the loan, it is usually presented as an additional fee rather than a separate product. The cost may vary, depending on the type of insurance, but in general these insurance products are similar to term life insurance, which is payable only on the condition of death within the given period of time (i.e., the loan period).[1] For example, as mentioned in the opening vignette of the chapter, DENA took 1 percent on every loan as an insurance premium for the duration of the loan. Someone getting a loan of Rs 10,000, for example, would pay Rs 100 for insurance. The insurance covered the repayment of the loan in case of the borrower or her guarantor's death. While DENA's internal insurance covered only repayment of the loan, other insurance policies offered additional benefits to the family of the deceased. For instance, a different MFI had a tie-in with ICICI Prudential, costing 2.44 percent of the loan amount (e.g., a fee of Rs 244 for a loan of Rs 10,000), which would pay a sum of Rs 30,000 to the nominee of the policyholder in case of death.

To claim the insurance, the surviving borrower or guarantor has to produce the death certificate, as well as a letter from the group acknowledging the death. This was not always straightforward. For example, family members often have difficulty getting the death certificate, having to bribe officials to get the documents processed. Or, as in the case of the family who declined the insurance, getting the documents can cause other kinds of problems in borrowers' social worlds. In one case, the family was still waiting for a death certificate following a borrower's accidental death. DENA staff had accepted the cremation receipt in its place to go ahead with closing out the loan and returning the margin money to the borrower's family.

Life insurance tied to microfinance loans has also been normalized among, and indeed desired by, borrowers. For instance, while discussing microfinance in an auto-rickshaw with staff from an SHG-model microfinance organization, the driver turned around to ask about what kind of loans they offered. "I have eighty thousand rupees already in loans from Bandhan and others," he said proudly. After inquiring about the amount the SHG offered in loans, he proceeded to ask, "Do you have *bima*? You know, if something happens to the borrower?" This SHG did not offer any such insurance; however, it was telling to see how life insurance had been absorbed into standard microfinance practices and sought out by borrowers. Life insurance allowed borrowers to avoid passing on debts to family members in case of death and a reprieve from payments following the loss of a household member and her income.

INSURANCE AND OVERCOMING RISK

Historically, life insurance emerged in Europe around the fifteenth century but was relegated to the commercial sphere. Nevertheless, due to its association with gambling on life, life insurance was widely banned in much of Europe, although French and English merchants used it for their slave cargoes. In England, the proliferation of insurance services in the early eighteenth century—to protect against everything from highway robbery to cuckolding—signaled the effects of calculability and manageability of risks (Clark 1999). Insurance was about both speculation and prudence; it was about conquering chance and betting on it.

Insurance more broadly became popular—and indeed possible—with growing calculability through the documentation of statistics. On the one hand, risk and insurance entail a new blaming system by which, as Mary Douglas suggests, we "treat every death as chargeable to someone's account, every accident as caused by someone's criminal negligence, every sickness a threatened prosecution" (1992, 15). On the other hand, risk is not just about apportioning blame. Rather than "something to be avoided, spread, or otherwise managed," argue Tom Baker and Jonathan Simon, risk is now "something to be encouraged or embraced" (2002, 20), as demonstrated by the increasing encouragement of risk-seeking behavior (e.g., stock market, extreme sports). The contradictory ideologies of risk as both something to be avoided and taken mark modernity.

Against the notions of pure speculation and risk taking, there is an increasing move toward precaution. More than risk taking, François Ewald (2002) suggests, the age of *precaution* is about finding the "zero-risk" option that avoids the occurrence of a threat.[2] It is better to avoid risk altogether through precautionary measures than to try to find adequate forms of compensation. Similarly, Karen Ho (2010) has argued that risk has been misrepresented in the analysis of Wall Street. Thus, rather than believe they had taken on more risk, bankers believed they had "mastered risk" by offsetting risky assets through hedges. In effect, the "value at risk" was thought—wrongly—to be zero. Despite the continued relation to gambling, finance is less about taking risk than about having conquered it through the powers of calculation.

With insurance as a precautionary tool, the risks of life can be brought under control, quantified, and financialized through calculative techniques. Insurance objectivizes events as risks, making "what was previously an obstacle into a possibility. Insurance assigns a new mode of existence to previously dreaded events" (Ewald 1991, 200). Insurance has grown in both public areas of life (e.g., Social Security, universal medical care) and the private domain (e.g. health, life, property, tort liability). The former has meant both the spreading of risk among the population to address social problems (e.g., unemployment, poverty), while the latter attempts to make individuals more accountable for themselves (Baker and Simon 2002). In the context of economic development, insurance is often offered as a tool for the poor who are seen as particularly vulnerable or "least able to cope with risk and shocks" (Dercon 2005, 2). These shocks must be dealt with through "income smoothing" or "consumption smoothing" mechanisms. Insurance policies—as well as credit—are seen as ways, or "risk-coping strategies," to address gaps in income and consequent effects on consumption (ibid., 12). The popularization of life insurance emerges from this tension between the social and individual accountability for various risks.

INSURING LIFE

While there are various forms of insurance that protect against "unpleasant contingencies," *life* insurance raises a particularly critical set of issues in raising questions of life and death (Ranade and Ahuja 1999, 203). Life insurance protects a household from the premature or untimely death of its income-earning member, most often the male head of household. The emergence of life insurance with that of capitalism marks "a new and unregulated form of property: property in the very fabric of human life" (Clark 1999, 60). Significantly, it was modern life insurance, "using the actuarial tables of average life expectancy and the likely career trajectory and wage income of a person in a given occupation" (Pietz 1997, 107), that was best able to articulate this monetary compensation for human life from a capitalist perspective and the normalization of the wage earner. Insurance became a particularly capitalist form of mediating and valuing death, as ideas about property and responsibility changed.

The expansion of life insurance to popular classes was also a key component in the expansion of capitalism. Daniel Defert argues that "popular" life insurance originates in mutual societies that provided support for workers. Under political suspicion, both employers and insurance companies attacked this form of mutualism as precursor to socialism. Contemporary insurance emerges from the "demutualization of [the] workers' movement" and the success of "employers' philanthropic paternalism" and "financiers' insurance companies" (Defert 1991, 227–228). The growth of popular life insurance marks the expansion of capitalism and moves away from mutual societies, providing greater social support, but it also marks the early stages of financialization of welfare as insurance companies replaced more socialized forms of support (Kar 2017a).

The growth and acceptance of life insurance, however, is not a straightforward march of capitalism. Viviana Zelizer (1978, 1979) has written of the emergence and acceptance of life insurance in the United States in the nineteenth century. These new institutions "were primarily concerned with death as a major financial episode. Their business was to make people plan and discuss death in monetary terms" (Zelizer 1978, 594). Yet such commercialization of human life was not readily accepted. The growth of life insurance required what Zelizer explains is the ritualization of life insurance. Life did not become profane; rather, insurance became sacred—part and parcel with a "good death" (ibid., 603). With increasing urbanization in the nineteenth century, women and children became increasingly dependent on the husband/father's role as wage earner, who was now also responsible for providing for his family in case of his death. Providing for one's family through financial investment in insurance became a measure of a "good death" in an increasingly nuclearized family, where "a man was judged posthumously by his financial foresight as much as by his spiritual qualities" (ibid.). Significantly, moving away from risk analysis alone, the acceptance of life insurance requires changes in the cultural understanding of death. Beyond the statistical and mathematical modeling of actuarial sciences, what is being assessed and protected through life insurance is subject to "moral and ethical evaluation" of life and value (Maurer 2005b, 152).

Given the importance of local cultural understanding of life and death in insurance and the origins of life insurance in the West, how, as Cheris Sun-ching Chan asks, "can this business be globalized and expanded to places with different cultural traditions?" (2009, 276). Across cultural contexts, social and kin networks, as well as mutual associations and government programs, have traditionally provided support in case of death of a head of household or primary income earner. As they do with credit, however, commercial financial institutions increasingly provide such services from within the market to the poor through life insurance policies.[3] In short, while life insurance marks the deepening of financial rationality through actuarial abstraction, it is simultaneously always already marked by existing social and cultural ideas of life and value.

LIFE INSURANCE IN INDIA

The history of insurance in India marks similar tensions between the expansion of finance capital and paternalistic protectionism, of risk aversion and the embrace of risk. The modern system of insurance in India originated in the nineteenth century under British colonial rule, with the Oriental Life Insurance Company set up in 1818, the Bombay Assurance Company in 1823, and the Madras Equitable Life Insurance Society in 1829. While operating in India, these companies insured only European lives. Once they did start insuring Indians, they were usually charged extra premiums of 20 percent or more (Sinha 2002). It was only in 1871 that the Bombay Mutual Life Assurance Society began offering "fair value" policies to Indians. By 1938, there were 176 insurance companies operating in India. The Indian Life Assurance Companies Act was the first statutory measure to regulate the life insurance sector in 1912, followed by a series of acts through to independence in 1947 (IRDA 2007).

In 1956, the insurance sector in India was nationalized by Finance Minister S. D. Deshmukh under the Life Insurance Corporation Act of India, bringing together two hundred or so individual insurance companies. Similar to bank nationalization, which actually came later, life insurance was brought under government control under the premise that private insurance could not extend sufficient benefits to the poor, particularly in rural areas (Sinha 2002). Insurance premiums to the state-owned insurance behemoth LIC were also supposed to provide the government greater access to private savings and investment funds for state-led development projects.

Unlike banking, insurance was not immediately liberalized in 1991. It was only in 1999, following a series of reports from government commissions, that the Insurance Regulatory Act opened the insurance market to the private sector, including foreign partnerships. Changing social and demographic norms in India, such as the decrease in joint families, which traditionally provided financial support after the death of a family member, as well as an increasingly aging population, have shaped the growth of life insurance in India (Ranade and Ahuja 1999). Insurance has also been brought into the ambit of the government's financial inclusion policies. In 2005, IRDA announced the Obligation of Insurers to Rural or Social Sectors, requiring insurance companies to increase outreach to rural areas and underserved populations.[4]

In discussing life insurance policies with borrowers, microfinance loan officers were often uncomfortable talking about what it was insuring against: death. They often chose to say, "If something happens" (*kichu hole*) rather than "in case of death" when explaining life insurance. *Bima* was the commonly used Bengali term borrowers and MFI staff used to refer to the insurance product. Stemming from Persian, *bima* broadly refers to "insurance against risk" and is not particular to death (Steingass 2005, 29). In China, Chan (2009) found that insurance was referred to as "money management" rather than "risk management" as a way of evading the taboo subject of sudden death by formulating life insurance as an investment. Likewise, in India, insurance companies often refer to insurance as *suraksha*, a Sanskrit word meaning "security" or "protection." Rather than refer to the event of death— even coded as life—Indian life insurance tends to be focused on notions of protection and security.

COLLATERALIZING LIFE

Credit and insurance have long been associated with each other: As credit networks became crucial to English commercial society in the eighteenth century, life insurance became a collateralizing device that "helped to lessen the costs of credit by reducing the risks of lending, thereby attracting more capital into the financial marketplace" (Clark 1999, 9). From its early uses, insurance became a way to collateralize loans. This intertwining of credit and insurance is not unusual in contemporary credit practices, including insurance sold for credit cards and mortgages.[5]

The lack of material collateral in providing credit to the poor has been one of the primary rationales for having microfinance as an alternative. In place of material capital, social capital through the use of JLGs was supposed to provide adequate assurance to lenders that they would be able to recuperate their capital in the case of a default. Nevertheless, a growing number of MFIs, including DENA, have moved from the JLGs to the individual liability method (ILM), in which the individual is liable for repaying the loan, but the group structure is retained as a way of reducing the transaction costs of lending to the poor (Giné and Karlan 2014). Under ILM, the group is no longer responsible for paying back the loan of the individual. Although the default of one borrower can have negative consequences for the perceived creditability of the group for subsequent loans, the group is not contractually obliged to pay back the loan of the defaulting borrower. Moreover, there is increasing evidence from studies of microfinance that it is not always social capital from the group (whether pressure or support) that induces people to pay back but the incentive of future loans that ensures people continue to maintain a good credit history (Bond and Rai 2009; Sadoulet 2005). The argument is that it is the "non-refinancing threats" on the part of MFIs that induce borrowers, expecting future loans, to repay (Armendáriz and Morduch 2000, 403).

In my own fieldwork, loan officers repeatedly pointed to this aspect, particularly as the crisis tightened their ability to offer larger subsequent loans. For example, one morning as I arrived at the branch office, Anand, the branch manager, was explaining to his staff that he had just received a message from the head office that they would have to stop disbursals of all new loans due to the lack of liquidity. This meant that not only would they not be able to take on new borrowers but also existing borrowers would not be able to get new loans.[6] Throughout the rest of the day, as we made the rounds to the group meetings, whenever the borrowers asked about new loans, Anand told them it was a new policy. On occasion, when the women challenged him, saying he was just saying that without sufficient reason or that he was misleading them, he pulled out his mobile phone, reading aloud the English text message from the head office: "Stop all disbursals until further notice."

Exhausted from this repeated conversation, on our way back to the office, Anand said, "This is the problem with no new loans; there will be no 'motivation' [for the women to repay]. This is going to ruin the groups." Along with peer pressure, high rates of loan recovery required that women believe they would get future loans. If they no longer believed that the MFI would provide loans in the future, they would not be motivated to repay their current loan. In other words, with the shift to the ILM, social capital is no longer the primary substitute for material capital in lending to the poor. Yet the MFI cannot lend without some kind of risk management strategy. If social capital is no longer the basis of collateral in microfinance, what then *is* being collateralized that enables MFIs to continue to take the risk of lending to poor borrowers?

Life insurance enables people to both reduce and embrace risk. The life insurance policies that microfinance borrowers take out (often without an option to do otherwise) enable MFIs to continue to lend to individuals—to take the added risk of lending to the poor— while simultaneously offsetting this risk through insurance. Insurance is about a certain understanding of temporality: of relations between the past and present to the future. Intertwined with risk analysis, insurance practices also lead to what Anthony Giddens terms the "colonization of the future," or the way in which the future "becomes a new terrain—a territory of counterfactual possibility" (1991, 111). Insurance comes to give new meaning to people's lived present, as death looms in the near future—the one-year term of the loan.

Life and death then become part of the calculation of risk in microfinance. Pregnant women are not given new loans by DENA (though they are required to continue to repay existing ones) because of the perceived higher mortality risks of pregnant women (Kar 2017c). Responding to my question about the need for "age proof" documents, a loan officer explained: "We only give loans to women from the ages of twenty to fifty." "Why?" I inquired. "Well, there's the usual, you know, people get sick or can't attend meetings, and . . . ," he trailed off. The unsaid here was that older women would have higher mortality rates. Ironically, death was often left unsaid in discussions about life insurance. As Anand, going over the details of life insurance to a group stated, "If you or your guarantor, the person in your joint photo, dies— and we don't like to think of these things—then you don't have to pay off the loan."

Without being spoken of or by referring to it as "something," life insurance constantly signals the possibility of death, suffering, and loss in the near future. Geeta Patel describes the purchase of insurance as the "desire for care, hope for change and intimacy through loss" (2007, 110). In other words, it is only through loss—whether of a person, of health, of property—that one can access insurance and gain benefits. Similarly, for Ewald, "what is insured is not the injury that is actually lived, suffered and resented by the person, but a capital against whose loss the insurer offers a guarantee" (1991, 204). In this formulation, the loss itself cannot be compensated; it cannot be transformed into a financial value. However, following Ewald, insurance can be understood as being about managing the risk of something else to start with: capital itself. What matters is not the loss of life (or health) but the capital that is seen to be inherent to the healthy, laboring body.

To return to an earlier question, what is it that is being collateralized when life insurance is taken as part of credit? It is the capital possibilities of the living, laboring borrower. For poor borrowers who do not have material collateral, it is the possibility that one can always work to pay off a loan *as long as one is alive* that enables MFIs and banks to take the risk of lending without material collateral. However, I would like to take one step back. In positing life insurance as collateral for microfinance borrowers, I examine the idea of collateral itself.

The basic definition of collateral is property or assets that a debtor puts up to secure a loan. In the case of default, the creditor can seize the collateral in its place. Collateral addresses the risk of a market exchange that occurs over a period of time. As Annelise Riles points out, in the duration of this exchange the fates of the two parties—the creditor and debtor— "are intermingled. Their fortunes influence one another, and their actions have consequences for one another" (2011, 163). Thus, a lender is concerned about the well-being of the borrower insofar as she can repay the loan—the risk that the lender has taken to make a return on interest. Collateral becomes a tool for "foreclosing those uncertainties, those risks. Collateral is a tool for *placing limits* on those mutual entanglements" (ibid., 164; emphasis in original). In other words, posting collateral becomes a way of ensuring a return of some sort to the lender even if the borrower defaults on the loan. Yet given the temporal dimensions, ownership of the collateral is not clearly defined: "Collateral is a kind of temporally delineated commons. . . . In the near future—that is, for a set period of time in the future delineated by the time when the debt is to be repaid—there are two hands on the baton" (165). Nevertheless, it is the creditor, not the debtor, who is in a more powerful situation in this relationship, for the debtor cannot escape the debt obligation without paying at least the collateral. Given this analytical framework for understanding collateral, what are the consequences for using life insurance as de facto collateral?

Following Ewald and Patel, I have argued that what life insurance compensates is not the injury or loss but the circulating capital value of the loan. When microfinance borrowers buy life insurance as part of the loan, there is no compensation for the experience of loss itself. What then is it that it insures? Primarily, it is the recovery of the loan by the creditor. Life insurance comes to stand in as the capital that the borrower has "posted" in the absence of material collateral. Thus, following Riles, for the duration of the loan, both the MFI and the borrower are invested in the collateralizing device: the life insurance. Such comingling of interests on the collateral can have complicated outcomes—discussed in the following vignette—as borrowers and lenders manage the uncertainties of the present and future.

The group met in Jaya's modest one-bedroom apartment. The meeting was in the bedroom, though by the time everyone arrived, the group had spilled into the hallway. Spread out on the bed were numerous notebooks with the name of a private school. "My son's just been admitted," said Jaya, indicating the pile of books. As we waited for the other women to arrive, she asked Anand if DENA offered any educational loans. "We've just enrolled our son in school, and it's been an expense," she said, explaining her need for a loan. As we were waiting, Jaya brought out her passbook as well as that of her sister, who also belonged to the group. "Why isn't she here?" demanded Anand. "Her husband is very sick. He has cancer," replied Jaya. "There isn't anyone else, and she has to look after him. He hasn't been able to eat anything recently . . . ," she trailed off. "Have they known for long?" asked Anand, picking up the passbook and opening it to the photo. "This is him, right?" Jaya nodded, "They've known for about two years and he's been getting worse. It's been very expensive." Anand held the book up for me to see the joint photo of the woman and her cancer-stricken husband before making a quick note in his book.

The moment marked the reality that loans from microfinance are not typically for building or expanding business. Both sisters needed their loans for other everyday necessities: education and health care. While Anand was sympathetic, his quick movement from learning about Jaya's brother-in-law's condition to picking up the passbook marked the way in which he immediately recognized the connection between the illness and its effect on the borrower's loan. As the loan's guarantor, Jaya's brother-in-law was covered by life insurance. Nevertheless, because he was the primary income earner, his illness could affect the loan recovery. Financial technologies, such as insurance, work to mitigate future risks. This emphasis on hedging future risks can render the future more certain than the present. Given this "colonization of the future" (Giddens 1991, 111) through risk assessment, how do we contend with the uncertainty of the present? For a collateralized life, the implications of an unhealthy body are highly problematic. In making this observation, I do not suggest that the MFI staff with whom

I worked ever preferred the death of borrowers or their guarantors. However, the financial preemption of risk through life insurance can complicate the relationship between a costly life and an insured death.

NARRATIVES OF SUICIDE

As noted previously, SERP, a service-delivery organization under the Department of Rural Development, Government of Andhra Pradesh, prepared a report on alleged harassment of microfinance borrowers in October 2010.[7] Of the 123 documented cases of harassment, there were fifty-four microfinance-related suicides. Suicide and attempted suicide noted in this report included cases in which defaulting borrowers had their possessions confiscated and houses locked by MFI staff, as well as a borrower encouraged by loan officers to go into prostitution to repay the loan and a case of harassment that triggered domestic violence.[8] Though the media, politicians, and regulators focused on the Andhra Pradesh crisis and related suicides,[9] I found over the course of fieldwork that microfinance-related suicide was also prevalent, if less visible, in Kolkata. As one borrower, interrupting an MFI staff member's recounting of the Andhra Pradesh case observed, "There are suicides here as well," going on to recount the case where the husband of a borrower had recently drunk poison. Narratives of suicide abounded during my fieldwork.

We were headed to a group meeting in the north of the city, near Clive House, once the residence of Lord Clive, the British officer who defeated Siraj ud-Daulah, the last nawab (prince/governor) of Bengal in the Battle of Plassey in 1757. Like Clive House, which had become a makeshift shelter for Bangladeshi refugees, many of the houses in the area were old and crumbling. It was early and the first meeting of the day, though there were a large number of absentees from the group. Displeased with the turnout, Putul demanded to know where everyone was. "It's the older members who don't come," said one woman. "You know, mostly people that Shilpa-*Didi* had brought in," she added. I noted some tension in the group at the mention of Shilpa, but I thought it was a not an uncommon situation where members did not get along. Later that day, as Putul and I were walking back from a house verification, I asked her why there were so many problems with the earlier group. Putul responded:

> You know they mentioned Shilpa-*Didi*? Well, the meeting used to be at her place, and she had started the group. But she always had problems paying back the loan—her husband didn't work, and she had a number of loans. She had brought people in, but a lot of times, money would go missing, and it was usually attributed to Shilpa-*Didi*. She committed suicide [*suicide koreche*] recently. Of course, her loan was covered by the insurance, so they didn't have to pay the rest of it off, but there are the others that she brought into the group who sometimes don't turn up or pay. So we're waiting for them to finish this loan cycle—they probably won't get another loan. We're going to try to move the center away from here—maybe to the house where the woman we just visited lives. She's said she has some more women in her neighborhood who want to borrow, so they can start another group and we'll disband the older one.

I asked why Shilpa had committed suicide and whether it because she was under pressure from all the loans. "Her husband didn't work, and they had problems," answered Putul.

Recovering the subaltern voice of the suicidal figure always remains fractured, and partial (Spivak 1988).[10] That is, Shilpa's suicide, like many of the other microfinance-related suicides, is read into the existing social and cultural narratives of death and suicide. In the South Asian context, suicide is incorporated into hegemonic local understandings of sacrifice, honor, and shame. Recognizing the impossibility of retrieving the subaltern voice of women who have taken their own lives, I do not attempt to disentangle in my analysis *why* particular individuals committed suicide. Each case is tragic, and without sufficient information on each of the women, such explications would not do justice to the individual lives. Rather, I focus on the narratives of these suicides as they circulate among borrowers and MFI staff.

In his classic study of suicide, Émile Durkheim (2006) argues that there are social causes for suicide, identifying them as egoistic, altruistic, anomic, and fatalistic.[11] While Durkheim's analysis shows why individuals commit suicide given certain social conditions (e.g., the cause), I am interested in how the discourse of suicide circulates and its social productivity (see Chua 2014). In other words, I am interested in understanding what James Staples argues are the "cultural contexts in which suicide becomes a meaningful act" (2012a, 20) and how the suicidal figure is read through the discourses of debt by members of the community.

The MFI staff suspected that Shilpa had taken a "syndicate loan," having others borrow on her behalf. In a syndicate loan, the primary borrower would still be servicing all of the loans simultaneously. Thus, one person could end up with Rs 40,000 loan if she and three other borrowers got even Rs 10,000 (on the low end) each. This means that at a 12.5 percent flat interest rate, the syndicate borrower must pay Rs 1,000 every week to service four loans (i.e., Rs 250 per loan) or Rs 4,000 every month—a significant debt burden for borrowers whose monthly income may be about Rs 10,000–15,000. By mentioning the syndicate loan, Putul revealed the way in which burdensome debt had to be acknowledged in Shilpa's death. Yet when asked about whether the debt was the reason for the suicide, Putul attributed it to other reasons: Shilpa's husband's unemployment and marital arguments.[12] For MFI staff and other borrowers trying to make sense of the suicide, debt, unemployment, and marital problems are entangled. While the mounting loans are one part of the puzzle, they cannot be read apart from the multiple points of undoing in a borrower's life.

The SERP report also included the case of Manjula, who had a loan of Rs 16,000, which caused marital discord with her husband over repayment. Faced with "unbearable harassment," Manjula committed suicide, though the case was treated as domestic violence. As in the case of Shilpa, Manjula's suicide was "embedded in a set of intimacies" (Garcia 2010, 152). That is, it was read not simply in terms of the individualized financial burden of the loan but also in the ways in which debt animates various points of social life and breakdown, whether through institutional or peer pressure or through domestic violence.

FAILURE AND THE MORALITY OF DEBT

There had been a suicide in the idyllically named Picnic Garden neighborhood of Kolkata. News of the death had traveled to the group meeting I was attending at the eastern edge of the city. One of the group members had heard the news through another MFI. After the meeting, I asked Anand if he knew of this case. He nodded, "Yes, she had a loan from DENA as well." In addition to having loans from multiple MFIs, she had a syndicate loan, with five people taking loans on her behalf. A few weeks later, her story reappeared at another meeting. One of the group members had loaned her Rs 3,000. "She said she was going to buy an ambulance. But just the next day she went and tied a rope around her neck [*Golaye dori badlo*]." Her blunt manner of recounting the story surprised me; her sympathy was tempered by the fact that she would not recover the personal loan she had made. The Picnic Garden suicide did not make the news, a fact unsurprising for a poor woman from the slums. But I was struck by the matter-of-fact way that her death—and the microfinance suicide cases in general—was discussed among other borrowers and MFI staff.

Even though the microfinance-related suicides were tied to various social factors of women's lives, blame for being unable to cope with the burden of the debt was often placed squarely backs on the borrowers themselves. Dinesh, a loan officer, explained:

> The AP [Andhra Pradesh] crisis and suicides happened because people took loans larger than their capacity. The fault is with those who take and not those who give. The situation now is that if we don't give loans, people will commit suicide instead. The motivation for suicide is that people took loans for two *lakhs* [200,000]. They don't have the capacity to repay, and so they commit suicide. If you can't utilize the money, then you have to commit suicide. It is the fault of the taker.

The reason for borrowers committing suicide is recast as one of individual responsibility. The moral of this narrative is that one should take only what one can pay back. Dinesh's frankness in saying "they don't have the capacity to repay, and so they commit suicide" was jarring. What is striking about his commentary is that the reasoning is also turned back on itself: people will commit suicide for *not* getting a loan, so MFIs cannot simply roll back on lending. Yet if there is little questioning of why borrowers were given these loans in the first place, there is even less concern about why the women needed loans beyond their capacity or that capacity could change due to unforeseen events such as illness or accident. To borrow beyond what you can repay is the fault of the borrower, just as the obligation to return is an absolute.

Until 2014, when the government moved to decriminalize it, attempted suicide was considered a criminal offense under the Indian Penal Code, Section 309, with a possible prison sentence of up to a year. Abetment of suicide (Section 306 of the Indian Penal Code) is also considered a criminal offense, with a possible prison term of up to ten years. Abetment here means not just directly aiding someone in the act of suicide but in causing a person to be suicidal.[13] To the extent that abetment of suicide can be considered a criminal offense, MFI staff members who may have harassed borrowers for repayment can also be considered liable. Because of the legal implications, there is a concerted effort on the part of MFI staff not to be implicated in abetting borrower suicides. Doing so can involve, as Dinesh does, shifting the entirety of the blame for the failure to the borrower rather than assuming any responsibility for the death.

In popular representations, the failures of microfinance are often glossed over in favor of the successful entrepreneurs who pull themselves out of poverty. In India, the neoliberal promise of a consumerist future is repeatedly made unattainable to millions of people living in enduring conditions of poverty. Failure in such conditions has made suicide thinkable: "a possible and appropriate response to being shamed, a means of communication when other means had failed, and a release from an otherwise intractable status quo" (Staples 2012b, 141–142). As Julie Livingston writes of suicide in Botswana, what is at stake in that economy with new forms of investment, risk, and self-determination is the "loneliness and rage . . . when such strategies fail" (2009, 654). Or, as Julia Elyachar (2005b, 211) observes in Cairo, every failure of empowerment debt reinforces the legitimacy of the market while placing the blame squarely on individuals. Insistence on debt repayment is constructed as a moral rather than an economic argument (Graeber 2011a; Peebles 2010). The morality of monetary debt repayment is absolute; the burden of failure is transferred to the debtor, who must repay regardless of its costs on her quality of life, regardless of whether the loan may cost the borrower her life. In this celebration of the market and condemnation of failed entrepreneurs emerges a new form of loneliness and marginality. While life insurance can extricate MFIs from the financial burden of this failure, it also turns inward to the individual who has put her life up as collateral rather than locate problems in the wider social structures.

THE CASE OF FARMER SUICIDES

Farmer suicides, particularly in the states of Andhra Pradesh, Karnataka, Kerala, and Maharashtra, have received widespread attention. Since 1997, an estimated two hundred thousand farmers have killed themselves, and in December 2011 the National Human Rights Commission of India demanded reports from three of the states on the issue.[14] While farmer suicides in India continue to grab headlines, a BBC report found that in 2014, the suicide rate of housewives in India was more than twice that of farmers, with limited attention to their cause (Biswas 2016). This is not to say that farmer suicides are not an important problem; rather, I want to explore why farmer suicides in particular get politicized over other everyday forms of suffering.

Indebtedness due to the cost of seeds and fertilizers has been the leading cause of farmer suicides, particularly in years of bad harvests.[15] In 2008, the United Progressive Alliance (UPA) government announced the Rs 600 billion Agricultural Debt Waiver and Debt Relief Scheme through Finance Minister P. Chidambaram's budget speech (2008; RBI 2008). The scheme would waive all loans overdue as of December 31, 2007, that remained unpaid for marginal farmers (holding up to one hectare of land) and provide a one-time settlement through a rebate for other farmers. By signing the debt waiver or debt relief, farmers would be eligible for fresh agricultural loans. Conservative critics of the scheme argued that this populist measure would ruin the "credit culture" of farmers by forgiving loans (Anup Roy 2012). Although the program has not been renewed in subsequent budgets, these critics argue that the expectation of future waivers reduces the incentive for loan repayment among small farmers. Other critics have noted that the scheme fails to address the indebtedness of poor farmers who had borrowed from moneylenders and not from the formal banking sector, which is overseeing the waiver.

The extent to which farmer suicides have become a hot-button political issue was reflected in the 2010 release of *Peepli Live*. Directed by first-time director Anusha Rizvi and produced by Bollywood superstar Aamir Khan, *Peepli Live* is a dark comedy about farmer suicides and government and media response to it. The film opened over Independence Day weekend in August to critical acclaim and box office success, grossing around Rs 402 million—a significant feat for a small-budget movie with a largely unknown cast. Additionally, there was a special screening for Prime Minister Manmohan Singh and other members of Parliament to raise awareness about farmer suicides.

Yet one of the ironies is that while it was hailed as a film about farmer suicides, there is no suicide in *Peepli Live*, although there are two deaths. The film is set in the village of Peepli in a fictional northern state. Two brothers, who are facing the loss of their farmland to the bank, come up with the plan for Natha—the younger and easily manipulated brother—to commit suicide to access government support for families of farmers who have killed themselves. When word of this plan gets out via a local reporter, Natha becomes the center of a political and media firestorm.

Throughout the film there is a silent figure that constantly appears in the background: a landless farmer, laboring away on backbreaking work. As the elite, urban media reporters focus on whether or not Natha will commit suicide, Rakesh Kapoor, the young local reporter who first broke the news about Natha, starts to notice the landless farmer. Eventually, Rakesh learns that the silent farmer has died of starvation and overwork. The second death is that of Rakesh, who disillusioned but still in pursuit of the suicide story, ends up in the barn where Natha is hiding from politicians and the media. Rakesh is killed in an accidental fire in the barn, but confusion over the body leads to the assumption that it is Natha who is killed. Natha escapes to the city, believing that his family can now claim compensation for his supposed death. This too falls apart, as the accidental nature of the fire means that it was not suicide; therefore, his family is not eligible for relief. In the end, we see Natha working in a major city as a construction worker; he is another dispossessed farmer who must labor silently.

What the satire points out is that despite the media hoopla over the planned suicide, it is the ongoing silent suffering that goes by unnoticed. The film gestures at this issue through the deaths of the already landless farmer and the reporter who tries to tell this story. Nevertheless, what is remarkable is perhaps that life imitates art. In its reception, the story of the landless farmer is almost erased, despite his presence throughout the film. In its reviews, *Peepli Live* is considered a story about Natha and farmer suicides. The structural parallels between the dispossessed landless farmer and Natha's final transformation into a dispossessed landless farmer in the city is a powerful critique of contemporary India. Moreover, the political focus on farmer suicides has tended to underestimate its prevalence in urban areas, which have encountered liberalization with the downsizing of the public-sector workforce (Parry 2012). Yet the "horror" (Asad 2007, 81) that the suicidal event evokes renders invisible the much more mundane forms of existence that can make life unlivable.[16] Political and media attention on suicide alone—whether of farmers or MFI borrowers—transforms the everyday deaths at the margins matter of fact, not something that must also be attended to.

TEMPORAL DISJUNCTURES
OF PRECARIOUS LABOR

On our way to the group meeting, Mukul, Tania, and I passed a Sitala temple. Sitting atop a donkey, the goddess of smallpox, carrying healing objects in each of her four arms, is popular in the slums of Kolkata. She is primarily worshipped by the urban poor, who suffer most from the infectious diseases that plague the city.[17] The numerous Sitala-*mandirs* (temples/altars) is telling of the everyday insecurities that confront the slum neighborhoods. When we arrived at the meeting center, Panchali, another of the loan officers, was already present. As we sat down, some of the members started whispering to Mukul that one of the members had received a loan from another MFI. As the meeting commenced, it became apparent why this was a problem: the same member, Ruma, had refused to repay her loan to DENA.

Ruma—introduced in Chapter 3—had been a borrower for three years. She had never had a problem before but had recently become unable to repay her loan of Rs 22,000. Her financial situation had changed when her husband had to retire from his job. With only one of her two sons employed, making just Rs 500 per week, she maintained that she could afford to repay only Rs 1,000 per month, or less than half of what she was supposed to pay. The DENA staff wanted the other members of the group to cover Ruma's weekly payment, and she would owe the members the monthly payment. In effect, they wanted the group to refinance Ruma's loan. However, Ruma would become heavily indebted to other borrowers, and the other members were unwilling to take the risk. They pointed to the rumors that Ruma had a new loan from another MFI to argue that she had enough money to pay off her existing loan. Other than explaining what she could pay, Ruma remained largely silent.

The meeting ran well past its set time, and still there was no resolution to the issue. But the DENA staff had come prepared for this very situation. Mukul instructed Panchali to stay with the group until they resolved the issue, and nobody would be let off until then. Many of the women complained about this situation, with children needing to be picked up from school or food to be cooked or taken off the stove. On our way back from the next meeting, which was nearby, Mukul checked back in on the meeting with Ruma, and the women were finally allowed to leave. "We just needed to put some pressure on her," explained Mukul about the whole event. "We got news that she got a loan from Bandhan and that she's paying back at other places. The others told us to put some pressure on her. She can pay; she's just trying not to."

The loss of her husband's income, one son's uncertain income, and another's unemployment marked the realities of Ruma's life. Trying to disentangle the real story of whether Ruma was trying to not pay her loan to DENA is not my goal in recounting this encounter. Rather, it is to point to the set of choices individuals have to make when there is a constant lack of money. The loan from the other MFI was seen as a possible source for repaying the DENA loan; yet to use that loan to pay off the one from DENA would only mark the way in which borrowers became trapped in debt cycles: borrowing from one lender to pay off another. Ruma's silence as she encountered the anger of the group members and the MFI staff pointed to a dilemma: How do you pay off debts when you have no money? Moreover, her position pointed to the temporal disjunctures between the regularized repayment of loans and the everyday realities of existence in the informal economy where income is often irregular, with little to put aside for sudden fluctuations in expenses.

In response to my questions about monthly and weekly repayments, one of the repeated complaints of borrowers was that it did not reflect their income flows. In particular, borrowers distinguished between those who depended on monthly salaries and those who had businesses or daily wages, with income that was more spread out but also at times more uncertain. For borrowers with monthly incomes, securing weekly payment meant putting aside enough money to ensure repayment every week, even when money became tight at the end of the month. For borrowers with small businesses, while income flows were more regular throughout the month, periods of bad business could severely affect the ability to repay the weekly loans. As one borrower explained the condition of repaying weekly loans, if she invested the loan in something, it would take a while to recover her investment, making it difficult to pay back the loan every week. With the current situation, she explained, the next week's payment comes up as soon as one week is paid up. "It is like we are just taking and giving [*nichi ar dichi*]." The experience of the loans is less of stability than of constant circulation.

When I asked another borrower, Payal, about her experience with microfinance loans, she explained:

> We are able to increase business. We are poor people, and nobody else will give us the money. So we are able to get loans from here. We aren't wasting [*khachina*] the money; we are using it to increase business. If we had larger

loans, we would be able to increase business more. Weekly payments are good because there's no money at the end of the month.

Payal's comments mark the many ambiguities and ironies of microfinance and its form of regularized repayment among poor borrowers. The loan offers the opportunity to increase business, yet loans do not seem to fundamentally change the problem of the shortage of money at the end of the month.

Loan repayments also change people's engagement with temporality. In his study of industrialization in England, E. P. Thompson traces how the development of the clock, the "small instrument which regulated the new rhythms of industrial life was at the same time one of the more urgent needs which industrial capitalism called forth to energize its advance" (1967, 69). Timekeeping technologies, therefore, not only regulated and discipline wage labor but also helped shape the moral and cultural sensibilities surrounding time. Recent anthropological and sociological work on finance and contemporary economic practices has similarly shown how conceptions of temporality are shaped by financial technologies and conceptions of the market (e.g., Knorr Cetina 2005; Miyazaki 2003; Zaloom 2006). For borrowers who must now constantly negotiate weekly payments, there is a heightened experience of the relation between time and money. Yet new forms of temporal regulation are often at odds with the realities of working in the informal economy. With the regularized repayment of microfinance loans, timely repayment constantly meets untimely expenses.

The need to repay can also have physical manifestations: borrowers often described the weekly repayments as "headaches" (*matha batha*). While *matha batha* can colloquially mean a "hassle," it still marks the way in which repayment produces a constant state of anxiety. Others said that they experience "tension" in making sure that they had enough money to repay the loans. The English term "tension" has gained popularity in India, signifying stress and anxiety.[18] There are often there are real physical consequences for such forms of stress—what Clara Han in her ethnography of debt in Chile explains is "neoliberal depression" (2012, 129). Being able to repay is a constant source of worry and anxiety as the need to maintain creditworthiness becomes increasingly important in being able to make ends meet.

Good borrowers are those who do not simply use up their loans—even in times of need—but invest them to create more wealth in the future. Payal's comments also emphasize the fact that they did not "waste" (*khachina*) the money but put it to use to increase their business. The term Payal used was *taka ta khachina*, which translates literally as "we don't eat the money." Other borrowers also commented that the loans did not go to their stomachs (*pete porena*); in other words, they did not consume the loans. It is the possibilities of a future loan that matters, not the present hunger, illness, or obligations. In an era of finance capital, the quest to constantly circulate money means that borrowers are expected to "invest" and not "use" money, even if it means going hungry or being unable to pay a doctor's bill. There is always the promise that invested wealth will return profits to the borrower.

Such language of not wasting or using the loan for consumption purposes highlights the ways in which microfinance requires the circulation of money, the ways in which exchange rather than use value of money is deemed central to its success. By and large, microfinance loans are meant to be for production rather than consumption purposes, despite the overwhelming need to make ends meet through loans.[19] As production loans, they are meant to enable borrowers to start or enhance a business. Consumption loans, on the other hand, are meant to be used without the expectation that they will create returns in the form of profits. The productive and consumptive uses of loans align with Marx's (1978) definition of use value and exchange value: while the consumption loan is meant to be used up, the productive loan is meant to be used only insofar as it creates more capital. Where money is most needed to pay for everyday needs, capital is increasingly extracted through financialized loans to be circulated in the global financial system.

THE COST OF LIVING

Parul wanted the meeting to end quickly. She had to rush out right after the meeting to pick up her children from school. We were in her apartment talking about microfinance—what she liked, didn't like. "Do you like the weekly repayments?" I asked. I had repeatedly come across debates over whether monthly or weekly repayments would be better for borrowers. "Weekly is better," replied Parul. "With monthly, you would have to put money aside to make a large payment at the end of the month. But what would happen if the children get sick? Of course, I would use that money to pay to see the doctor. So it's better to pay every week."

Parul's comments reflected the multiple claims on money that has been saved or kept at home. They highlight the choices that borrowers have to make every day when money is scarce: Do you pay for a doctor's bill? Or do you repay the loan so you can maintain access to credit in the future for other necessary expenses? The answers to these questions are rarely about economically deterministic rational choice but about confronting "ordinary ethics" (Lambek 2010) in everyday life.[20] For many of the borrowers I interviewed, microfinance loans helped structure the practices of care and providing for family members (see Han 2012).

At the end of a meeting, one woman hung back to ask Anand a question regarding loan repayments. "What happens," she wanted to know, "if the borrower and guarantor are both sick? How can they pay back? Or what about if the income earner is sick, then the other person has to take care of him?" Her series of questions reflected the fact that there are few contingency plans for when illness strikes a family, particularly an income earner. Yet, as the borrower asks, illness is not just about the individual but about the family members—particularly in the absence of affordable health-care facilities—who must attend to the patient. Anand replied that that was a great question, but they did not have anything like that at DENA. After the meeting, however, he and the loan officer laughingly discussed the impossibility of letting people off for illness, saying that once they allowed it, people would be coming with ailments all the time. And even if they required a letter from a doctor, it would be easy enough to get one forged in Kolkata, that it would not be a hindrance.

Yet the borrower's question points to a critical issue of managing the costs of living, where seemingly the only certainty is that there are constant expenses. Illness was present throughout my fieldwork: many borrowers or their family members were often sick, creating difficulties in repayment. The constant negotiations between paying for health care and trying to make ends meet could seem highly detached from emotional care. Nevertheless, these "choiceless decisions" (Aretxaga 1997, 60) about caregiving and indebtedness were being shaped by the larger political economy and structural inequalities (Scheper-Hughes 1992).

Consider, for instance, the case of Aruna, her arm wrapped in a blue cast when I encountered her at a group meeting. She had broken her arm recently after falling down. "In two hours they took three thousand rupees!" she exclaimed. It cost about Rs 300 just to see the doctor at the private Ruby Hospital. But her son had recently been injured as well when he had fallen into the public toilet. But with his school exams, she had to take him to school and back in a hired car. As she bemoaned her hard times, Mithun tried to console her by explaining how he liked hard times: "It just means that things can't get worse and good days are ahead!" he said encouragingly. Aruna raised her eyebrows and looked unconvinced.

Health care has been one of the main areas of privatization since the liberalization of the Indian economy in 1991. There have been massive cuts to the public sector for health care, along with privatization of medical care (Berman 1998; Qadeer 2000). While the Supreme Court of India has ruled that private hospitals (in Delhi) built on concessional land have to reserve 10 percent of beds and 25 percent of outpatient services for free treatment to the poor, most private hospitals have continuously failed to do so.[21] Yet, like credit to the poor, health care in India has been identified as an investment opportunity (O'Donohoe, Leijonhufvud, and Saltuk 2010). Similarly, a report on emerging markets from PricewaterhouseCoopers notes:

> Healthcare is one of India's largest sectors, in terms of revenue and employment, and the sector is expanding rapidly. . . . Today the total value of the

sector is more than $34 billion. This translates to $34 per capita, or roughly 6% of GDP. By 2012, India's healthcare sector is projected to grow to nearly $40 billion. The private sector accounts for more than 80% of total healthcare spending in India. Unless there is a decline in the combined federal and state government deficit, which currently stands at roughly 9%, the opportunity for significantly higher public health spending will be limited. (Pate et al. 2007, 1)

In the absence of good public facilities, private hospitals have increasingly emerged, especially in the urban areas, as the only option for the poor to obtain good or immediate access to health care. Loans, including from MFIs, become ways of managing these privatized expenses for those who are often least able to afford it. As more and more people are enfolded into global finance, there is a larger system that relies on ensuring the expansive circulation of capital. The regularity of repayment required for such loans and systemic stability conflicts with the very precariousness of life at the margins.

HAUNTING DEBTS

It was almost a year since Amina had stopped repaying her loan when I encountered her name. I was accompanying Joy, the loan officer, to a group meeting in North Kolkata. Having climbed a series of unlit stairs of an old apartment building, we arrived at the roof where, instead of open space, we found a series of rooms had been added, seemingly ad hoc. Some of the women were late arriving at the meeting, as there had been a disturbance the night before: "a husband-wife issue," as it was explained. The police had been called and they had been making inquiries late into the night, causing delays with the residents' morning schedules.

"There is one OD in this group," said Joy, with the ledger on his lap, as we waited for all the women to arrive. Hearing him mention the outstanding loan, one of the women, Farah, spoke up: "We used to have problems with her [Amina]. She was always late with payments, so we put a lock on her door, so she couldn't go in [to her home] until she paid her loan. After that she ran away. We managed to contact her natal home and got news that she had gone to Bombay. We heard she did this and that she was over there, but then we got the news that she had taken *bish* [poison/pesticide] and died. I still see her two boys around sometimes. . . . I feel bad for them."

"We can't do anything about it," added Joy. "We don't have a death certificate or anything for her. Without the documents [necessary to claim insurance], her loan is still OD." Amina had died indebted; the loan in her name remained on the books as unpaid. A few weeks later, Farah told me that Amina had taken Rs 3,000 from her as a personal loan, which she had also not paid back. Added to the tragedy of Amina's death was the fact that she had not escaped her debts even in death, despite the life insurance on her loan. The precariousness of Amina's life meant that there was no record of her death, no documentation to claim insurance, her final means of paying off her debt.

In this chapter, I have shown how the dilemma of collateral manifests itself with the increasing financialization of microfinance lending. Recent work on risk has shown how excessive risk taking is simultaneously mediated by attempts to hedge or offset this risk. In the case of microfinance, the question of collateral—of managing the risk of lending—has always been an issue. Not only has the concept of social capital standing in for material capital been problematic; MFIs have increasingly moved away from the group lending model toward individual lending as they have "scaled up" their services. In the absence of both material and social capital, life insurance has become the new solution to the problem of collateral. Although financial institutions can try to mitigate these risks, cases such as Amina's show that uncertainty in borrowers' lives can exceed the attempts to financially preempt risk. Without the necessary documents certifying her death, Amina's insured loan remained unpaid; it was a weekly reminder that haunted the accounting books.

When considering what it is that this insurance collateralizes, we increasingly see the laboring body of the poor as central to this formulation. Yet when poor borrowers face the precarity of the present, where wages and indeed health can be subject to sudden changes, the regularity of debt repayments can cause painful disjunctures with lived reality. While the tragic cases of suicide mark moments when this pain becomes unbearable, emphasis on these deaths alone can foreclose the ways of seeing and addressing the conditions that make debt both necessary and unbearable in the informal economy.

I ASKED AMIT, a loan officer, if he thought microfinance helped. He had, after all, joined DENA after learning about and being inspired by Muhammad Yunus and the Grameen Bank. "After I joined, I'm not so sure anymore. It's just a business," he said with a wry smile. "And for the borrowers?" I asked. "Getting loans had become an addiction," Amit replied. Did he think that microfinance was doing anything to help the poor? "Maybe for ten percent; for the rest, it doesn't do anything," he concluded. After working in microfinance for a few years, loan officers like Amit had few expectations that the small loans from DENA had serious developmental impact. If the MFI was "doing well"—as just a business—it was less clear if it was "doing good," as the loans fed into debt cycles of the poor.

In looking at microfinance as a social business, I have tried to unpack what corporatized development looks like. That is, can developmental goals such as social and economic empowerment be fulfilled by the incentivized for-profit sector? From the perspective of loan officers like Amit, there is little scope for social change through for-profit microfinance, when ultimately, it is run as a business with, most important, a financial bottom line. While the culture of entrepreneurship encourages corporations to "do well by doing good" and individuals to raise themselves out of poverty, the state has receded in its responsibility to take the risk of providing real and substantial change.

With MFIs raising capital through commercial debt from banks, as well as through investments, IPOs, and securitization, they increasingly financialize poverty. Banking on the poor, however, is tied to multiple attempts at hedging the risk even while taking new ones. Ultimately, such forms of risk management stabilize forms of inequality and hierarchy through a process of systemic enfolding. Throughout this book, I have shown how financial risk management is constantly at the edges of speculation.

For Amit, the borrowers had developed an addiction to credit; though perhaps it is more accurate to consider the loans a necessity to make ends meet in India's precarious informal economy. Partho, the husband of a borrower, for instance, commented on the dearth of loans for the urban poor: "Banks have housing loans, educational loans, agricultural loans, but nothing really for [poor] people in the city. For us, there are only business loans, and you need to have documents or a mortgage to get those." For the urban poor, there are few options for formal-sector credit other than microfinance. Yet expenses in the city are high. The urban poor increasingly pay for private-sector services—from health to education—that are likewise financialized, drawing more and more capital from the poor into circulation for financial gain rather than for poverty reduction.

Growing more animated, Partho pointed to the ways in which microfinance failed to account for the precariousness of everyday life:

> Also, you are always under pressure to pay back the loan. But sometimes people take loans when things are good, but what happens when there is a problem? I have to travel around a lot to work, including to rural areas for work, and see these things there as well. For example, people might be promised a job through NREGA [National Rural Employment Guarantee Act],[1] but what happens if they don't get work? Or if someone is a *rickshaw-wallah* [rickshaw driver] and there is a *bandh* [strike]. Suddenly they don't have a day's income. But then they still have to pay back the loan, even though they have no money to do so. People always need money, but when they get the

loans, they have to show that [it] is for a business purpose, even if they are
borrowing for other reasons, like a wedding.

Partho highlights here the conditions of perpetual lack and financial insecurity—of constantly needing to make ends meet—under which people take these loans and the mounting pressures to pay them back.

Illness or a *bandh* could upend a family's income and indeed their family credit history. Partho had sustained his injuries when he fell from the third floor of his house, which was under construction. He had gone up early one morning when it was still dark to see the work that had been done the day before. But he slipped, falling first onto telephone lines, trees, and bushes before hitting the ground. Remarkably, his injuries, while serious, were not life threatening. Microfinance recognizes the risks of high mortality among poor borrowers through the inclusion of life insurance policies. However, even as life itself is collateralized through insurance, it cannot account for the uncertainties of everyday life. The regular repayments have been a hallmark of microfinance, yet this very regularity is out of synch with the realities of working in India's informal economy.

Loans were also needed for social obligations such as weddings—as Partho noted—and for contributions to neighborhood festivals and holidays. While microfinance loans are meant to help people grow their businesses, many need the money to cover other consumption costs, particularly ones that allow the poor to attain signs of a good life. While loan application forms documented business purposes of loans, in conversations women admitted they needed the lump sums of money to pay for their daughters' weddings, to pay for community festivals, or to buy clothes for their children during Durga Puja. MFI staff recognize these different uses and assess the creditworthiness of borrowers, not so much on the possible success or failure of the stated loan purpose but on the more qualitative knowledge of people's capacity to repay.

"Another demerit [of microfinance]," Partho continued, "is that the interest rate is actually higher than banks'. Anyone with a little bit of education can do the math to see that they are paying such high inter-

est rates. But since there is no other option, we have to turn to this." It
is often the poor, who both most need credit and are least able to afford it, who are burdened with the highest rates of interest.[2] The ideological discourse of social entrepreneurship and bottom of the pyramid is accepted much more readily by elites than by actual consumers
of microfinance like Partho and loan officers like Amit, who are aware
of its exploitative dimensions. For both the borrowers and MFI staff
on the ground, there is no great curtain to pull back and reveal to borrowers that they are not, in fact, the beneficiaries of companies "doing
well while doing good."

While banks and MFIs continue to capitalize on poverty, the 2010
Indian microfinance crisis revealed how a sudden liquidity crunch
could curtail people's access to credit, on which they have come to rely
as means of making do. Like the 2008 subprime crisis in the United
States, it is a reminder that effects are not always "downstream," but
failure to attend to the difficulties of the borrowers in repaying can
have "upstream" systemic consequences for national and global economies. It becomes increasingly necessary to recognize both that the
poor are good borrowers and that their everyday lives are precarious.
By systemically enfolding the poor into global finance, financial institutions not only expose the poor to financial crises, but they themselves must pay closer attention to the lived realities of the poor.

Even as the limits of microfinance are known, by accounting for
the "sense of lived poverty and the everyday survival strategies of the
economically marginalized" (L. Fernandes 2010, 266), we can come
closer to understanding the ways in which structural inequality is reproduced, often by the very measures meant to counter them. Writing
of empire, Catherine Lutz notes that, as ethnographers, we can trace
"how people and groups come to grips with empire and how ideological change might happen" (2006, 607). Likewise, recognizing the labor of both MFI staff and of women seeking out and repaying loans
defetishizes credit, or capital as commodity. Defetishizing credit is important because it suggests that the spread of finance is not inevitable.
Rather, financialization as a process is peopled; thus, it offers points

and places at which we encounter the moral limits of the market (Sandel 2012).

The critical approach to microfinance in this book is neither an argument to make microfinance better by comparing the Indian commercial sector to other models (Kar and Schuster 2016) nor to say that credit to the poor should be abandoned. Rather, this is an argument to identify microfinance as a form of working-class credit and to consider how these loans are actually being used, rather than treat microfinance as primarily a tool of development. Ethnographic accounts can demonstrate more than high repayment records: they reveal what happens in the moments of interaction between people; they attest not only to the stated business purpose of a loan but also the ways in which the loans fill gaps in everyday household incomes and untimely expenses.

Microfinance loans fulfill a purpose, though it is not the purpose that is so widely circulated in the popular imagination and policy circles of producing entrepreneurial housewives. Rather, people's use of microfinance signifies not only a lack in income but also the lack of affordable and adequate social services such as education, housing, and health care. The growth of microfinance in India should indicate not that poor people need credit—something that seems to be stating the obvious—but that they are increasingly using these loans to make do. Development policy, should, in other words, use the case of microfinance and other sources of indebtedness of the poor to highlight the areas of lack in poor households rather than assume that credit will fill these gaps.

In attending to the disappointments people express in terms of the promise of microfinance, I do not mean to undermine the power or role of hope in the lives of many of my informants, including urban poor borrowers, MFI staff, state regulators, and institutional representatives. Indeed, hope for a better future for themselves, for their children, and for the nation shape the actions and lives of these diverse individuals. These hopes for a better future reflect, perhaps, not what microfinance has achieved but its very limitations as people find that access to credit is not a silver bullet solution to problems of persistent inequalities. These gaps mark places for the "ethical imagination" (H. Moore 2011) and possibilities for social change. Individuals who use loans to pay for medical care or private schools or to tide them over during times of un- and underemployment say more about the state's limited provision of health-care services, education, and precarious labor than the use of credit to create a billion entrepreneurs. These desires, often revealed in ethnographic encounters, can provide important insight into the deficiencies of current development policies or models.

Finally, the analysis of microfinance offers insight into the government's ongoing programs of financial inclusion. Most recently, financial inclusion in India has been precipitated by the government's new scheme, the *Pradhan Mantri Jan Dhan Yojana* (the Prime Minister's People's Wealth Scheme). Rolled out by the Modi government in 2014, the new financial inclusion program has been aimed at giving people access to no-frills bank accounts, including an indigenous Ru-Pay debit card and the possibility of an overdraft. The aim of the program—which claims that 90 percent of households now have access to finance—is to eventually transfer welfare payments through bank accounts. Simultaneously, the government has also rolled out a number of low-cost insurance schemes for life and accident coverage, expanding the market for insurance companies in India (Kar 2017a).

As these programs expand, the poor are further enfolded into global financial networks. Financial inclusion, now often touted as a form of welfare, masks the ways in which poor people's money is increasingly circulated in global circuits of finance. Yet ethnographic analysis of microfinance shows the financial limitations and requirements of households. More than offer new financial products or create bank accounts that sit empty, the state ultimately needs to provide the social services that poor people increasingly seek out in the private sector, including primary and higher education and a reliable health-care system.

INTRODUCTION

1. Names have been changed to maintain anonymity, unless otherwise indicated.

2. *Didi* (elder sister) is a Bengali honorific and was used to refer to all borrowers by MFI staff, regardless of age.

3. While it was estimated that around 60 percent of the Indian population did not have access to formal financial services, in 2014 the Modi government introduced the Pradhan Mantri Jan Dhan Yojana (PMJDY) scheme to push for 100 percent financial inclusion in India. This has meant requiring banks to open zero-balance accounts with minimal know-your-customer (KYC) requirements.

4. In 2005, Tufts University announced the Omidyar-Tufts Microfinance Fund. Omidyar gave US$100 million to Tufts University to be invested in a microfinance initiative, with 50 percent of returns to be used by the university and the remaining 50 percent to be reinvested in microfinance (Arenson 2005). In 2009, the Bill and Melinda Gates Foundation (2009) awarded US$700,000 to the Microcredit Summit Campaign to measure the campaign's progress in alleviating poverty. In 2010, the Gates Foundation (2010) announced US$38 million in new grants for microfinance institutions.

5. In 2010, the *New York Times* reported that with less availability of credit cards since the recession and the declining value of real estate against which borrowers could get credit, small businesses have turned to MFIs to access loans, typically less than US$35,000 with an interest rate ranging from 5 to 18 percent (Shevory 2010).

6. For instance, Sean O'Connell (2009), Avram Taylor (2002), and Melanie Tebbutt (1983) have all written about the ways in the working class make do through various sources of credit in the UK context.

7. The financial system, as defined by Karin Knorr Cetina and Alex Preda, is what "controls and manages credit" (2005, 1). While the end users of capital rely on investors to provide funds, investors seek profits at a later time through the transfer of money as shares, bonds, or derivatives in the financial system.

8. Frederic Jameson (1997) argues that new forms of abstraction emerge from the logics of finance capital and come to shape cultural production. For example, with the intensified competition in the film industry for viewership, previews now encompass the entirety of the film, reflecting the increasingly fragmentary nature of cultural production. Or as Randy Martin argues, finance has emerged from behind the closed doors of banks to the ticker tape showing stock prices on twenty-four-hour

news channels "as if the modulations of equity prices were an EKG to the global body" (2009, 118). See also Martin (2002) and Spivak (1999).

9. In other words, social scientific knowledge is performative in the sense that J. L. Austin (1975) formulated certain phrases to have illocutionary force. For example, a phrase such as "I now pronounce you" not only describes the act but also "performs" the act in its statement. In a parallel manner, while economic theory describes the market, in its articulation it also actively shapes it. As Donald MacKenzie (2007) shows in his analysis of the Black-Scholes-Merton model for options pricing, prices followed the model in part because of its very existence.

10. See, for example, Beunza and Stark (2004), Garcia-Parpet (2007), and Mac-Kenzie (2007) on the performativity of finance. However, as critics of economic performativity such as Daniel Miller argue, this perspective ends up producing "a defence of the economists' view of the world and a rejection of the evidence of how actual economies operate as available to anthropologists and sociologists" (2002, 219). Performativity of finance effectively brackets out power and the ideological foundations of the economic theories he studies and accepts the easy translation of theory into reality.

11. See, for instance, Fisher (2012) on gender and finance; Fisher and Downey (2006), Ho (2009), Lepinay (2011), Maurer (2002), Miyazaki (2013), Riles (2011) and Zaloom (2006) on ideologies and practices of financial actors; and Holmes (2014) and Lee and LiPuma (2004) on linguistics and banking.

12. Ankie Hoogvelt (1997) similarly refers to the process of growing global inequalities as one of financial deepening.

13. In *Capital: Volume III*, Marx notes that in interest-bearing capital, which is at the heart of finance, "we have the irrational form of capital, the misrepresentation and objectification of the relations of production, in its highest power . . . the capital mystification in the most flagrant form" (1993a, 516). See also Comaroff and Comaroff (2001) on millennial capitalism and the rise of speculation.

14. See De Goede (2005) on the depoliticization of finance. See Graeber (2011b) and Ho (2012) on finance and the politics of the Occupy movements.

15. Ethnographic studies of debt relationships include Bourdieu (1977); Elyachar (2005b); Han (2012); James (2015); Langford (2009); Malinowski (2002); Munn (1992); Roitman (2005); Schuster (2015); and Shipton (2010). Theoretical and historical overviews of debt and anthropology include Graeber (2011a); Mauss (2000); and Peebles (2010).

16. See Granovetter (1985) and Polanyi (1957) on the embeddedness of the economy. See also Krippner's (2001) critique on what it means to analyze economic embeddedness.

17. For instance, see Maurer (2005a) on qualitative forms of assessment in due diligence. Similarly, Julia Elyachar (2005b) argues that it is not simply that "traditional" economies are embedded, while those in the "modern" economy are not. Rather, there is a concerted effort to conceptually transform embedded relationships into a new kind of resource.

18. See Maurer's review of the anthropology of money (2006). Moreover, people earmark money differently, signifying not equal value but different kinds of social and moral values (Zelizer 1994). Jessica Cattelino (2008), meanwhile, argues that "popular and scholarly theories of money's abstracting and deculturalizing force blind us to the ways that people undertake political acts of valuation in the course of exploiting money's fungibility" (2008, 3).

19. Whether expressed in terms of economic inequality or class distinction, structural inequality highlights what Pierre Bourdieu terms the "race in which, after a series of bursts in which various runners forge ahead or catch up, the initial gaps are maintained" (1984, 160–161). Structural inequality can also be identified in terms of other forms of social difference, including race or ethnicity (Balibar and Wallerstein 1991). See also Farmer (2004) on structural violence.

20. See Poon (2009) on "downstream" effects of credit risk analysis.

21. In the draft 2011 Microfinance Bill introduced in the lower house of Parliament (Lok Sabha), microfinance was designated to have systemic importance. However, the 2012 bill that was finally tabled had excluded the provision for the microfinance sector to be monitored in terms of systemic risk.

22. Roitman argues that the term "crisis" "establishes the conditions of possible histories" (2014, 11). Rather than deny crisis, it becomes necessary to "*take note of the effects of the claim to crisis, to be attentive to the effects of our very accession to that judgment*" (2014, 12; emphasis in original).

23. As Weston argues, there are never corpses, funerals, or cadavers in discussions of economic ill health. Rather, "the body of the economy-as-patient is always alive, though perhaps just hanging on. It is a body awaiting a cure, and so, of course, its policy physicians" (2013, S35).

24. Calcutta was the center of the nineteenth-century movement known as the Bengal Renaissance, which included social reform movements, literary and artistic work, and nationalist activities.

25. See Chakrabarty (1989) and L. Fernandes (1997) on the working class and the jute industry in West Bengal.

26. See Kohli's discussion of social-democratic politics in West Bengal (2012, 206).

27. In 2007, fourteen people were killed by state violence in the village of Nandigram over the creation of a Special Economic Zone for an Indonesian chemical plant. The same year, popular protests mobilized against land acquisition for the Tata car factory led to the closure of the factory for the world's cheapest car and its transfer to a different state. See Banerjee et al. (2007); Chandra (2008); and Patnaik (2007).

28. According to the Census of India (2011), an urban agglomeration is defined as "a continuous urban spread constituting a town and its adjoining outgrowths, or two or more physically contiguous towns together with or without outgrowths of such towns." Further, it identifies a mega city as an urban agglomeration of more than 10 million. Mumbai (18.4 million) and Delhi (16.3 million) are the two other mega cities in India.

29. See Ghertner's (2011) discussion on governance of Indian cities under the aesthetic notion of "world class." In Kolkata, there have been a number of city "beautification" projects that include the demolition of street vendor stalls (Partha Chatterjee 2004; Ananya Roy 2003). These movements reflect what Arvind Rajagopal describes as "the confrontation between the majority, who dwell and make their livelihood on the street, and the minority, who view the streets as but the circuitry of the formal economy in which they themselves work" (2001, 92). See also Anjaria (2011) on the contested urban spaces.

30. As Tithi Bhattacharya argues, "'Bhadralok' as a historical term expresses [a] legacy of theoretical disagreements in its definitions" (2001, 162). There is an extensive literature on the constitution, historical legacy, and contemporary role of this group in shaping Kolkata. See, for example, Partha Chatterjee (1993, 2004); Donner (2008); Ghosh (2004); Karlekar (1986); Kaviraj (1997); Ray and Qayum (2009); and Sarkar (1992).

31. See McKinsey's report *India's Urban Awakening: Building Inclusive Cities, Sustaining Economic Growth* (Shirish Sankhe et al. 2010).

32. The Hard-Core Poor program at Bandhan is a grant-based program that offers beneficiaries training and asset transfer (e.g., livestock) to set up a small business. Once successful, the beneficiaries are expected to graduate into borrowers.

CHAPTER 1

1. This is sometimes called the triple bottom line, including the environment. For the purposes of microfinance, it is called the double bottom line.

2. While the interview is publicly available, I have not included its reference to protect the anonymity of Mr. Ray.

3. *Banker to the Poor* (2003) follows Muhammad Yunus's transformation from an academic economist to the founder of the bank that serves the poor in Bangladesh and its eventual growth worldwide.

4. After graduating from Tufts University, US-born Akula moved to India to work at an NGO that provided microcredit. Upon returning to the United States, Akula embarked on a PhD in political science at the University of Chicago. During his time as a graduate student Akula founded SKS Microfinance as a profit-driven microfinance venture.

5. Examining the person-to-person microlending website Kiva, Shameem Black (2009) argues that sentimentality in the stories of potential poor borrowers is key to raising funds from rich lenders by creating emotional linkages across distance.

6. See Subramanian (2015) on the ways that caste continues to play a role in seemingly meritocratic settings, such as universities.

7. Through karmic reincarnation, action in the current life shapes the future of the spirit, and one can assure a better future by performing caste duty (Keyes 1983).

8. For instance, there is a 2010 business book *Gandhi, CEO: 14 Principles to Guide & Inspire Modern Leaders* by Alan Axelrod. Challenging capitalist development, Gandhi championed alternative development based on village life. Gandhi's

vision, however, was overturned by Nehru's belief in large-scale industry (Chatterjee 1993).

9. Karen Ho (2009) has traced the increasing valuation of shareholder value in corporations, over, for example, employees, leading to an overemphasis on the financial side of corporations.

10. Like Prahalad, Muhammad Yunus has also advocated the role of for-profit businesses in alleviating poverty. In *Creating a World without Poverty: Social Business and the Future of Capitalism*, Yunus, however, criticizes mainstream free-market theory for envisioning people as "one-dimensional" profit maximizers (2007, 18). Yunus sees the social business as a "non-loss, non-dividend business" (ibid., 24). That is, while investors can recoup their investment, the profit is reinvested *in* the business rather than shared with investors. This is a key difference from Vikram Akula (2011), who describes investor returns as key to scaling up the business.

11. See also Benson (2012) on CSR in the tobacco industry; Welker (2009) on the mining industry; and Shever (2010) on the oil industry.

12. For example, see Dolan (2007); Goodman (2004); and Lyon and Moberg (2010). See also Hilton and Daunton (2001) on fair trade and consumer politics.

13. In his argument of development as freedom, Amartya Sen (1999) differentiates between the means, or instrumental aspects, and the ends of development. For Sen, freedom, as an intrinsic value, is both a means and an end of development.

14. The data in this table were collected by asking every member of a new group (ninety-two groups total) that I visited the stated purpose of their loan.

15. Keith Hart argues that urban economies that lack significant industrial development "must grant a place to the analysis of informal as well as formal structures" (1973, 89). See Breman (1996) and De Neve (2005) on the Indian informal economy.

16. See also Bagchi (1998) and Pedersen (2001) on industrial decline in West Bengal. See Gooptu (2007) and Mukhopadhyay (1998) on its impacts on Kolkata.

17. The informal economy is not separate from, but sustains forms of, production and circulation in the formal sector and ultimately links to the global economy (Nordstrom 2001).

18. As Loïc Waquant finds in US ghettos, mass unemployment, chronic underemployment, and inadequate welfare support mean that most residents have "little choice but to 'moonlight' on jobs, to 'hustle' for money through a diversity of schemes, or to engage in illegal commerce of various kinds (including the most dangerous and potentially lucrative of them, drug retail sale), in order to 'make that dollar' day to day'" (2008, 62).

19. *Lakh* is the indigenous term for 100,000.

20. As Kath Weston writes, both the industrialized global North and the industrializing South are subject to nostalgia: "One case may enlist future-directed nostalgia, the other memory-driven nostalgia, but it is nostalgia all the same. Nostalgia, in each case, for a less precarious existence" (2012, 432).

21. See Gooptu (2007) and L. Fernandes (2006) on the new middle-class politics. Despite the rhetoric of liberalization, the Indian state remains involved in the

economy. However, the policy trend has been of "a rightward drift in which the embrace of business continues to grow warmer, leaving many others out in the cold" (Kohli 2004, 285).

22. For instance, conflict between workers and management of car manufacturer Maruti Suzuki at the Manesar, Haryana, plant, erupted in 2012 and led to the death of a plant manager. While the protests allegedly stemmed from a caste-based slur by the manager, they were also the culmination of long-brewing dissatisfaction over labor conditions, including the use of contract workers who lacked job security. The state, however, has responded with violent repression of workers, including mass imprisonment and labeling workers as "Maoists" (Teltumbde 2012).

CHAPTER 2

1. In examining empowerment in debt in Cairo, Julia Elyachar writes of the need to first answer a set of technical questions: "Who gave money for empowerment debt? To whom did they give that money? How was that money transferred, how was it distributed, and how was it used?" (2005b, 197). Elyachar points to the intermediary role of local banks between international organizations and microfinance institutions.

2. For an extensive history of banking and its colonial history in India, see Amiya Kumar Bagchi's multivolume work on the State Bank of India (1987, 1989, 1997).

3. Charging rates over those stipulated in Vedic scriptures is considered usury and a sin in Hinduism (Gregory 1997, 216–217).

4. However, rather than credit being a kind of trap to capture property, economic historian Tirthankar Roy argues that informal lenders lent money to peasants because "they had a reasonable chance of making money from the interest income." That is, moneylender as creditor "hoped the debtor would repay rather than fail to repay the loan" (2010, 205).

5. The RBI's 1951–1952 stratified sample survey of indebtedness of rural households found borrowing from the informal sector to be 90 percent of total rural credit (Chandavarkar 1983, 798).

6. See Foucault (1991) and Mitchell (2002) on the historical transformation of economy into a site of governance. See also Peebles (2008) on the historical emergence of national currencies in the nineteenth and twentieth centuries, whereby citizens are increasingly dependent on the state to safeguard economic value. Janet Roitman (2005) similarly demonstrates the role and importance of the economic relationship between citizens and the state through fiscal regulation.

7. In 2015 Narendra Modi replaced the Planning Commission by a think tank–like entity known as the National Institution for Transforming India (NITI) Aayog.

8. One of the early experiments with microfinance was the Mahila SEWA Cooperative Bank established in 1973. Part of the Self-Employed Women's Association (SEWA), founded by activist Ela Bhatt, the bank was established by around six thousand members of SEWA buying shares of Rs 10 each. In its original mission, the

SEWA Bank aimed not only to provide loans for productive purposes but also to help "redeem women's pawned jewelry, mortgaged house or land, redeem old debts from brokers, moneylenders or landholders" (Bhatt 2005, 102–103). As a cooperative bank, the SEWA Bank does not use group lending; rather, there are Bank *Sathis* (bank workers from the local communities) who assess creditworthiness and collect repayment. As a cooperative bank, SEWA Bank faces greater regulatory scrutiny than microfinance institutions that have emerged since.

9. Many of the large MFIs in India were founded in the late 1990s and early 2000s, including BASIX, SKS, Spandana Sphoorty, Ujjivan, and Bandhan.

10. Based on reports from the *Telegraph* (Calcutta), the *Economic Times*, and *Business World*.

11. Rakesh Khurana has argued that there has been a shift in corporate leadership from one of "managerial capitalism" to charismatic authority of CEOs, who, observes Khurana, have transcended the profane task of making money and have been portrayed in various ways from visionary to role model (2002, 68).

12. In comparison, annual compensation in FY2009–2010 for the CEO and managing director of the privately owned ICICI Bank was about Rs 20 million (*Rediff Business* 2010).

13. The SERP report was obtained by and published in *Microfinance Focus* (2010).

14. SHGs have increasingly been developed and mobilized by political parties in India to further particular interests (Khape 2009; Kumar 2010; *Times of India* 2012). Groups formed for loan purposes can be more easily accessed by politicians. Some SHGs have taken on particular political hues, such that members of another party cannot join the SHG. MFI groups tend to be less politically driven because funding is not tied to political interests. However, since groups often overlap between MFIs and SHGs, there may be some effects on the MFI groups.

15. The term "culture of non-repayment" was used by Richard Weingarten, managing director, Norwegian Microfinance Initiative at the National Microfinance Conference in 2011.

16. In 2014, Hyderabad became the capital of the newly formed state Telangana when Andhra Pradesh was divided into two states.

17. Numbers reflected in the Microfinance Map of India on Sa-Dhan's website: http://www.sa-dhan.net/files/Sa-dhan-indian-map.htm. The website was last visited in February 2012 but is no longer available online.

18. An NBFC-MFI is a company that "provides financial services pre-dominantly to low-income borrowers with loans of small amounts, for short-terms, on unsecured basis, mainly for income-generating activities, with repayment schedules which are more frequent than those normally stipulated by commercial banks and which further conforms to the regulations specified on that behalf" (Malegam 2011, sec. 4.2).

19. This means that MFIs cannot charge a security deposit, and any existing security deposits should be returned. See Section 8.7 of Malegam Committee Report (2011).

20. However, one participant pointed out that while the Malegam Committee

only recommended that borrowers have a right to ask for monthly or weekly options, the MFI still retains the right to refuse the chosen option if it deems the borrower unable to repay the monthly amount.

21. Reportedly, while the Finance Ministry wanted to include the lower cap, the Law Ministry did not. In order to not further delay the bill, the credit limit was raised significantly higher than the original recommendation (Rajshekhar 2012).

22. For overviews and analyses on the US subprime crisis, see McLean and Nocera (2011), Rajan (2010), and Tett (2009).

23. Begoña Aretxaga writes that a critical rupture "is a tear in the fabric of everyday life. . . . Such a rupture forces us to see a dimension of the real that we do not generally see and which seems intolerable and inexpressible, unsymbolizable and which therefore has a shocking effect" (2005, 128).

CHAPTER 3

A version of Chapter 3 was published as 'Recovering Debts: Microfinance Loan Officers and the Work of "Proxy-Creditors,"' *American Ethnologist* 30, no. 3 (2013): 480–493.

1. I draw on E. P. Thompson's (1991) definition of the moral economy whereby customs and traditions determine a form of distribution that is deemed socially acceptable.

2. Daniel Beunza and David Stark (2004) write of the links, not only between traders but also between traders and their tools. Similarly, Karin Knorr-Cetina (2005) describes how the introduction of computerized screen quotes in 1981 meant that "the market" is no longer situated as a network of many places but identically and simultaneously represented on the screen in all places. Financial technologies, therefore, work to reshape the ways in which space and time are experienced in everyday life. See also Callon (1998) and MacKenzie, Muniesa, and Siu (2007).

3. Aminur Rahman (1999, 5) argues that this referential system reinforces the hierarchical structure of the Grameen Bank model of microcredit lending in which the power of the male bank workers over the women borrowers is reinforced.

4. Rs 5,000 is about US$100, approximately the salary level for full-time drivers.

5. As Laurence Harris (1976, 160) notes, for Marx, capital as commodity occurs when the money capitalist lends to the industrial capitalist, who converts money to its use value, to be used in production (see Marx 1991).

6. See Marx (1978, 320) on fetishism. See also Taussig (1980, 1987). Note that Michael Taussig (1987) has written of "debt fetishism" in reference to the system of debt-peonage, whereby it is the debt that is fetishized and not the commodity. While Taussig emphasizes the difference between the debt and commodity, I am interested in looking at how the debt operates *as* commodity under financialization.

7. In the film, Radha's mother-in-law takes a loan from Sukhilala to pay for her son's wedding. When Radha's husband is injured in an accident and unable to work, he abandons the family. Burdened with the loan, Radha struggles as a peasant woman with two young sons in newly independent India. In the end, the younger

of Radha's sons, Birju, realizes that they have been exploited by Sukhilala because they are not literate and therefore do not understand how the interest has been compounded. Bent on revenge, Birju kills the moneylender, recovers his mother's wedding bangles, and kidnaps Sukhilala's daughter. In a final act of sacrifice, Radha, symbolically embodying *Mother India*, kills her own son to protect the chastity of the young woman.

8. In other words, office work would offer greater levels of cultural capital than the work of loan collections (see Bourdieu 1984).

9. Against representations of money as free from quality (following Georg Simmel), Viviana Zelizer notes how money attains meaning beyond its utilitarian value. For example, Zelizer notes that "identical quantities of money do not 'add up' in the same way" (1989, 352). That is, $1,000 is not the same in meaning if it is from a paycheck, stolen, or given as a gift. See also Graeber (2001) on money and value.

CHAPTER 4

1. During Bangladesh's liberation war to gain independence from Pakistan in 1971.

2. The intellectual history of social capital can be traced to the eighteenth-century Scottish Enlightenment on the role of society in regulating markets (Woolcock 1998). More recently, Pierre Bourdieu's (1986) study on the material benefits derived through social networks and James Coleman's work on the social context of persistent inequality have been influential (Fine 2010; Portes 1998). See also Granovetter (1985) on embedded social relationships and Putnam (1993) on civic life.

3. See Harriss and De Renzio (1997) and Fukuyama (2001) on perspectives of social capital coming from the left and from the right, respectively.

4. Modernization theory posits that societies move from tradition to modernity (Valenzuela and Valenzuela 1978). Development, premised on modernization, has been on "a linear path, directed toward a goal, or a series of goals separated by stages" (Partha Chatterjee 1993, 204).

5. Economist Ester Boserup's work helped bring women back into mainstream economic development. Boserup's analysis of agriculture in Sub-Saharan Africa critiqued development policies that instituted "Western notions about what constituted 'appropriate' female tasks" (Razavi and Miller 1995, 4), leading to male monopoly of new farming technologies and displacing women from the traditionally more equal positions in agricultural economies.

6. The first point on its mission statement was empowerment aimed at "removing all the obstacles to women's active participation in all spheres of public and private life through a full and equal share in economic, social, cultural and political decision-making" (UN Women 1995).

7. Naila Kabeer (1999) has described empowerment as the process by which those who are denied the ability to make choices gain that ability.

8. In the seminal work on gender in anthropology, *Women, Culture and Society*, Michelle Rosaldo identifies the "domestic" and "public" as "the basis of a structural

framework necessary to identify and explore the place of male and female in psychological, cultural, social, and economic aspects of human life" (1974, 23). It is only when women "transcend domestic limits" (ibid., 41) and enter the public sphere that women can challenge unequal power structures of gender relations. Sylvia Yanagisako and Jane Collier (1990) have pointed to the analytical limits of this dichotomy, including the problematic universalization of gender roles and domestic activities.

9. Fraser draws on Habermas's model of the public sphere "in which political participation is enacted through the medium of talk" (1992, 110). She argues that the historically constructed public sphere was "not simply an unrealized utopian ideal; it was also a masculinist ideological notion that functioned to legitimate an emergent form of class rule" (ibid., 116).

10. DENA stopped giving new business loans around December because of the crisis.

11. For a discussion of the politics surrounding access to water in urban India, see Nikhil Anand (2011) on "hydraulic citizenship."

12. For lower grades, school is often only a few hours in the morning rather than the entire day.

13. This research was conducted before the launch of the Aadhaar biometric card, which now offers another form of identity card.

14. Atul Kohli argues that the CPM is "communist in name only and is essentially social-democratic in its ideology, social program, and policies." The CPM consolidated lower-income groups with some redistributive policies but largely "adopted a nonthreatening approach toward property-owning groups" (1990, 267).

15. Studies of the new middle class include Donner (2009); L. Fernandes (2006); Fernandes and Heller (2006); Mazzarella (2003); Oza (2006); and Radhakrishnan (2011).

16. Piya Chatterjee shows in her ethnography of women working in tea plantations how tribal women's bodies become iconic of "wildness and primitivism. Her essence demands a civilizing and disciplining mission" (2001, 8).

17. Deborah James (2015) has argued in the South African context that new sources of debt have become ways for post-apartheid South Africans to attain middle-class aspirations.

18. In the 1980s, the CPM introduced a policy for Bengali-only education in government primary schools, a move that was unpopular with the middle class. The unpopular policy was eventually overturned in 1999 (see Scrase 2002).

19. This desire for credentials in the form of an English education can perhaps be understood as misrecognition of the value of such cultural capital, or what Bourdieu calls *allodoxia* (1984, 155). This is seen in the continuing unemployment and underemployment of educated young people in India (Jeffrey 2010).

20. Saba Mahmood contends that "agentival capacity is entailed not only in those acts that resist norms but also in the multiple ways in which one *inhabits* norms." Therefore, we have to understand the "discursive and practical conditions within

which women come to cultivate various forms of desire and capacities of ethical action" (2005, 15), which do not necessarily coincide with liberal feminist politics.

CHAPTER 5

1. Caitlin Zaloom's (2006) ethnography of the commodity exchange market in Chicago shows the transformation of trading from the physical pits to computer-based trading. Similarly, writing of currency exchange, Karin Knorr Cetina observes the shift from markets based on "network architecture" reliant on social networks to "flow architecture," which uses technical systems, such as computer screens (2005, 39). These technologies transform the ways in which space and scale are imagined as well as forms of social interactions.

2. In his analysis of genomics, Kausik Sunder Rajan argues that healthy patients are transformed into "patients-in-waiting." Speculation about the future allows for interventions in the present and ensures the creation of a market of not just "patients-in-waiting" but "consumers-in-waiting" (2005, 24). Calculation of these future risks both in terms of disease and profits and losses determines market decisions.

3. The *Financial Times* reported that Deutsche Bank aided the US-based Finca International (with international operations) in creating a US$21.2 million CDO (O'Connor and Grene 2009). Prior to the financial meltdown, Citibank, Credit Suisse, and others had been involved in microfinance CDOs.

4. According to report by the Consultative Group to Assist the Poor (CGAP), over half of cross-border funding to MFIs comes from MIVs (Gahwiler and Negre 2011).

5. MFIs that are regulated as NBFC-MFIs will be able to use external commercial borrowing (ECB) to get funds from multilateral institutions (e.g., Asian Development Bank), regional financial institutions, international banks, and foreign equity holders (*The Hindu* 2011).

6. The parameters and the weights given to each were as follows: character (35 percent), capacity (35 percent), collateral (10 percent), loan officer (10 percent), and evaluator (10 percent). The character of the borrower is based on her reputation among other borrowers in the group, as well as her interaction with branch office staff. Capacity refers to the borrower's income and hence ability to repay. Collateral (which is officially not required by MFIs) indicates the material possessions that reflect the net worth of a borrower. The weightings of the loan officer and the evaluator (i.e., the branch officer) are meant to address any biases or problems on the institutional side.

7. Grameen Foundation is a nonprofit organization headquartered in the United States that helps promote the "Grameen philosophy" worldwide. IFMR Trust invests in companies that work on financial inclusion.

8. For a fee, the Grameen "growth guarantee" covers the principal lent by local commercial banks to MFIs through a Citibank standby letter of credit.

9. As Robert Desjarlais suggests, our subjective, phenomenological experiences are themselves shaped by our social worlds. Critiquing the "ease with which anthro-

pologists have assessed foreign realities" (1992, 16–17), Desjarlais argues for the need to "bear in mind that subjective experiences of this sort [trances] are deeply patterned by long-standing cultural context forming and informing one's identity" (ibid., 17). My inability to "smell" was marked by my own distance from the social world and context that drew the negative response to beef.

10. The politics of beef are present in other aspects of Indian social life (e.g., Sarkar and Sarkar 2016; Staples 2017).

11. As defined by Bourdieu, taste, "the propensity and capacity to appropriate (materially or symbolically) a given class of classified, classifying objects or practices, is the generative formula of life-style, a unitary set of distinctive preferences which express the same expressive intention in the specific logic of each of the symbolic subspaces, furniture, clothing, language or body hexis" (1984, 173).

12. The Twelfth Five-Year Plan by the Planning Commission of India (2013) notes that the Muslim minority lags in most major human development indices. This includes education, where literacy rates for the Muslim minority is 67 percent (the national rate is 75 percent, and 76 percent for Hindus), and health, with Muslim mothers least likely to have access to a health facility for births (33 percent) or to have postnatal checkups.

13. Historically, the partition of India and Pakistan, which coincided with the independence of the two nation-states, reinscribed religion with new meaning in South Asia. The creation of Pakistan for a Muslim majority called into question the loyalties of Muslims who remained in India (Pandey 1999). Though founded as a secular state, contemporary India continued to be influenced by partition and the related preindependence movements (Tejani 2008).

14. Scholars have extensively examined and debated the caste system of (predominantly though not exclusively) Hindu India, identified as a distinctly South Asian form of social stratification. The Portuguese-derived term "caste" refers to "two distinct concepts of corporate affiliation: the jati (birth group) and the varna (order, class or kind)" (Bayly 1999, 8). While there is a profusion of birth groups, they are largely limited by geographical area. Drawing on Hindu scriptures, *varna* refers to the division of Hindu society into four units: Brahmans, Kshatriyas, Vaishyas, and Shudras. The so-called untouchables or Dalits "occupy an ambivalent place below, outside or parallel to this varna scheme" (ibid., 9). The intersections and different meanings of caste broadly, as well as the intersections of *jati* and *varna* in everyday life in South Asia have been subject to vigorous anthropological debate.

15. See Jaffrelot (2003) on lower-caste politics.

16. See Bourdieu (1991) on the symbolic power of the linguistic norm. There are also political consequence of linguistic differences between Bengali and non-Bengali speakers (Kohli 1990).

17. Syndicate borrowing refers to a borrower having other people take out loans on her behalf. In other words, one person bears the cost of all the loans, but the loans are in the names of other people.

18. In the context of rural Bangladesh, Lamia Karim (2011) has written of the

way in which microfinance NGOs have appropriated existing clientelist relations in their practices. See also Ito (2003) on clientelism. Alpa Shah (2010) has written of forms of patronage in rural India.

19. The RBI (2004, 5) outlines KYC norms for preparing customer profiles to include social/financial status and the nature of and information about a client's business activity. The RBI advises that banks should seek only information relevant to the risk category and that is not intrusive.

20. The RBI released the Malegam Committee report in 2011 in response to the microfinance crisis. Based on its findings, the committee offered directives for regulating the microfinance sector. See Chapter 2 for further analysis of the report.

21. Writing of the state apparatus, Louis Althusser argues that individuals are "always already" subjects that "constantly practice the rituals of ideological recognition" (1971, 172). For Althusser, ideological state apparatuses such as education, religion, and media contribute to the ways in which individuals come to submit freely to their subjection.

CHAPTER 6

1. This is in contrast to whole life insurance, which insures the entirety of a person's life.

2. Ewald gives the example of the shift toward "zero-risk" in military strategy, comparing current risk analysis of lowering the risk of losing soldiers to the situation in the First and Second World Wars where men were sent en masse to battle in the field (2002, 297).

3. See, for example, Bähre (2011) and Golomski (2015) on life insurance in South Africa.

4. The IRDA (2005) requires that by the sixth financial year of operation, at least 18 percent of life insurance companies and 5 percent for non–life insurance companies be in the rural sector and that twenty-five thousand new lives be covered in the social sector.

5. In March 2012, the United Kingdom's Financial Services Authority ordered banks and insurance brokers to inform customers that they may have been missold payment protection insurance (PPI) for credit cards, personal loans, or mortgages and that these premiums could be reclaimed (E. Moore 2012).

6. The day before, on February 14, 2011, the *Times of India* reported that banks had refused to extend lending to MFIs beyond what they had committed to by December 30, 2010, at a meeting between MFIs and the Indian Bankers' Association (Singh 2011).

7. In February 2012, the Andhra Pradesh government reopened investigations into suicides related to SKS Microfinance following the Associated Press report (Kinetz 2012) that more than two hundred people committed suicide in the state in late 2010.

8. Cases documented in the SERP report included (1) the suicide of a man whose scooter was confiscated and house locked by MFI staff due to failure to re-

pay a loan of Rs 18,000; (2) a woman who attempted suicide and was hospitalized after MFI staff told her to go into prostitution for failing to repay a loan of Rs 15,000; and (3) a woman who committed suicide following harassment that led to a feud in the family over failure to repay a loan of Rs 16,000. The case, however, was treated as one of domestic violence.

9. Andhra Pradesh, and South India more generally, has one of the highest suicide rates in India and globally (Aaron et al. 2004). See also Jocelyn Chua's (2014) and Murphy Halliburton's (1998) work on suicide in the southern state of Kerala, which paradoxically has the highest suicide rate in India, despite being a model for development with high rates of education and life expectancy.

10. In her seminal piece *Can the Subaltern Speak?* Gayatri Chakravarty Spivak (1988) analyzes the case of Bhuvaneswari Bhaduri, who committed suicide while menstruating. This timing puzzled people, for menstruation symbolized the fact that it was not the case of an illicit pregnancy. It was not until the discovery of Bhaduri's membership in a militant group that it was assumed that her suicide related to her being unable to go through with a political assassination in the armed struggle for Indian independence. Yet the suicidal woman in India always already exists in the narrative of *sati*, widow immolation (see Mani 1998; R. Sunder Rajan 1993). Spivak argues that Bhuvaneswari's death is a "displacing gesture" (1988, 308) that also reverses the interdict of menstruating (and thereby ritually impure) widows from immolating themselves. Nevertheless, the hegemonic, masculine narrative forecloses these multiple meanings of Bhuvaneswari's death.

11. For Durkheim (2006), egotistic suicide occurs due to excessive individualism, and altruistic suicide is a result of excessive integration into society. Anomic suicide occurs at times of social change, when there is a flux in social regulation, while fatalistic suicide is the result of oppressive social conditions.

12. On a methodological note, I did not follow up directly with Shilpa's family on her suicide. Given my affiliation with the MFI, I did not want cause any added stress to the surviving family.

13. The Andhra Pradesh government charged employees of MFIs with abetment of suicide (Kinetz 2012).

14. The National Human Rights Commission (2011) sent notices to the state governments of Maharashtra, Andhra Pradesh, and Kerala following media reports on farmer suicides in the state. Media reports suggest that 680 farmers committed suicide in six districts of Maharashtra in 2011, 90 farmers in six districts of Andhra Pradesh between October and November, and 8 cases in Kerala's Wayanad district in November. *India Today* reported in January 2012 that 29 farmers had killed themselves over debt woes in just a few months in West Bengal (Bhabani 2012).

15. The privatization of seed production has led to increasing levels of indebtedness for farmers who have to buy hybrid seeds as well as chemical fertilizer (Shiva et al. 2000). While these trends have emerged since the 1970s, they have intensified since the liberalization of the Indian economy in 1991. Though technological innovations have led to a rise in the production of cash crops such as cotton, these yields

have fluctuated annually, depending on variations in rainfall, often leading to farmers being unable to pay off their debts (Mohanty and Shroff 2004). Small farmers have also become particularly vulnerable to price shifts with the agrarian integration into global markets since the 1990s (Mohanakumar and Sharma 2006).

16. Writing of suicide bombing, Asad argues that horror is "a state of being" rather than a "matter of interpretation" and is something that "requires no discursive effort" (2007, 81). What horrifies "is not just dying and killing (or killing by dying) but the violent appearance of something that is normally disregarded in secular modernity" (ibid., 91).

17. As Sudipta Kaviraj argues, "Even gods in modern Calcutta are divided in strictly intelligible class terms," with the middle class worshipping Durga, while the working class worship "appropriately lower forms of divine life like Shitala, the goddess of smallpox, or Manasa, goddess of snakes" (1997, 103).

18. Murphy Halliburton (2005) has noted the emergence and proliferation of mental health categories such as "tension" in India as a more universal and portable term of allopathic medicine, as well as a way to describe emerging experiences of subjective illness.

19. See Brett (2006) on sacrificing food to repay loans.

20. Ethics, argues Michael Lambek, is an integral part of the human condition: Human beings cannot avoid being subject to ethics, speaking and acting with ethical consequences, evaluating our actions and those of others, acknowledging and refusing acknowledgment, caring and taking care, but also being aware of our failure to do so consistently (2010, 1).

21. Reported in the *Times of India* (2011). The Kolkata Municipal Corporation has offered similar incentives to private hospitals (Ganguly 2009).

EPILOGUE

1. The Mahatma Gandhi National Rural Employment Guarantee Act (MGNREGA) was introduced by the central government in 2005 to offer livelihood security in rural areas by guaranteeing one hundred days of wage labor in a fiscal year.

2. See Williams (2004) on how credit cards in the United States punish the poor with the highest interest rates while offering wealthier users perks such as points.

REFERENCES

Aaron, Rita, Abraham Joseph, Sulochana Abraham, Jayaprakash Muliyil, Kurian George, Jasmine Prasad, Shantidani Minz, Vinod Joseph Abraham, and Anuradha Bose. 2004. "Suicides in Young People in Rural Southern India." *Lancet* 363 (9415): 1117–1118.

Abedal, Rawi. 2007. *Capital Rules: The Construction of Global Finance.* Cambridge, MA: Harvard University Press.

Aiyar, Swaminathan. 2010. "Killing Microfinance Will Help Moneylenders." *Economic Times* (Kolkata), October 24, 18.

Akula, Vikram. 2011. *A Fistful of Rice: My Unexpected Quest to End Poverty through Profitability.* Boston: Harvard Business Review Press.

Allison, Anne. 1994. *Nightwork: Sexuality, Pleasure and Corporate Masculinity in a Tokyo Hostess Club.* Chicago: University of Chicago Press.

———. 2012. "Ordinary Refugees: Social Precarity and Soul in 21st Century Japan." *Anthropological Quarterly* 85 (2): 345–370.

Althusser, Louis. 1971. *Lenin and Philosophy and Other Essays.* New York: Monthly Review Press.

Anand, Nikhil. 2011. "Pressure: The PoliTechnics of Water Supply in Mumbai." *Cultural Anthropology* 26 (4): 542–564.

Anderson, Robert T. 1966. "Rotating Credit Associations in India." *Economic Development and Cultural Change* 14 (3): 334–339.

Anjaria, Jonathan. 2011. "Ordinary States: Everyday Corruption and the Politics of Space in Mumbai." *American Ethnologist* 38 (1): 58–72.

Appadurai, Arjun. 1988. "Introduction: Commodities and the Politics of Value." In *The Social Life of Things: Commodities in Cultural Perspective*, ed. Arjun Appadurai, 3–63. Cambridge: Cambridge University Press.

———. 1996. *Modernity at Large: Cultural Dimensions of Globalization.* Minneapolis: University of Minnesota Press.

———. 2015. *Banking on Words: The Failure of Language in the Age of Derivative Finance.* Chicago: University of Chicago Press.

Arenson, Kate. 2005. "Tufts Is Getting Gift of $100 Million, with Rare Strings." *New York Times*, November 4.

Aretxaga, Begoña. 1997. *Shattering Silence: Women, Nationalism, and Political Subjectivity in Northern Ireland.* Princeton, NJ: Princeton University Press.

———. 2005. *States of Terror: Begoña Aretxaga's Essays.* Edited by Joseba Zulaika. Reno: University of Nevada Press.

Armendáriz de Aghion, Beatriz, and Jonathan Morduch. 2000. "Microfinance beyond Group Lending." *Economics of Transition* 8 (2): 401–420.

Arrighi, Giovanni. 2010. *The Long Twentieth Century: Money, Power, and the Origins of Our Times*. London: Verso.

Arun, T. G, and J. D. Turner. 2002. Financial Sector Reforms in Developing Countries: The Indian Experience. *World Economy* 25 (3): 429–445.

Asad, Talal. 2007. *On Suicide Bombing*. New York: Columbia University Press.

Austin, J. L. 1975. *How to Do Things with Words*. Cambridge, MA: Harvard University Press.

Auyero, Javier. 2012. *Patients of the State: The Politics of Waiting in Argentina*. Durham, NC: Duke University Press.

Bacchetta, Paola. 2004. *Gender in the Hindu Nation: RSS Women as Ideologues*. New Delhi: Women Unlimited.

Bagchi, Amiya Kumar. 1987. *The Evolution of the State Bank of India: The Roots, 1806–1876*. New Delhi: State Bank of India and Sage Publications.

———. 1989. *The Presidency Banks and the Indian Economy, 1876–1914*. New Delhi: State Bank of India and Sage Publications.

———. 1997. *The Evolution of the State Bank of India: The Era of the Presidency Banks, 1876–1920*. New Delhi: State Bank of India and Sage Publications.

———. 1998. "Studies on the Economy of West Bengal since Independence." *Economic and Political Weekly* 33 (47/48): 2973–2978.

Bähre, Erik. 2011. "Liberation and Redistribution: Social Grants, Commercial Insurance, and Religious Riches in South Africa." *Comparative Studies in Society and History* 53 (2): 371–392.

Baker, Tom, and Jonathan Simon. 2002. "Introduction." In *Embracing Risk: The Changing Culture of Insurance and Responsibility*, ed. Tom Baker and Jonathan Simon, 1–25. Chicago: University of Chicago Press.

Balibar, Étienne, and Immanuel Wallerstein. 1991. *Race, Nation, Class: Ambiguous Identities*. New York: Verso.

Banerjee, Abhijit, Pranab Bardhan, Kaushik Basu, Mrinal Datta Chaudhury, Maitreesh Ghatak, Ashok Guha, Mukul Majumdar, Dilip Mookherjee, and Debraj Ray. 2007. "Beyond Nandigram: Industrialisation in West Bengal." *Economic and Political Weekly* 42 (17): 1487–1489.

Banerjee, Abhijit, and Esther Duflo. 2011. *Poor Economics: Rethinking Poverty and the Ways to End It*. Noida, India: Random House India.

Banerjee, Banashree. 2002. "Security of Tenure in Indian Cities." In *Holding Their Ground: Secure Land Tenure for the Urban Poor in Developing Countries*, ed. Alain Durand-Lasserve and Lauren Royston, 37–58. London: Earthscan.

Bansal, Rashmi. 2011. *I Have a Dream: The Inspiring Stories of 20 Social Entrepreneurs Who Found New Ways to Solve Old Problems*. New Delhi: Westland.

Barry, Andrew. 2004. "Ethical Capitalism." In *Global Governmentality: Governing International Spaces*, ed. Wendy Larner and William Walters, 195–211. London: Routledge.

Basu, Amrita. 1992. *Two Faces of Protest: Contrasting Modes of Women's Activism in India*. Berkeley: University of California Press.

Bayly, Susan. 1999. *Caste, Society and Politics in India: From the Eighteenth Century to the Modern Age*. Cambridge: Cambridge University Press.

Bear, Laura, Karen Ho, Anna Tsing, and Sylvia Yanagisako. 2015. "Gens: A Feminist Manifesto for the Study of Capitalism. Theorizing the Contemporary." *Cultural Anthropology*, March 30. https://culanth.org/fieldsights/652-gens-a-feminist -manifesto-for-the-study-of-capitalism.

Beck, Ulrich.1992. *Risk Society: Towards a New Modernity*. London: Sage.

———. 2006. "Living in the World Risk Society." *Economy and Society* 35 (3): 329–345.

Benson, Peter. 2012. *Tobacco Capitalism: Growers, Migrant Workers, and the Changing Face of a Global Industry*. Princeton, NJ: Princeton University Press.

Berlant, Lauren. 2006. "Cruel Optimism." *Differences* 17 (3): 20–36.

Berman, Peter. 1998. "Rethinking Health Care Systems: Private Health Care Provision in India." *World Development* 26 (8): 1463–1479.

Beunza, Daniel, and David Stark. 2004. "Tools of the Trade: The Socio-technology of Arbitrage in a Wall Street Trading Room." *Industrial and Corporate Change* 13 (2): 369–400.

Bhabani, Soudhriti. 2012. "Mamata Banerjee Oblivious to Farmer's Suicide in West Bengal." *India Today*, January 30.

Bhagat, R. B. 2011. "Emerging Pattern of Urbanisation in India." *Economic and Political Weekly* 46 (34): 10–12.

Bhatt, Ela. 2005. *We Are Poor but So Many: The Story of Self-Employed Women in India*. New Delhi: Oxford University Press.

Bhattacharya, Tithi. 2001. "In the Name of Culture." *South Asia Research* 21 (2): 161–187.

Birla, Ritu. 2009. *Stages of Capital: Law, Culture, and Market Governance in Late Colonial India*. Durham, NC: Duke University Press.

Biswas, Soutik. 2016. "Why Are India's Housewives Killing Themselves?" *BBC*, April 12. http://www.bbc.co.uk/news/world-asia-india-35994601.

Black, Shameem. 2009. "Microloans and Micronarratives: Sentiment for a Small World." *Public Culture* 21 (2): 269–292.

Boholm, Åsa. 2003. "The Cultural Nature of Risk: Can There Be an Anthropology of Uncertainty?" *Ethnos* 68 (2): 159–178.

Boltanski, Luc, and Ève Chiapello. 2005. *The New Spirit of Capitalism*. New York: Verso.

Bond, Phillip, and Ashok Rai. 2009. "Borrower Runs." *Journal of Development Economics* 88 (2): 185–191.

Bose, Purnima, and Laura Lyons, eds. 2010. *Cultural Critique and the Global Corporation*. Bloomington: Indiana University Press.

Bourdieu, Pierre. 1977. *Outline of a Theory of Practice*. Cambridge: Cambridge University Press.

———. 1984. *Distinction: A Social Critique of the Judgment of Taste*. Cambridge, MA: Harvard University Press.

———. 1986. "The Forms of Capital." In *Handbook of Theory and Research for the Sociology of Education*, ed. J. Richardson, 81–93. Westport, CT: Greenwood Press.

———. 1991. *Language & Symbolic Power*. Cambridge: Polity Press.

Breman, Jan. 1996. *Footloose Labour: Working in India's Informal Economy*. Cambridge: Cambridge University Press.

Brenner, Suzanne. 1998. *The Domestication of Desire: Women, Wealth, and Modernity in Java*. Princeton, NJ: Princeton University Press.

Brett, John. 2006. "'We Sacrifice and Eat Less': The Structural Complexities of Microfinance Participation." *Human Organization* 65 (1): 8–19.

Brown, Wendy. 2005. *Edgework: Critical Essays on Knowledge and Politics*. Princeton, NJ: Princeton University Press.

———. 2015. *Undoing the Demos: Neoliberalism's Stealth Revolution*. Brooklyn, NY: Zone Books.

Business Standard. 2010. "Gurumani Can Continue as SKS Director: Court." October 9. http://www.business-standard.com/article/companies/gurumani-can -continue-as-sks-director-court-110100900088_1.html.

———. 2011. "MFIN Launches Credit Bureau for Microfin Client Data." March 3. http://www.business-standard.com/article/finance/mfin-launches-credit-bureau -for-microfin-client-data-111030300003_1.html.

Bystrom, Hans. 2008. "The Microfinance Collateralized Debt Obligation: A Modern Robin Hood?" *World Development* 36 (11): 2109–2126.

Callon, Michel. 1998. "Introduction: The Embeddedness of Economic Markets in Economics." *Sociological Review* 46 (S1): 1–57.

———. 2007. "What Does It Mean to Say That Economics Is Performative?" In *Do Economists Make Markets?*, ed. Donald MacKenzie, Fabian Muniesa, and Lucia Siu, 311–357. Princeton, NJ: Princeton University Press.

Cattelino, Jessica. 2008. *High Stakes: Florida Seminole Gaming and Sovereignty*. Durham, NC: Duke University Press.

Census of India. 2011. "Urban Agglomerations and Cities." http://censusindia.gov .in/2011-prov-results/paper2/data_files/India2/1.%20Data%20Highlight.pdf.

Chakrabarty, Dipesh. 1989. *Rethinking Working Class History: Bengal 1890–1940*. Princeton, NJ: Princeton University Press.

Chakravorty, Sanjoy. 2000. "From Colonial City to Globalizing City? The Far-from-Complete Spatial Transformation of Calcutta." In *Globalizing Cities: A New Spatial Order?*, ed. Peter Marcuse and Ronald van Kempen, 56–77. Malden, MA: Blackwell.

Chan, Cheris Shun-Ching. 2009. "Creating a Market in the Presence of Cultural Resistance: The Case of Life Insurance in China." *Theory and Society* 38 (3): 271–305.

Chandavarkar, A. G. 1983. "Money and Credit (1858–1947)." In *The Cambridge Economic History of India*, ed. Dharma Kumar and Desai Meghnad, 762–803. Cambridge: Cambridge University Press.

Chandra, Nirmal Kumar. 2008. "Tata Motors in Singur: A Step towards Industrialisation or Pauperisation?" *Economic and Political Weekly* 43 (50): 41–51.

Chatterjee, Partha. 1993. *The Nation and Its Fragments: Colonial and Postcolonial Histories*. Princeton, NJ: Princeton University Press.

———. 2004. *The Politics of the Governed: Reflections on Popular Politics in Most of the
World*. New York: Columbia University Press.

Chatterjee, Piya. 2001. *A Time for Tea: Women, Labor, and Post/Colonial Politics on an
Indian Plantation*. Durham, NC: Duke University Press.

Chidambaram, P. 2008. "Budget Speech." Ministry of Finance, Government of India. http://indiabudget.nic.in/ub2008-09/bs/speecha.htm.

Chu, Julie. 2010. *Cosmologies of Credit: Transnational Mobility and the Politics of Destination in China*. Durham, NC: Duke University Press.

Chua, Jocelyn Lim. 2014. *In Pursuit of the Good Life: Aspiration and Suicide in Globalizing South India*. Berkeley: University of California Press.

Clark, Geoffrey. 1999. *Betting on Lives: The Culture of Life Insurance in England, 1695–
1775*. Manchester, UK: Manchester University Press.

Collier, Stephen, Andrew Lakoff, and Paul Rabinow. 2004. "Biosecurity: Towards an
Anthropology of the Contemporary." *Anthropology Today* 20 (5): 3–7.

Collins, Daryl, Jonathan Morduch, Stuart Rutherford, and Orlanda Ruthven. 2009.
Portfolios of the Poor: How the World's Poor Live on $2 a Day. Princeton, NJ: Prince-
ton University Press.

Comaroff, Jean, and John Comaroff, eds. 2001. *Millennial Capitalism and the Culture
of Neoliberalism*. Durham, NC: Duke University Press.

Corbridge, Stuart, and John Harriss. 2000. *Reinventing India: Liberalization, Hindu
Nationalism and Popular Democracy*. Cambridge: Polity Press.

Cross, Jamie. 2010. "Neoliberalism as Unexceptional: Economic Zones and the
Everyday Precariousness of Working Life in South India." *Critique of Anthropology* 30 (4): 355–373.

Damodaran, Harish. 2008. *India's New Capitalists: Caste, Business, and Industry in a
Modern Nation*. New York: Palgrave.

Das Gupta, Ananda. 2010. *Ethics, Business, and Society: Managing Responsibly*. New
Delhi: Response Books.

Das, Veena, and Deborah Poole. 2004. *Anthropology in the Margins of the State*. Santa
Fe, NM: School of American Research Press.

Davala, Sarath, Renana Jhabvala, Soumya Kapoor Mehta, and Guy Standing. 2015.
Basic Income: A Transformative Policy for India. London: Bloomsbury.

Davis, Mike. 2006. *Planet of Slums*. London: Verso.

De Goede, Marieke. 2005. *Virtue, Fortune and Faith: A Genealogy of Finance*. Minneapolis: University of Minnesota Press.

De Neve, Geert. 2005. *The Everyday Politics of Labour: Working Lives in India's Informal Economy*. New Delhi: Social Science Press.

De Quidt, Jonathan, Thiemo Fetzer, and Maitreesh Ghatak. 2016. "Group Lending without Joint Liability." *Journal of Development Economics* 121 (July): 217–236.

Defert, Daniel. 1991. "'Popular Life' and Insurance Technology." In *The Foucault Effect: Studies in Governmentality*, ed. Graham Burchell, Colin Gordon, and Peter Miller, 211–233. Chicago: University of Chicago Press.

Dercon, Stefan. 2005. "Risk, Insurance, and Poverty: A Review." In *Insurance against Poverty*, ed. Stefan Dercon, 9–37. Oxford: Oxford University Press.

Desjarlais, Robert. 1992. *Body and Emotion: The Aesthetics of Illness and Healing in the Nepal Himalayas*. Philadelphia: University of Pennsylvania Press.

Devji, Faisal. 2011. "The Paradox of Nonviolence." *Public Culture* 23 (2): 269–274.

Di Leonardo, Micaela. 1987. "The Female World of Cards and Holidays: Women, Families and the Work of Kinship." *Signs* 12 (3): 440–453.

Dickey, Sara. 2016. *Living Class in Urban India*. New Brunswick, NJ: Rutgers University Press.

Dieckmann, Robert. 2007. "Microfinance: An Emerging Investment Opportunity." *Deutsche Bank Research*. https://www.db.com/usa/docs/Emerging_Investment _Opportunities.pdf.

Dolan, Catherine. 2007. "Market Affections: Moral Encounters with Kenyan Fairtrade Flowers." *Ethnos* 72 (2): 239–261.

Dolan, Catherine, Christina Garsten, and Dinah Rajak. 2011. "Introduction: Ethnographies of Corporate Ethicizing." *Focaal—Journal of Global and Historical Anthropology* 60 (Summer): 3–8.

Donner, Henrike. 2008. *Domestic Goddesses: Maternity, Globalization and Middle-Class Identity in Contemporary India*. Aldershot, UK: Ashgate.

Douglas, Mary. 1992. *Risk and Blame: Essays in Cultural Theory*. New York: Routledge.

Dowla, Asif, and Dipal Barua. 2006. *The Poor Always Pay Back: The Grameen II Story*. Bloomfield, CT: Kumarian Press.

Dube, Leela. 1988. "On the Construction of Gender: Hindu Girls in Patrilineal India." *Economic and Political Weekly* 23 (18): WS11–WS19.

Duménil, Gérard, and Dominique Lévy. 2011. *The Crisis of Neoliberalism*. Cambridge, MA: Harvard University Press.

Dunn, Elizabeth. 2004. *Privatizing Poland: Baby Food, Big Business and the Remaking of Labor*. Ithaca, NY: Cornell University Press.

Durkheim, Émile. 2006. *On Suicide*. Translated by Robin Buss. London: Penguin Classics.

Economic Times. 2010. "No Paper Tigers: Over 60 SKS Staffers Join Millionaire Club." October 29, 14.

———. 2011a. "Bank License Seekers Must Commit to Govt's Financial Inclusion Agenda: Subbarao." March 4, 1.

———. 2011b. "Dalits Open Their Own Chamber of Commerce in Mumbai." May 31, 16 (Kolkata).

———. 2011c. "Financial Inclusion Is Necessary for Poverty Alleviation." April 8, 22 (Kolkata).

———. 2011d. "L&T Fin Just Can't Wait, to Go Ahead with IPO." June 28, 8 (Kolkata).

———. 2012. "Large Corporate Houses Plan Big: Ambanis, Birlas and Others Pursuing Financial Services Sector Initiatives." April 22. https://economictimes .indiatimes.com/news/company/corporate-trends/large-corporate-houses-plan -big-ambanis-birlas-and-others-pursuing-financial-services-sector-initiatives /articleshow/12822474.cms.

Edelman, Marc. 2005. "Bringing the Moral Economy Back In . . . to the Study of 21st-Century Transnational Peasant." *American Anthropologist* 107 (3): 331–345.

Elyachar, Julia. 2005a. "Best Practices: Research Finance, and NGOs in Cairo." *American Ethnologist* 33 (3): 413–426.

———. 2005b. *Markets of Dispossession: NGOs, Economic Development, and the State in Cairo.* Durham, NC: Duke University Press.

———. 2012. "Next Practices: Knowledge, Infrastructure, and Public Goods at the Bottom of the Pyramid." *Public Culture* 24 (1): 109–130.

Escobar, Arturo. 1995. *Encountering Development: The Making and Unmaking of the Third World.* Princeton, NJ: Princeton University Press.

Ewald, François. 1991. "Insurance and Risk." In *The Foucault Effect: Studies in Governmentality,* ed. G. Burchell, C. Gordon, and P. Miller, 197–210. Chicago: University of Chicago Press.

———. 2002. "The Return of Descartes's Malicious Demon: An Outline of a Philosophy of Precaution." In *Embracing Risk: The Changing Culture of Insurance and Responsibility,* ed. Tom Baker and Jonathan Simon, 273–301. Chicago: University of Chicago Press.

Faier, Lieba. 2009. *Intimate Encounters: Filipina Women and the Remaking of Rural Japan.* Berkeley: University of California Press.

Farmer, Paul. 2004. "An Anthropology of Structural Violence." *Current Anthropology* 45 (3): 305–325.

Feigenberg, Benjamin, Erica Field, and Rohini Pande. 2013. "The Economic Returns to Social Interaction: Experimental Evidence from Microfinance." *Review of Economic Studies* 80 (4): 1459–1483.

Ferguson, James. 1994. *The Anti-politics Machine: Development, Depoliticization, and Bureaucratic Power in Lesotho.* Minneapolis: University of Minnesota Press.

———. 2015. *Give a Man a Fish: Reflections on the New Politics of Distribution.* Durham, NC: Duke University Press.

Fernandes, Kshama. 2011. "A Structured Finance Approach to Microfinance." In *The Euromoney Securitisation & Structured Finance Handbook 2011/12,* 56–64. London: Euromoney Yearbooks.

Fernandes, Leela. 1997. *Producing Workers: The Politics of Gender, Class, and Culture in Calcutta Jute Mills.* Philadelphia: University of Pennsylvania Press.

———. 2006. *India's New Middle Class: Democratic Politics in an Era of Economic Reform.* Minneapolis: University of Minnesota Press.

———. 2010. "The Violence of Forgetting." *Critical Asian Studies* 42 (2): 265–272.

Fernandes, Leela, and Patrick Heller. 2006. "Hegemonic Aspirations: New Middle

Class Politics and India's Democracy in Comparative Perspective." *Critical Asian Studies* 38 (4): 495–522.

Fine, Ben. 1999. "The Developmental State is Dead—Long Live Social Capital?" *Development and Change* 30 (1): 1–19.

Fisher, Melissa. 2012. *Wall Street Women*. Durham, NC: Duke University Press.

Fisher, Melissa, and Greg Downey. 2006. *Frontiers of Capital: Ethnographic Reflections on the New Economy*. Durham, NC: Duke University Press.

Foucault, Michel. 1991. "Governmentality." In *The Foucault Effect: Studies in Governmentality*, ed. Graham Burchell, Colin Gordon, and Peter Miller, 87–104. Chicago: University of Chicago Press.

Fox, Richard G. 1967. "Family, Caste, and Commerce in a North Indian Market Town." *Economic Development and Cultural Change* 15 (3): 297–314.

Fraser, Nancy. 1992. "Rethinking the Public Sphere: A Contribution to the Critique of Actually Existing Democracy." In *Habermas and the Public Sphere*, ed. C. Calhoun, 56–80. Cambridge, MA: MIT Press.

———. 2003. "From Discipline to Flexibilization? Rereading Foucault in the Shadow of Globalization." *Constellations* 10 (2): 160–171.

———. 2013. *Fortunes of Feminism: From State Managed Capitalism to Neoliberal Crisis*. London: Verso.

Freeman, Carla. 2000. *High Tech and High Heels in the Global Economy: Women, Work and Pink-Collar Identities in the Caribbean*. Durham, NC: Duke University Press.

Fruzzetti, Lina. 1982. *The Gift of the Virgin: Women, Marriage and Ritual in a Bengali Society*. New Brunswick, NJ: Rutgers University Press.

Fruzzetti, Lina, and Ákos Östör. 2003. *Calcutta Conversations*. New Delhi: Chronicle Books.

Fukuyama, Francis. 2001. "Social Capital, Civil Society and Development." *Third World Quarterly* 22 (1): 7–20.

Fukuzawa, Hiroshi. 1983. "Agrarian Relations: Western India." In *The Cambridge Economic History of India*, ed. Dharma Kumar and Meghnad Desai, 177–206. Cambridge: Cambridge University Press.

Gahwiler, Barbara, and Alice Negre. 2011. *Trends in Cross-border Funding*. Washington, DC: CGAP.

Galema, Rients, Robert Lensink, and Laura Spierdijk. 2011. "International Diversification and Microfinance." *Journal of International Money and Finance* 30 (3): 507–515.

Ganapati, Priya. 2003. "India Inc Rediscovers Mahatma Gandhi." *Rediff*, April 11. http://www.rediff.com/money/2003/apr/11spec2.htm.

Gandhi, Indira. 1975. "Re-orientation of Credit Policies." In *The Years of Endeavor: Selected Speeches of Indira Gandhi, August 1969–August 1972*. New Delhi: Publications Division, Ministry of Information and Broadcasting, Government of India.

Ganguly, Deepankar. 2009. "SOPs for Hospitals to Treat Poor." *The Telegraph* (Calcutta), May 23.

Garcia, Angela. 2010. *The Pastoral Clinic: Addiction and Dispossession along the Rio Grande*. Berkeley: University of California Press.

Garcia-Parpet, Marie-France. 2007. "The Social Construction of a Perfect Market: The Strawberry Auction at Fontaines-en-Sologne." In *Do Economists Make Markets?*, ed. Donald MacKenzie, Fabian Muniesa, and Lucia Siu, 20–53. Princeton, NJ: Princeton University Press.

Gates Foundation. 2009. "Microcredit Summit Campaign to Expand Efforts to Document Success of Microfinance." Press release. https://www.gatesfoundation .org/Media-Center/Press-Releases/2009/01/Microcredit-Summit-Campaign-to -Expand-Efforts-to-Document-Success-of-Microfinance.

———. 2010. "Grants Signal New Movement toward Savings Accounts for the Poor." Press release. https://www.gatesfoundation.org/Media-Center/Press-Re leases/2010/01/Grants-Signal-New-Movement-Toward-Savings-Accounts-for -the-Poor.

Ghate, Prabhu. 2007. *Indian Microfinance: The Challenges of Rapid Growth*. New Delhi: Sage.

———. 2008. *Microfinance in India: A State of the Sector Report, 2007*. New Delhi: Sage.

Ghertner, Asher. 2011. "Rule by Aesthetics: World-Class City Making in Delhi." In *Worlding Cities: Asian Experiments and the Art of Being Global*, ed. Ananya Roy and Aihwa Ong, 279–306. Malden, MA: Blackwell.

Ghosh, Parimal. 2004. "Where Have All the 'Bhadraloks' Gone?" *Economic and Political Weekly* 39 (3): 247–251.

Giddens, Anthony. 1991. *Modernity and Self-Identity: Self and Society in the Late Modern Age*. Stanford, CA: Stanford University Press.

Giné, Xavier, and Dean Karlan. 2014. "Group versus Individual Liability: Short and Long Term Evidence from Philippine Microcredit Lending Groups." *Journal of Development Economics* 107 (March): 65–83.

Goetz, Ane Marie, and Rina Sen Gupta. 1996. "Who Takes the Credit? Gender, Power, and Control over Loan Use in Rural Credit Programs in Bangladesh." *World Development* 24 (1): 45–63.

Golomski, Casey. 2015. "Compassion Technology: Life Insurance and the Remaking of Kinship in Swaziland's Age of HIV." *American Ethnologist* 42 (1): 81–96.

Goodman, Michael. 2004. "Reading Fair Trade: Political Ecological Imaginary and the Moral Economy of Fair Trade Foods." *Political Geography* 23 (7): 891–915.

Gooptu, Nandini. 2007. "Economic Liberalisation, Work and Democracy: Industrial Decline and Urban Politics in Kolkata." *Economic and Political Weekly* 42 (21): 1922–1933.

Graeber, David. 2001. *Toward an Anthropological Theory of Value: The False Coin of Our Own Dreams*. New York: Palgrave.

———. 2011a. *Debt: The First 5000 Years*. New York: Melville House.

———. 2011b. "Occupy Wall Street Rediscovers the Radical Imagination." *The Guardian*, September 25.

Granovetter, Mark. 1985. "Economic Action and Social Structure: The Problem of Embeddedness." *American Journal of Sociology* 91 (3): 481–510.

Gregory, C. A. 1997. *Savage Money: The Anthropology and Politics of Commodity Exchange*. Amsterdam: Psychology Press.

Guérin, Isabelle, Bert D'Espallier, and Roy Mersland. 2013. "Focus on Women in Microfinance Institutions." *Journal of Development Studies* 49 (5): 589–608.

Halliburton, Murphy. 1998. "Suicide: A Paradox of Development in Kerala." *Economic and Political Weekly* 33 (36/37): 2341–2345.

———. 2005. "'Just Some Spirits': The Erosion of Spirit Possession and the Rise of 'Tension' in South India." *Medical Anthropology* 24 (2): 111–144.

Han, Clara. 2012. *Life in Debt: Times of Care and Violence in Neoliberal Chile*. Berkeley: University of California Press.

Hansen, Thomas Blom. 1999. *The Saffron Wave: Democracy and Hindu Nationalism in Modern India*. Princeton, NJ: Princeton University Press.

Hanson, James. 2003. "Indian Banking: Market Liberalization and the Pressures for Institutional and Market Framework Reform." In *Reforming India's External, Financial, and Fiscal Policies*, ed. Anne O. Krueger and Sajjid Z. Chinoy, 97–125. Stanford, CA: Stanford University Press.

Harris, Laurence. 1976. "On Interest, Credit and Capital." *Economy and Society* 5 (2): 145–177.

Harriss, John, and Paolo De Renzio. 1997. "'Missing Link' or Analytically Missing? The Concept of Social Capital." *Journal of International Development* 9 (7): 919–937.

Harriss-White, Barbara. 2002. *India Working: Essays on Society and Economy*. Cambridge: Cambridge University Press.

Hart, Keith. 1973. "Income Opportunities and Urban Employment in Ghana." *Journal of Modern African Studies* 11 (1): 61–89.

Harvey, David. 2003. *The New Imperialism*. Oxford: Oxford University Press.

Henaff, Marcel. 2010. *The Price of Truth: Gift, Money and Philosophy*. Translated by Jean Louis Morhange. Stanford, CA: Stanford University Press.

Hilton, Matthew, and Martin Daunton, eds. 2001. *The Politics of Consumption: Material Culture and Citizenship in Europe and America*. Oxford: Berg.

The Hindu. 2011. "MFIs Can Tap ECBs." December 19. http://www.thehindu.com /business/Economy/mfis-can-tap-ecb/article2729442.ece.

Ho, Karen. 2009. *Liquidated: An Ethnography of Wall Street*. Durham, NC: Duke University Press.

———. 2010. "Outsmarting Risk: From Bonuses to Bailouts." *Anthro Now* 2 (1): 1–9.

———. 2012. "Occupy Finance and the Paradox / Possibilities of Productivity." *Cultural Anthropology*, May 15, 3–6. http://culanth.org/?q=node/573.

Hochschild, Arlie. 1983. *The Managed Heart: Commercialization of Feeling*. Berkeley: University of California Press.

Holmes, Douglas. 2014. *Economy of Words: Communicative Imperatives in Central Banks*. Chicago: University of Chicago Press.

Holvoet, Nathalie. 2005. "The Impact of Microfinance on Decision-Making Agency: Evidence from South India." *Development and Change* 36 (1): 75–102.

Hoogvelt, Ankie. 1997. *Globalization and the Postcolonial World: The New Political Economy of Development*. Baltimore: Johns Hopkins University Press.

Hutnyk, John. 1996. *The Rumour of Calcutta: Tourism, Charity and the Poverty of Representation*. London: Zed Books.

Illouz, Eva. 2007. *Cold Intimacies: The Making of Emotional Capitalism*. Malden, MA: Polity Press.

IRDA (Insurance Regulatory and Development Authority). 2005. *(Micro-Insurance) Regulations*. https://irdai.gov.in/ADMINCMS/cms/frmGeneral_NoYearList.aspx?DF=RL&mid=26.1.

———. 2007. *History of Insurance in India*. https://irdai.gov.in/ADMINCMS/cms/NormalData_Layout.aspx?page=PageNo4&mid=2.

Ito, Sanae. 2003. "Microfinance and Social Capital: Does Social Capital Help Create Good Practice?" *Development in Practice* 13 (4): 322–332.

Jaffrelot, Cristophe. 2003. *India's Silent Revolution: The Rise of Lower Castes in North India*. New York: Columbia University Press.

James, Deborah. 2015. *Money from Nothing: Indebtedness and Aspiration in South Africa*. Stanford, CA: Stanford University Press.

Jameson, Frederic. 1997. "Culture and Finance Capital." *Critical Inquiry* 24 (1): 246–265.

Jeffrey, Craig. 2010. *Timepass: Youth, Class, and the Politics of Waiting in India*. Stanford, CA: Stanford University Press.

Jeffrey, Craig, and Stephen Young. 2014. "Jugād: Youth and Enterprise in India." *Annals of the Association of American Geographers* 104 (1): 192–195.

Jenq, Christina, Jessica Pan, and Walter Theseira. 2015. "Beauty, Weight, and Skin Color in Charitable Giving." *Journal of Economic Behavior & Organization* 119 (November): 234–253.

Jordan, William. 1993. *Women and Credit in Pre-industrial and Developing Societies*. Philadelphia: University of Pennsylvania Press.

Joshi, Deepali Pant. 2006. *Social Banking: Promise, Performance and Potential*. New Delhi: Foundation Books.

Kabeer, Naila.1999. "Resources, Agency, Achievements: Reflections on the Measurement of Women's Empowerment." *Development and Change* 30:435–464.

Kar, Sohini. 2017a. "Austerity Welfare: Social Security in the Era of Finance." *Anthropology Today* 33 (5): 12–15.

———. 2017b. "Crisis, Again: On Demonetization and Microfinance," *Cultural Anthropology*, September 27. https://culanth.org/fieldsights/1213-crisis-again-on-demonetization-and-microfinance.

———. 2017c. "Relative Indemnity: Risk, Insurance, and Kinship in Indian Microfinance." *Journal of the Royal Anthropological Institute* 23 (2): 302–319.

———. 2018. "Securitizing Women: Gender, Precaution, and Risk in Indian Finance." *Signs: Journal of Women in Culture and Society* 43 (2): 301–325.

Kar, Sohini, and Caroline Schuster. 2016. "Comparative Projects and the Limits of Choice: Ethnography and Microfinance in India and Paraguay." *Journal of Cultural Economy* 9 (4): 347–363.

Karim, Lamia. 2011. *Microfinance and Its Discontents: Women in Debt in Bangladesh*. Minneapolis: University of Minnesota Press.

Karlekar, Malavika. 1986. "Kadambini and the Bhadralok: Early Debates over Women's Education in Bengal." *Economic and Political Weekly* 21 (17): WS25–WS31.

Karmakar, K. G. 1999. *Rural Credit and Self-Help Groups: Micro-finance Needs and Concepts in India*. New Delhi: Sage.

Karnani, Aneel. 2007. "Microfinance Misses Its Mark." *Stanford Social Innovation Review* 35 (Summer): 34–40.

Karunakaran, Naren. 2011. "Dalit Entrepreneurs Make a Mark in New Age India Inc." *Economic Times* (Kolkata), May 1, 1.

Kaviraj, Sudipta. 1997. "Filth and the Public Sphere: Concepts and Practices about Space in Calcutta." *Public Culture* 1 (1): 83–113.

Kazmin, Amy. 2014. "Strong Demand Fuels Renaissance of India Microfinance." *Financial Times*, October 9.

———. 2015. India Microlenders Upgrade to Banks. *Financial Times*, September 17.

Kelkar, Govind, Dev Nathan, and Rownok Jahan. 2004. "Redefining Women's 'Samman': Microcredit and Gender Relations in Rural Bangladesh." *Economic and Political Weekly* 39 (32): 3627–3640.

Keyes, Charles. 1983. "Introduction: The Study of Popular Ideas of Karma." In *Karma: An Anthropological Inquiry*, ed. Charles Keyes and E. V. Daniel, 1–24. Berkeley: University of California Press.

Khan, H. R. 2005. *Report of the Internal Group to Examine Issues Relating to Rural Credit and Microfinance*. Mumbai: Reserve Bank of India.

Khape, Anil. 2009. "Self-Help Groups: New Vehicle for Political Outreach." *Indian Express*, October 8.

Khurana, Rakesh. 2002. *Searching for a Corporate Savior: The Irrational Quest for Charismatic CEOs*. Princeton, NJ: Princeton University Press.

Kinetz, Erika. 2012. "AP Impact." *Associated Press*, February 24.

Knorr Cetina, Karin. 2005. "How Are Global Markets Global? The Architecture of a Flow World." In *The Sociology of Financial Markets*, ed. Karin Knorr Cetina and Alex Preda, 38–61. Oxford: Oxford University Press.

Knorr Cetina, Karin, and Alex Preda. 2005. *The Sociology of Financial Markets*. Oxford: Oxford University Press.

Kohli, Atul. 1989. *The State and Poverty in India*. Cambridge: Cambridge University Press.

———. 1990. *Democracy and Its Discontent: India's Growing Crisis of Governability*. Cambridge: Cambridge University Press.

———. 2004. *State-Directed Development: Political Power and Industrialization in the Global Periphery*. Cambridge: Cambridge University Press.

———. 2012. *Poverty amid Plenty in the New India*. Cambridge: Cambridge University Press.

Krauss, Nicolas, and Ingo Walter. 2009. "Can Microfinance Reduce Portfolio Volatility?" *Economic Development and Cultural Change* 58 (1): 85–110.

Krippner, Greta. 2001. "The Elusive Market: Embeddedness and the Paradigm of Economic Sociology." *Theory and Society* 30 (6): 775–810.

———. 2011. *Capitalizing on Crisis: The Political Origins of the Rise of Finance*. Cambridge, MA: Harvard University Press.

Kumar, R. K. 2010. "Political Parties Woo SHGs." *The Hindu*, December 30, 11–12.

Lamb, Sarah. 1997. "The Making and Unmaking of Persons: Notes on Aging and Gender in North India." *Ethos* 25 (3): 279–302.

Lambek, Michael, ed. 2010. *Ordinary Ethics: Anthropology, Language, and Action*. New York: Fordham University Press.

Langford, Jean M. 2009. "Gifts Intercepted: Biopolitics and Spirit Debt." *Cultural Anthropology* 24 (4): 681–711.

Lazar, Sian. 2004. "Education for Credit: Development as Citizenship Project in Bolivia." *Critique of Anthropology* 24 (3): 301–319.

Lee, Benjamin, and Edward LiPuma. 2002. "Cultures of Circulation: The Imaginations of Modernity." *Public Culture* 14 (1): 191–213.

———. 2004. *Financial Derivatives and the Globalization of Risk*. Durham, NC: Duke University Press.

Lemire, Beverly, Ruth Pearson, and Gail Campbell. 2001. *Women and Credit: Researching the Past, Refiguring the Future*. Oxford: Berg.

Lepinay, Vincent. 2011. *Codes of Finance: Engineering Derivatives in a Global Bank*. Princeton, NJ: Princeton University Press.

Leyshon, Andrew, Paola Signoretta, David Knights, Catrina Alferoff, and Dawn Burton. 2006. "Walking with Moneylenders: The Ecology of the UK Home-Collected Credit Industry." *Urban Studies* 43 (1): 161–186.

Leyshon, Andrew, and Nigel Thrift. 2007. "The Capitalization of Almost Everything: The Future of Finance and Capitalism." *Theory, Culture & Society* 24 (7–8): 97–115.

Li, Tania. 2014. *Land's End: Capitalist Relations on an Indigenous Frontier*. Durham, NC: Duke University Press.

Livingston, Julie. 2009. "Suicide, Risk, and Investment in the Heart of the African Miracle." *Cultural Anthropology* 24 (4): 652–680.

Lutz, Catherine. 2006. "Empire Is in the Details." *American Ethnologist* 33 (4): 593–611.

Lutz, Catherine, and Donald Nonini. 1999. "The Economies of Violence and the Violence of Economies." In *Anthropological Theory Today*, ed. Henrietta Moore, 73–113. London: Polity Press.

Lyon, Sarah, and Mark Moberg, eds. 2010. *Fair Trade and Social Justice: Global Ethnographies*. New York: New York University Press.

MacKenzie, Donald. 2007. "Is Economics Performative? Option Theory and the

Construction of Derivatives Markets." In *Do Economists Make Markets? On the Performativity of Economics*, ed. Donald MacKenzie, Fabian Muniesa, and Lucia Siu, 54–86. Princeton, NJ: Princeton University Press.

MacKenzie, Donald, Fabian Muniesa, and Lucia Siu, eds. 2007. *Do Economists Make Markets? On the Performativity of Economics*. Princeton, NJ: Princeton University Press.

Mader, Philip. 2013. "Rise and Fall of Microfinance in India: The Andhra Pradesh Crisis in Perspective." *Strategic Change* 22 (1–2): 47–66.

———. 2015. *The Political Economy of Microfinance: Financializing Poverty*. Basingstoke, UK: Palgrave Macmillan.

Mahajan, Vijay. 2011. "Operation Successful—Patient Dead." *Financial Express*, January 21.

Mahmood, Saba. 2005. *Politics of Piety: The Islamic Revival and the Feminist Subject*. Princeton, NJ: Princeton University Press.

Majumdar, Diptos. 2010. "Jyoti Basu, the Last Bhadralok Communist." *News18*, January 18. http://www.news18.com/blogs/india/diptosh-majumdar/jyoti-basu-the-last-bhadralok-communist-14010-744722.html.

Malegam, Y. H. 2011. *Report of the Sub-committee of the Central Board of Directors of Reserve Bank of India to Study Issues and Concerns in the MFI Sector*. Mumbai: Reserve Bank of India.

Malinowski, Bronislaw. 2002. *Argonauts of the Western Pacific*. New York: Routledge.

Mani, Lata. 1998. *Contentious Traditions: The Debate on Sati in Colonial India*. Berkeley: University of California Press.

Martin, Randy. 2002. *Financialization of Daily Life*. Philadelphia: Temple University Press.

———. 2009. "The Twin Towers of Financialization: Entanglements of Political and Cultural Economies." *Global South* 3 (1): 108–125.

Marx, Karl. 1978. *The Marx-Engels Reader*. 2nd ed. Edited by Robert Tucker. New York: W. W. Norton.

———. 1991. *Capital: A Critique of Political Economy, Vol. 3*. London: Penguin Classics.

Maurer, Bill. 2002. "Repressed Futures: Financial Derivatives' Theological Unconscious." *Economy and Society* 31 (1): 15–36.

———. 2005a. "Due Diligence and 'Reasonable Man,' Offshore." *Cultural Anthropology* 20 (4): 474–505.

———. 2005b. *Mutual Life, Limited: Islamic Banking, Alternative Currencies, Lateral Reason*. Princeton, NJ: Princeton University Press.

———. 2006. "The Anthropology of Money." *Annual Review of Anthropology* 35:15–36.

Mauss, Marcel. 2000. *The Gift: The Form and Reason for Exchange in Archaic Societies*. New York: W. W. Norton.

Mazzarella, William. 2003. *Shoveling Smoke: Advertising and Globalization in Contemporary India*. Durham, NC: Duke University Press.

McLean, Bethany, and Joe Nocera. 2011. *All the Devils Are Here: The Hidden History of the Financial Crisis.* New York: Penguin.

Menon, Shailesh. 2010. "MFIs Increasingly Raising Money through Securitisation." *Economic Times*, August 30.

Metcalf, Thomas. 1962. "The British and the Moneylender in Nineteenth-Century India." *Journal of Modern History* 34 (4): 390–397.

Mian, Atif, and Amir Sufi. 2015. *House of Debt: How They (and You) Caused the Great Recession, and How We Can Prevent It from Happening Again.* Chicago: University of Chicago Press.

Microfinance Focus. 2010. "Exclusive: 54 Microfinance-Related Suicides in AP, SERP Report." http://www.microfinancefocus.com/content/exclusive-54-micro finance-related-suicides-ap-says-serp-report (site discontinued).

Millar, Kathleen. 2014. "The Precarious Present: Wageless Labor and Disrupted Life in Rio de Janeiro, Brazil." *Cultural Anthropology* 29 (1): 32–53.

Miller, Daniel. 2002. "Turning Callon the Right Way Up." *Economy and Society* 31 (2): 218–233.

Miller, Margaret. 2003. *Credit Reporting Systems and the International Economy.* Cambridge, MA: MIT Press.

Mitchell, Timothy. 2002. *Rule of Experts: Egypt, Techno-politics, Modernity.* Berkeley: University of California Press.

Miyazaki, Hirokazu. 2003. "The Temporalities of the Market. *American Anthropologist* 105 (2): 255–65.

———. 2013. *Arbitraging Japan: Dreams of Capitalism at the End of Finance.* Berkeley: University of California Press.

Mohanakumar, S., and R. K. Sharma. 2006. "Analysis of Farmer Suicides in Kerala." *Economic and Political Weekly* 41 (16): 1553–1558.

Mohanty, B. B., and Sangeeta Shroff. 2004. "Farmers' Suicides in Maharashtra." *Economic and Political Weekly* 39 (52): 5599–5606.

Mohanty, Chandra Talpade. 1991. "Under Western Eyes: Feminist Scholarship and Colonial Discourses." In *Third World Women and the Politics of Feminism*, ed. Chandra Talpade Mohanty, Ann Russo, and Lourdes Torres, 51–80. Bloomington: Indiana University Press.

Molé, Noelle. 2012. "Hauntings of Solidarity in Post-Fordist Italy." *Anthropological Quarterly* 85 (2): 371–396.

Molyneux, Maxine. 2002. "Gender and the Silences of Social Capital: Lessons from Latin America." *Development and Change* 33 (2): 167–188.

Moodie, Megan. 2008. "Enter Microcredit: A New Culture of Women's Empowerment in Rajasthan?" *American Ethnologist* 35 (3): 454–465.

Moore, Elaine. 2012. "Banks Face £3bn Bill in PPI Scandal." *Financial Times*, March 6.

Moore, Henrietta. 2011. *Still Life: Hopes, Desires and Satisfactions.* Cambridge: Polity Press.

Mother India. 1957. Directed by Mehboob Khan. Bombay: Mehboob Productions.

Muehlebach, Andrea. 2011. "On Affective Labor in Post-Fordist Italy." *Cultural Anthropology* 26 (1): 59–82.

Muehlebach, Andrea, and Nitzan Shoshan. 2012. "Post-Fordist Affect: Introduction." *Anthropological Quarterly* 85 (2): 317–344.

Mukherjee, Pranab. 2010. "Union Budget Speech 2010–2011." Government of India, February 26. http://indiabudget.nic.in/ub2010-11/bs/speecha.htm.

Mukhopadhyay, Ishita. 1998. "Calcutta's Informal Sector: Changing Pattern of Labour Use." *Economic and Political Weekly* 33 (47/48): 3075–3080.

Munn, Nancy. 1992. *The Fame of Gawa: A Symbolic Study of Value Transformation in a Massim Society.* Durham, NC: Duke University Press.

NABARD (National Bank for Agriculture and Rural Development). n.d. *A Handbook on Forming Self-Help Groups (SHGs).* Mumbai: NABARD.

Nair, Tara. 2009. "Urban Microfinance in the Context of Urban Poverty." In *India Urban Poverty Report*, ed. Ministry of Housing and Poverty Alleviation, Government of India, 114–128. New Delhi: Oxford University Press.

Nandy, Ashis. 1990. "The Politics of Secularism and the Recovery of Religious Tolerance." In *Mirrors of Violence*, ed. Veena Das, 69–93. New Delhi: Oxford University Press.

———. 2001. *An Ambiguous Journey to the City: The Village and Other Odd Ruins of the Indian Imagination.* New Delhi: Oxford University Press.

Nash, June. 1994. "Global Integration and Subsistence Insecurity." *American Anthropologist* 96 (1): 7–30.

National Human Rights Commission. 2011. *NHRC Issues Notices to the Maharashtra, Andhra Pradesh and Kerala Governments on Farmers' Suicide.* New Delhi: NHRC.

Nayak, Gayatri. 2010. "For-Profit MFIs Worse Than Money Lenders." *Economic Times*, November 23.

Nordstrom, Carolyn. 2001. "Out of the Shadows." In *Intervention and Transnationalism in Africa: Global-Local Networks of Power*, ed. Thomas Callaghy, Ronald Kassimir, and Robert Latham, 216–239. Cambridge: Cambridge University Press.

O'Connell, Sean. 2009. *Credit and Community: Working-Class Debt in the UK since 1880.* Oxford: Oxford University Press.

O'Connor, Sarah, and Sophia Grene. 2009. "Microfinance Group in CDO Scheme." *Financial Times*, November 11.

O'Donohoe, Nick, Christina Leijonhufvud, and Yasemin Saltuk. 2010. *Impact Investments: An Emerging Asset Class.* J. P. Morgan Global Research, November 29. https://www.jpmorganchase.com/corporate/socialfinance/document/impact_investments_nov2010.pdf.

Ong, Aihwa. 2006. *Neoliberalism as Exception: Mutations in Citizenship and Sovereignty.* Durham, NC: Duke University Press.

O'Reilly, Kathleen. 2006. "'Traditional' Women, 'Modern' Water: Linking Gender and Commodification in Rajasthan, India. *Geoforum* 37:958–972.

Oza, Rupal. 2006. *The Making of Neoliberal India: Nationalism, Gender, and the Paradoxes of Globalization.* New York: Routledge.

Pandey, Gyanendra. 1999. "Can a Muslim Be an Indian?" *Comparative Studies in Society and History* 41 (4): 608–629.

Pandian, Anand. 2008. "Devoted to Development: Moral Progress, Ethical Work, and Divine Favor in South India." *Anthropological Theory* 8 (2): 159–179.

Parry, Jonathan. 1989. "On the Moral Perils of Exchange." In *Money and the Morality of Exchange*, ed. Jonathan Parry and Maurice Bloch, 64–93. Cambridge: Cambridge University Press.

———. 2012. "Suicide in a Central Indian Steel Town." *Contributions to Indian Sociology* 46 (1–2): 145–180.

Parry, Jonathan, and Maurice Bloch, eds. "Introduction." In *Money and the Morality of Exchange*, ed. Jonathan Parry and Maurice Bloch, 1–32. Cambridge: Cambridge University Press.

Pate, R. Carter, Jairaj Purandare, Wim Oosterom, and Todd Hall. 2007. *Healthcare in India: Emerging Market Report 2007*. London: PricewaterhouseCoopers.

Patel, Geeta. 2007. "Imagining Risk, Care and Security: Insurance and Fantasy." *Anthropological Theory* 7 (1): 99–118.

Patnaik, Prabhu. 2007. "In the Aftermath of Nandigram." *Economic and Political Weekly* 42 (21): 1893–1895.

Pedersen, Jurgen. 2001. "India's Industrial Dilemmas in West Bengal." *Asian Survey* 41 (4): 646–668.

Peebles, Gustav. 2008. "Inverting the Panopticon: Money and the Nationalization of the Future." *Public Culture* 20 (2): 233–265.

———. 2010. "The Anthropology of Credit and Debt." *Annual Review of Anthropology* 39:225–240.

Peepli Live. 2010. Directed by Anusha Rizvi. Mumbai: Aamir Khan Productions.

Petryna, Adriana. 2002. *Life Exposed: Biological Citizens after Chernobyl*. Princeton, NJ: Princeton University Press.

Pietz, William. 1997. "Death of the Deodand: Accursed Objects and the Money Value of Human Life." *Anthropology and Aesthetics* 31 (Spring): 97–108.

Pinto, Sarah. 2011. "Rational Love, Relational Medicine: Psychiatry and the Accumulation of Precarious Kinship." *Culture, Medicine and Psychiatry* 35 (3): 376–395.

Planning Commission, Government of India. 2008. *Eleventh Five-Year Plan*. Vol. 1. New Delhi: Oxford University Press.

———. 2009. *A Hundred Small Steps: Report of the Committee on Financial Sector Reforms*. New Delhi: Sage.

———. 2013. *Twelfth Five-Year Plan*. New Delhi: Sage.

Po, June, and S. V. Subramanian. 2011. "Mortality Burden and Socioeconomic Status in India." *PLoS ONE* 6 (2): 1–8.

Polanyi, Karl. 1957. *The Great Transformation: The Political and Economic Origins of Our Time*. New York: Beacon Press.

Poon, Martha. 2009. "From New Deal Institutions to Capital Markets: Commercial Consumer Risk Scores and the Making of Subprime Mortgage Finance. *Accounting, Organizations and Society* 34 (5): 654–674.

Poovey, Mary. 2008. *Genres of the Credit Economy: Mediating Value in Eighteenth- and Nineteenth-Century Britain*. Chicago: University of Chicago Press.

Portes, Alejandro. 1998. "Social Capital: Its Origins and Applications in Modern Sociology." *Annual Review of Sociology* 24:1–24.

Prahalad, C. K. 2010. *The Fortune at the Bottom of the Pyramid: Eradicating Poverty through Profits*. 5th anniversary ed. Philadelphia: Wharton School Publishing.

Prakash, Gyan. 2010. *Noir Urbanisms: Dystopic Images of the Modern City*. Princeton, NJ: Princeton University Press.

Press Information Bureau. 2014. *Rangarajan Report on Poverty*. Delhi: Planning Commission, Government of India.

PTI (Press Trust of India). 2014a. "Foreign Investor Stake in SKS Microfinance Hits Record High in September Quarter." *NDTV*, October 28.

———. 2014b. "RBI's Plan to Grant New Bank Licenses Could Increase Risks Banking Sector: S&P." *Economic Times*, October 28.

Puhazhendi, V., and K. C. Badatya. 2002. *SHG-Bank Linkage Programme for Rural Poor—an Impact Assessment*. Mumbai: NABARD.

Putnam, Robert. 1993. *Making Democracy Work: Civic Traditions in Modern Italy*. Princeton, NJ: Princeton University Press.

Qadeer, Imrana. 2000. "Health Care Systems in Transition III. India, Part I. The Indian Experience." *Journal of Public Health Medicine* 22 (1): 25–32.

Radhakrishnan, Smitha. 2011. *Appropriately Indian: Gender and Culture in a New Transnational Class*. Durham, NC: Duke University Press.

Rahman, Aminur. 1999. *Women and Microcredit in Rural Bangladesh: An Anthropological Study of Grameen Bank Lending*. Boulder, CO: Westview Press.

Rediff Business. 2010. "RBI for Higher Pay to PSU Bank CEOs." September 7. http://business.rediff.com/report/2010/sep/07/rbi-governor-for-higher-compensation-to-psb-staff.htm.

Rai, Vineet. 2010. "India's Microfinance Crisis Is a Battle to Monopolize the Poor." *Harvard Business Review*, November 4.

Rajagopal, Arvind. 2001. "The Violence of Commodity Aesthetics: Hawkers, Demolition Raids, and a New Regime of Consumption." *Social Text* 19 (3): 91–114.

Rajak, Dinah. 2011. *In Good Company: An Anatomy of Corporate Social Responsibility*. Stanford, CA: Stanford University Press.

Rajan, Raghuram. 2010. *Fault Lines: How Hidden Fractures Still Threaten the World Economy*. Princeton, NJ: Princeton University Press.

Rajshekhar, M. 2012. "Changes in Draft Microfinance Institutions Bill Shocks the Microfinance Sector." *Economic Times*, May 26.

Ranade, Ajit, and Rajeev Ahuja. 1999. "Life Insurance in India: Emerging Issues." *Economic and Political Weekly* 34 (3/4): 203–212.

Rangarajan, C. 2008. *Report of the Committee on Financial Inclusion*. Mumbai: NABARD.

Rankin, Katherine. 2001. "Governing Development: Neoliberalism, Microcredit, and Rational Economic Woman." *Economy and Society* 30 (1): 18–37.

————. 2002. "Social Capital, Microfinance, and the Politics of Development." *Feminist Economics* 8 (1): 1–24.

Ray, Atmadip. 2016. "Firms Are Now Looking to Invest in MFIs after RBI Awarded Small Finance Bank Licenses." *Economic Times*, April 20.

Ray, Rajat Kanta. 1995. "Asian Capital in the Age of European Domination: The Rise of the Bazaar, 1800–1914." *Modern Asian Studies* 29 (3): 449–554.

Ray, Raka, and Seemin Qayum. 2009. *Cultures of Servitude: Modernity, Domesticity, and Class in India*. Stanford, CA: Stanford University Press.

Ray, Utsa. 2010. "Aestheticizing Labour: An Affective Discourse of Cooking in Colonial Bengal." *South Asian History and Culture* 1 (1): 60–70.

Raychaudhuri, Ajitava, and Biswajit Chatterjee. 1998. "Pattern of Industrial Growth in West Bengal during Last Two Decades: Some Policy Suggestions." *Economic and Political Weekly* 33 (47/48): 3061–3065.

Razavi, Shahrashoub, and Carol Miller. 1995. *From WID to GAD: Conceptual Shifts in the Women and Development Discourse*. Geneva: United Nations Research Institute for Social Development (UNRISD).

RBI (Reserve Bank of India). 1991. *Committee on the Financial System, and M. Narasimham. Report of the Committee on the Financial System*. Mumbai: RBI.

————. 2001. *Committee on Banking Sector Reforms (Narasimham Committee II)—Action Taken on the Recommendations*. https://www.rbi.org.in/Scripts/Publication ReportDetails.aspx?ID=251.

————. 2004. *"Know Your Customer" (KYC) Guidelines—Anti Money Laundering Standards*. https://rbi.org.in/Scripts/NotificationUser.aspx?Id=9914&Mode=0.

————. 2006. *Financial Inclusion by Extension of Banking Services—Use of Business Facilitators and Correspondents*. https://www.rbi.org.in/scripts/BS_CircularIndex Display.aspx?Id=2718.

————. 2007. *Report of the Technical Group Set to Review Legislations on Money Lending*. https://rbi.org.in/scripts/PublicationReportDetails.aspx?UrlPage=&ID=513.

————. 2008. *Agricultural Debt Waiver and Debt Relief Scheme, 2008*. https://rbi.org .in/scripts/BS_CircularIndexDisplay.aspx?Id=4190.

————. 2011. *Basic Statistical Returns*. https://rbidocs.rbi.org.in/rdocs/Publications /PDFs/03HIGHBSRV390711.pdf.

————. 2013. *Guidelines for Licensing of New Banks in the Private Sector*. https://rbi .org.in/scripts/BS_PressReleaseDisplay.aspx?prid=28191.

————. 2014. "RBI Decides to Grant "In-Principle" Approval for Banking Licences." Press release. https://rbi.org.in/scripts/BS_PressReleaseDisplay.aspx?prid=30931.

Riles, Annelise. 2010. "Collateral Expertise: Legal Knowledge in the Global Financial Markets." *Current Anthropology* 51 (6): 795–818.

————. 2011. *Collateral Knowledge: Legal Reasoning in the Global Financial Markets*. Chicago: University of Chicago Press.

Robinson, Marguerite. 2001. *The Microfinance Revolution: Sustainable Finance for the Poor*. Washington, DC: World Bank Publications.

Rock, Paul. 1973. *Making People Pay*. London: Routledge & Kegan Paul.

Roitman, Janet. 2005. *Fiscal Disobedience: An Anthropology of Economic Regulation in Central Africa*. Princeton, NJ: Princeton University Press.

———. 2014. *Anti-crisis*. Durham, NC: Duke University Press.

Rosaldo, Michelle. 1974. "Woman, Culture and Society: A Theoretical Overview." In *Women, Culture and Society*, ed. Louise Lamphere and Michelle Rosaldo, 17–42. Stanford, CA: Stanford University Press.

Roy, Ananya. 2003. *City Requiem, Calcutta: Gender and the Politics of Poverty*. Minneapolis: University of Minnesota Press.

———. 2010. *Poverty Capital: Microfinance and the Making of Development*. New York: Routledge.

———. 2012. "Ethical Subjects: Market Rule in an Age of Poverty." *Public Culture* 24 (1): 105–108.

Roy, Anup. 2012. "The Farm Loan Waiver Continues to Destroy the Credit Culture in Rural India." *Livemint*, February 16. http://www.livemint.com/Opinion /1FEnH9OVJlyGweMNnsdaGO/Views—The-farm-loan-waiver-continues-to -destroy-the-credit.html.

Roy, Tirthankar. 2010. *Company of Kinsmen: Enterprise and Community in South Asian History 1700–1940*. New Delhi: Oxford University Press.

Rudner, David. 1994. *Caste and Capitalism in Colonial India: The Nattukottai Chettiars*. Berkeley: University of California Press.

Saavala, Minna. 2010. *Middle-Class Moralities: Everyday Struggle over Belonging and Prestige in India*. Hyderabad: Orient Blackswan.

Sadoulet, Loic. 2005. "Learning from Visa? Incorporating Insurance Provisions in Microfinance Contracts." In *Insurance against Poverty*, ed. Stefan Dercon, 387–421. Oxford: Oxford University Press.

Sandel, Michael. 2012. *What Money Can't Buy: The Moral Limits of Markets*. New York: Farrar, Straus and Giroux.

Sanyal, Paromita. 2009. "From Credit to Collective Action: The Role of Microfinance in Promoting Women's Social Capital and Normative Influence." *American Sociological Review* 74 (4): 529–550.

———. 2014. *Credit to Capabilities: A Sociological Study of Microcredit Groups in India*. Cambridge: Cambridge University Press

Sarkar, Radha, and Amar Sarkar. 2016. "Sacred Slaughter: An Analysis of Historical, Communal, and Constitutional Aspects of Beef Bans in India." *Politics, Religion & Ideology* 17 (4): 329–351.

Sarkar, Sumit. 1992. "'Kaliyuga,' 'Chakri' and 'Bhakti': Ramakrishna and His Times." *Economic and Political Weekly* 27 (29): 1543–1559.

Scheper-Hughes, Nancy. 1992. *Death without Weeping: The Violence of Everyday Life in Brazil*. Berkeley: University of California Press.

Schrader, Heiko. 1994. "Professional Moneylenders and the Emergence of Capitalism in India and Indonesia." *International Sociology* 9 (2): 185–208.

Schuster, Caroline. 2014. "The Social Unit of Debt: Gender and Creditworthiness in Paraguayan Microfinance." *American Ethnologist* 41 (3): 563–578.

———. 2015. *Social Collateral: Women and Microfinance in Paraguay's Smuggling Economy*. Berkeley: University of California Press.

Schwarcz, Steven. 2008. "Systemic Risk." *Georgetown Law Journal* 97 (1): 193–249.

Scott, James. 1976. *The Moral Economy of the Peasant: Rebellion and Subsistence in Southeast Asia*. New Haven, CT: Yale University Press.

Scrase, Timothy. 2002. "Globalisation and the Cultural Politics of Educational Change: The Controversy over the Teaching of English in West Bengal, India." *International Review of Education* 48 (5): 361–375.

Sen, Amartya. 1999. *Development as Freedom*. New York: Anchor.

Sen, Atreyee. 2007. *Shiv Sena Women: Violence and Communalism in a Bombay Slum*. Bloomington: University of Indiana Press.

Sengupta, Urmi. 2010. "The Hindered Self-Help: Housing Policies, Politics and Poverty in Kolkata, India." *Habitat International* 34 (3): 323–331.

Sethi, Raj Mohini. 1995. "Women's ROSCAs in Contemporary India." In *Money-Go-Rounds: The Importance of Rotating Savings and Credit Associations for Women*, ed. Shirley Ardener and Sandra Burman, 163–178. Oxford: Berg.

Shah, Alpa. 2010. *In the Shadows of the State: Indigenous Politics, Environmentalism, and Insurgency in Jharkhand, India*. New Delhi: Oxford University Press.

Sharma, Aradhana. 2008. *Logics of Empowerment: Development, Gender, and Governance in Neoliberal India*. Minneapolis: University of Minnesota Press.

Sharma, Shishir, and S. Chamala. 2003. "Moneylender's Positive Image: Paradigms and Rural Development." *Economic and Political Weekly* 38 (17): 1713–1720.

Shever, Elana. 2010. "Engendering the Company: Corporate Personhood and the 'Face' of an Oil Company in Metropolitan Buenos Aires." *PoLAR: Political and Legal Anthropology Review* 33 (1): 26–46.

Shevory, Kristina. 2010. "With Credit Tight, Microlending Blossoms." *New York Times*, July 28.

Shipton, Parker. 2010. *Credit between Cultures: Farmers, Financiers, and Misunderstanding in Africa*. New Haven, CT: Yale University Press.

Shirish Sankhe, Ireena Vittal, Richard Dobbs, Ajit Mohan, Ankur Gulati, Jonathan Ablett, Shishir Gupta, Alex Kim, Sudipto Paul, Aditya Sanghvi, and Gurpreet Sethy. 2010. *India's Urban Awakening: Building Inclusive Cities, Sustaining Economic Growth*. McKinsey Global Institute, April. https://www.mckinsey.com/global-themes/urbanization/urban-awakening-in-india.

Shirreff, David. 2004. *Dealing with Financial Risk*. London: Profile Books.

Shiva, Vandana, Afsar Jafri, Ashok Emani, and Manish Pande. 2000. *Seeds of Suicide: The Ecological and Human Costs of Globalisation of Agriculture*. New Delhi: Navdanya.

Singh, Namrata. 2011. "Banks Deny Credit to MFIs, Put Condition for Restructuring." *Times of India*, February 14.

Singh, Ramendra, Vaibhav Gupta, and Akash Mondal. 2012. "Jugaad—From 'Making Do' and 'Quick Fix' to an Innovative, Sustainable and Low-Cost Survival

Strategy at the Bottom of the Pyramid." *International Journal of Rural Management* 8 (1–2): 87–105.

Sinha, Janmejaya, and Arvind Subramanian. 2007. *The Next Billion Consumers: A Road Map for Expanding Financial Inclusion in India*. Boston: Boston Consulting Group.

Sinha, Tapen. 2002. "Privatization of the Insurance Market in India: From the British Raj to Monopoly Raj to Swaraj." University of Nottingham Centre for Risk & Insurance Studies (CRIS) Discussion Paper Series, X.

Smith, James. 2008. *Bewitching Development: Witchcraft and the Reinvention of Development in Neoliberal Kenya*. Chicago: University of Chicago Press.

Spivak, Gayatri Chakravorty. 1988. "Can the Subaltern Speak?" In *Marxism and the Interpretation of Culture*, ed. Cary Nelson and Lawrence Grossberg, 271–313. Champaign: University of Illinois Press.

———. 1999. *A Critique of Postcolonial Reason: Toward a History of the Vanishing Present*. Cambridge, MA: Harvard University Press.

Standing, Guy. 2009. *Work after Globalization: Building Occupational Citizenship*. Cheltenham, UK: Edward Elgar.

Staples, James. 2012a. "Suicide in South Asia: Ethnographic Perspectives." *Contributions to Indian Sociology* 46 (1–2): 1–28.

———. 2012b. "The Suicide Niche: Accounting for Self-Harm in a South Indian Leprosy Colony." *Contributions to Indian Sociology* 46 (1–2): 117–144.

———. 2017. "Beef and Beyond: Exploring the Meat Consumption Practices of Christians in India." *Ethnos* 82 (2): 232–251.

Steingass, Francis. 2005. *A Comprehensive Persian-English Dictionary*. Delhi: Asian Educational Services.

Stoll, David. 2013. *El Norte or Bust! How Migration Fever and Microcredit Produced a Financial Crisis in a Latin American Town*. Lanham, MD: Rowman & Littlefield.

Subramanian, Ajantha. 2015. "Making Merit: The Indian Institutes of Technology and the Social Life of Caste." *Comparative Studies in Society and History* 57 (2): 291–322.

Sunder Rajan, Kausik. 2005. "Subjects of Speculation: Emergent Life Sciences and Market Logics in the United States and India." *American Anthropologist* 107 (1): 19–30.

Sunder Rajan, Rajeswari. 1993. *Real and Imagined Women: Gender, Culture, and Postcolonialism*. London: Routledge.

Taussig, Michael. 1980. *The Devil and Commodity Fetishism in South America*. Chapel Hill: University of North Carolina Press.

———. 1987. *Shamanism, Colonialism, and the Wild Man: A Study in Terror and Healing*. Chicago: University of Chicago Press.

Taylor, Avram. 2002. *Working Class Credit since 1918*. New York: Palgrave Macmillan.

Tebbutt, Melanie. 1983. *Making Ends Meet: Pawnbroking and Working-Class Credit*. Leicester, UK: Leicester University Press.

Tejani, Shabnum. 2008. *Indian Secularism: A Social and Intellectual History 1890–1950.* Bloomington: Indiana University Press.

Teltumbde, Anand. 2012. "The Maoists of Manesar." *Countercurrents*, August 29. http://www.countercurrents.org/teltumbde290812.htm.

Tett, Gillian. 2009. *Fool's Gold: How Unrestrained Greed Corrupted a Dream, Shattered Global Markets and Unleashed a Catastrophe.* New York: Little, Brown.

Thomas, Frederic. 1996. *Calcutta Poor: Elegies on a City above Pretense.* New York: East Gate.

Thompson, E. P. 1967. "Time, Work-Discipline, and Industrial Capitalism." *Past and Present* 38 (1): 56–97.

———. 1971. "The Moral Economy of the English Crowd in the Eighteenth Century." *Past and Present* 50 (1): 76–136.

———. 1991. *Customs in Common.* New York: New Press.

Times of India. 2011. "Private Hospitals to Provide Free Treatment to Poor: Supreme Court." September 1.

———. 2012. "SHGs Hold Sway over Panchayat Elections." February 8.

Torri, Michelguglielmo. 1975. "Factional Politics and Economic Policy: The Case of India's Bank Nationalization." *Asian Survey* 15 (12): 1077–1096.

Tsai, Kellee. 2004. "Imperfect Substitutes: The Local Political Economy of Informal Finance and Microfinance in Rural China and India." *World Development* 32 (9): 1487–1507.

Tsing, Anna. 2005. *Friction: An Ethnography of Global Connection.* Princeton, NJ: Princeton University Press.

Udgirkar, Trushna. 2010. "Suresh Gurumani: Micro Manager to the Core." *Economic Times*, October 13.

UN (United Nations) Women. 1995. *The United Nations Fourth World Conference on Women: Platform for Action.* http://www.un.org/womenwatch/daw/beijing /platform/plat1.htm#objectives.

Valenzuela, Samuel, and Arturo Valenzuela. 1978. "Modernization and Dependency: An Alternative Perspective to the Study of Latin American Development." *Comparative Politics* 10 (4): 535–552.

Van der Veer, Peter. 2002. "Religion in South Asia." *Annual Review of Anthropology* 32:173–187.

Wacquant, Loïc. 2008. *Urban Outcastes: A Comparative Sociology of Advanced Marginality.* Cambridge: Polity Press.

Warner, Michael. 2005. *Publics and Counterpublics.* New York: Zone Books.

Weber, Heloise. 2004. "The 'New Economy' and Social Risk: Banking on the Poor?" *Review of International Political Economy* 11 (2): 356–386.

Weber, Max. 2001. *The Protestant Ethic and the Spirit of Capitalism.* New York: Routledge.

Weeks, Kathi. 2011. *The Problem with Work: Feminism, Marxism, Antiwork Politics, and Postwork Imaginaries.* Durham, NC: Duke University Press.

Weeratunge, Nireka. 2010. "Being Sadharana: Talking about the Just Business Person in Sri Lanka." In *Ordinary Ethics: Anthropology, Language and Action*, ed. Michael Lambek, 328–348. New York: Fordham University Press.

Weiner, Annette. 1985. "Inalienable Wealth." *American Ethnologist* 12 (2): 210–227.

Welker, Marina. 2009. "'Corporate Security Begins in the Community': Mining, the Corporate Social Responsibility Industry, and Environmental Advocacy in Indonesia." *Cultural Anthropology* 24 (1): 142–179.

Weston, Kath. 2012. "Political Ecologies of the Precarious." *Anthropological Quarterly* 85 (2): 429–456.

———. 2013. "Lifeblood, Liquidity, and Cash Transfusions: Beyond Metaphor in the Cultural Study of Finance." *Journal of the Royal Anthropological Institute* 19:S24–S41.

White, Hylton. 2012. "A Post-Fordist Ethnicity: Insecurity, Authority, and Identity in South Africa." *Anthropological Quarterly* 85 (2): 397–428.

Williams, Brett. 2004. *Debt for Sale: A Social History of the Credit Trap*. Philadelphia: University of Pennsylvania Press.

Woolcock, Michael. 1998. "Social Capital and Economic Development: Toward a Theoretical Synthesis and Policy Framework." *Theory and Society* 27 (2): 151–208.

Woolcock, Michael, and Deepa Narayan. 2000. "Social Capital: Implications for Development Theory, Research, and Policy." *World Bank Research Observer* 15 (2): 225–249.

Yanagisako, Sylvia, and Jane Collier. 1990. "The Mode of Reproduction in Anthropology." In *Theoretical Perspectives on Sexual Difference*, ed. Deborah Rhode, 131–144. New Haven, CT: Yale University Press.

Yang, Mayfair. 2000. "Putting Global Capitalism in Its Place: Economic Hybridity, Bataille, and Ritual Expenditure." *Current Anthropology* 41 (4): 477–509.

Yunus, Muhammad. 2003. *Banker to the Poor: Micro-lending and the Battle against World Poverty*. New York: PublicAffairs.

———. 2007. *Creating a World without Poverty: Social Business and the Future of Capitalism*. New York: PublicAffairs.

Zaloom, Caitlin. 2006. *Out of the Pits: Traders and Technology from Chicago to London*. Chicago: University of Chicago Press.

Zanini, Giovanni. 2001. *India: The Challenges of Development*. Washington, DC: World Bank.

Zelizer, Viviana. 1978. "Human Values and the Market: The Case of Life Insurance and Death in 19th-Century America." *American Journal of Sociology* 84 (3): 591–610.

———. 1979. *Morals and Markets: The Development of Life Insurance in the United States*. New York: Columbia University Press.

———. 1989. "The Social Meaning of Money: 'Special Monies.'" *American Journal of Sociology* 95 (2): 342–377.

———. 1994. *The Social Meaning of Money*. New York: Basic Books.

Page numbers in italic indicate material in figures or tables.

Abedal, Rawi, 80
"accumulation by dispossession," 13, 87
address proof, 126, 162. *See also* house
    verifications
Aditi (borrower), 53
"aesthetics of poverty," 140
affective/emotional labor, 97–101
agency houses, 60
age of precaution, 172
"age proof" documents, 179
aging population, 176
Agricultural Debt Waiver and Debt Re-
    lief Scheme, 187–188
agriculture: displacement of women
    from, 213n5; farmer debt and sui-
    cides, 187–189; harvest failures,
    droughts, 62; social banking and
    credit, 63
Aiyar, Swaminathan, 73
Ajanta (borrower), 44–45, 54
Akula, Vikram, 34–35, 40, 71–72,
    208n4, 209n10
alienation of debts by loan officers,
    82–86
Allison, Anne, 98
allodoxia, 214n19
Althusser, Louis, 217n21
Amina (borrower), 196–197
Amit (loan officer): dangers of his job,
    94; leaving early to free up kitchen,
    99; on microfinance, 199–200, 202;
    on need to be "Gandhian" with bor-

rowers, 93–94; on non-Bengali,
    Muslim borrowers, 156; searching
    out delinquent borrowers, 1–6
Anand (branch manager): behavior to-
    ward borrowers, 94, 105–106, 194;
    blaming RBI for lack of loans, 91–
    92; on borrower suicide, 185; class
    distinctions by, 139, 158–159; con-
    trasting MFIs with moneylenders,
    93; cooking habits as worthiness cri-
    terion, 158; explaining life insurance,
    179; during financial crisis, 177–178;
    giving money to borrower's child,
    81–82; and health of borrowers, 181–
    182, 194; on lack of meeting space,
    115; loan amount decisions by, 139–
    140; and Muslim borrowers, 155, 160;
    as poor but educated, 159; on urban
    borrowers, 160–161
Anand, Nikhil, 214n11
Andhra Pradesh Micro Finance Institu-
    tions Ordinance (2010), 72–75
anthropology: on capitalist encounter,
    38; on conceptions of temporality,
    192; on domestic/public dichotomy,
    113–114, 133, 163; of finance, 12, 43
antiwork politics, 53
APL (above the poverty line) house-
    holds, 24
Appadurai, Arjun, 36, 59
Arati (borrower), 120–121, 124, 139, 154
Aretxaga, Begoña, 195, 212n23

Arijul (husband of borrower), 48–50, 54
Armendáriz de Aghion, Beatriz, 177
Aruna (borrower), 195
Asad, Talal, 189, 219n16
Asian financial crisis (1997), 65
Austin, J. L., 206n9

Badatya, K. C., 68
Bajaj Allianz, 170
Baker, Tom, 172
balance of payments crisis (1991), 64
Bandhan Microfinance, 10, 24, 58, 79,
    103, 190, 208n32
Bangladesh Liberation War, 21
Banker to the Poor (Yunus), 34, 208n3
banking: bailouts, 13; colonialism and,
    59–62; licenses, 58, 65; offshore, 151;
    social control of, 63, 66
Banking Companies (Acquisition and
    Transfer of Undertakings) Ordi-
    nance, 57
Bansal, Rashmi, 36–37
Barua, Dipal, 141
basic income grants, 55
BASIX, 74, 77, 211n9
Basu, Jyoti, 131
Basu, Mr. (MFI founder), 33–35
Battle of Plassey, 19, 182
Beck, Ulrich, 147
beef, Hindu disgust over, 154–155,
    215–216n9
Beijing Platform, 112
Bengali culture: *bhadralok* identity in,
    22, 131–133, 135–137, 158, 208n30;
    gender/class conflicts, 133–135, 137;
    importance of class in, 22–23, 28;
    language differences within, 159–
    160, 214n18, 216n16; women defined
    by marriage, 129
Berlant, Lauren, 53
Beunza, Daniel, 212n2
bhadralok ("respectable folk") class, 22,
    131–133, 135–137, 158, 208n30

Bhaduri, Bhuvaneswari, 218n10
Bharat Financial Inclusion. *See* SKS
    Microfinance/Bharat Financial
    Inclusion
Bharti (borrower), 107–109
Bhatt, Ela, 210–211n8
Bhattacharya, Tithi, 208n30
bima. See life insurance/*bima*
Bina (borrower), 120–121
biosecurity, 142
BJP (Bharatiya Janata Party), 7, 78, 157
Black, Shameem, 34–35, 208n5
Black-Scholes-Merton model, 206n9
Bloch, Maurice, 14
Boholm, Åsa, 18
Boltanski, Luc, 38, 54
Bombay Mutual Life Assurance Soci-
    ety, 175
bookbinding, 48–49
BOP ("bottom-of-the-pyramid") capi-
    talism, 33, 40–43
borrowers/borrowers' groups: charg-
    ing rent for meetings, 117; credit-
    worthiness of all at risk, 5; diffi-
    culties of weekly payments, 191;
    displacing lack temporarily, 18;
    group leaders, 85; leaders' ability to
    deny loans, 125; learning about from
    neighbors, 119; limited understand-
    ing of finance, 11; procuring loans for
    husbands, 53; relationships affected
    by debt, 6. *See also* group meetings;
    life insurance/*bima*
Bose, Mr. (MFI founder), 31–32, 34–35
Bose, Purnima, 35
Boserup, Esther, 111, 213n5
bottom billion capitalism, 40–41, 43, 54
"bottom-of-the-pyramid" (BOP) capi-
    talism, 33, 40–43
Bourdieu, Pierre, 88, 123, 155, 207n19,
    213n2, 214n19, 216n11
BPL (below the poverty line) house-
    holds, 24, 91

branch managers (DENA), 25–26, 85, 141–142, 146–147. *See also* Anand; Mukul; Putul; Saurav
Brenner, Suzanne, 109
British colonial rule, 19, 59–60
Brown, Wendy, 54
"business ethics," 41
"business junkies," 36
bustee/slum, 163

Calcutta, 16, 19–21, 207n24. *See also* Kolkata
Callon, Michel, 12
Can the Subaltern Speak? (Spivak), 218
"capitalization of almost everything," 12
caste system, 216n14; and class, 157–159; discrimination within, 39; question on application, 150
casualization of labor, 20
catadores in Brazil, 54–55
categories of exclusion, 157–160
Cattelino, Jessica, 207n18
CDOs (collateralized debt obligations), 88, 143
CEOs, charismatic authority of, 211n11
CGAP think tank, 100
Chakrabarty, K. C., 39
Chakravorty, Sanjoy, 19–20
Chan, Cheris Shun-ching, 175, 176
Chandavarkar, A. G., 60–61
Charnock, Job, 19
Chatterjee, Partha, 21, 47, 133, 208n29, 213n4
Chatterjee, Piya, 214n16
Chiapello, Ève, 38, 54
Chidambaram, P., 66, 187
China, war with, 62
chit funds, 61
chotolok/lowly people, 131
Chua, Jocelyn, 218n9
CIBIL, 166
Citi, 10, 145
citizen role(s), 210n6; "citizenship

through labor," 52; creditworthiness as, 166; marked and unmarked, 157; poor as consumers not citizens, 43; versus shareholder/stakeholder roles, 38
Clark, Geoffrey, 173, 177
class: in Bengali culture, 22–23, 28, 131, 133–135, 137; *bhadralok*/"respectable folk," 22, 131–133, 135–137, 158, 208n30; cleanliness and, 158; distinctions by DENA staff, 139, 158–159; *madhyabitta*/middle, 131; poor as "emerging asset class," 43. *See also* middle class
'class,' having, 139
Clive, Lord, 182
clock, impact of the, 192
"cold" and "warm" money, 68
Coleman, James, 213n2
collateral: collateralized debt obligations, 88, 143; collateralizing of life, 168, 176–182; definition of, 179–180; land as, 61; life insurance as, 180; Muhammad Yunis on, 110
Collier, Jane, 214n8
"colonization of the future," 178, 181
Comaroff, Jean, 143
Comaroff, John, 143
commercialization: of feelings, 101; of human life, 174
commercial MFIs, 2, 27, 65
commercials on television, 101–102
Committee of Financial Sector Reforms, 66
commodity fetishism, 83, 88, 202
Communist Party, 20, 131, 134, 158
"competition States," 21
Congress Party, 7, 62–63
consultancies for MFIs, 101, 145
"consumers-in-waiting," 215n2
consumption loans, 90, 132, 137, 193, 201
"consumption smoothing" mechanisms, 173

"contingent relations" of neighborhood, 123

cooking habits as worthiness criterion, 158

Corbridge, Stuart, 21

corporations: concerns with staff/customer relationship, 102; corporate social responsibility (CSR), 8, 40–42; corporatized development, 199; "doing well by doing good," 32, 38, 40, 144, 199, 202; focus on shareholder value, 209n9; role of in society, 41

CPM (Communist Party of India (Marxist)), 20–21

credit: credit cards in United States, 219n2; "credit-work," 123; "credit-worthiness of purpose," 57–58; GDP ratio, 12; purpose versus use of, 137; risk analysis, 141–143, 146, 153; as source of capital, 11–12

credit bureau, 164–166

creditor, work of the, 84–86

creditworthiness: anxiety over, 193; credit bureau assessing, 166; future loans dependent on, 177; "of purpose," 57–58; social evaluations of, 16, 152–153

crisis discourse, 18, 207n22

"cruel optimism," 53

CSR (corporate social responsibility), 8, 40–42

"cultural articulations," 137

"cultural practices of valuation", 12

culture of entrepreneurship, 32–33; alternatives to, 53; in books, 36–37; centered on building a business, 54; "doing well by doing good," 199; in India, 38, 44, 48; limits of, 51; self-sufficiency over dependence, 35; on television, 35–36; treatment of small businesses, 50; what counts as labor in, 53

"culture of non-repayment," 74, 211n15

"Dalit capitalism," 39

Dalits ("untouchables"), 216n14

Das Gupta, Ananda, 41

Davis, Mike, 162

death: as "chargeable," 172; concept of "good death," 174; mediating and valuing, 173; rate of among poor borrowers, 169–170; as taboo subject, 176. *See also* life insurance/*bima*; suicide

debt as commodity, 87, 97

"debt fetishism," 212n6

debt relationships within MFIs, 14, 87–88; emotional labor of debt recovery, 97–101; as formalized loan products, 105; loan officer position within, 28, 84, 92–97, 102, 104–105; loan officers as proxies, 82, 87; as new form, 6; original inalienable, 106; as presented in commercials, 101–102

Deccan Agriculturalists Relief Act, 62

Deccan Riots, 61–62

Defert, Daniel, 173–174

De Goede, Marieke, 12

delinquent payments, follow-up on, 1

"demutualizing of workers' movement," 174

DENA: businesses of borrowers, *46*; "Code of Conduct," 100; credit risk analysis at, 146; documents needed for loans, 126–130 (*127*); expansion of, 70; fieldwork with, 25–26; and JLG structure, 110; KYC (know your customer) norms, 164; loan application form, 149–151; loan process, 48–49, 87, 147–153; printed pamphlets, 160; resources for repaying loans, 191; verification process, 45–47. *See also* branch managers (DENA); group meetings; house verifications; loan officers (DENA)

Dercon, Stefan, 173
Desai, Moraji, 63
Deshmukh, S. D., 175
Desjarlais, Robert, 215–216n9
development: as freedom, 209n13; as positive externality, 42
Devil and Commodity Fetishism in South America, The (Taussig), 83
Didi honorific, 85, 205n2
dignity of the poor, 40
Di Leonardo, Micaela, 122
Dinesh (loan officer), 33, 185–186
disaster management, 142
discourse of crisis, 18
"displacing gestures," 218n10
documents needed for loans, 126–130 (*127*)
"doing well by doing good," 32, 38, 40, 82, 144, 199, 202
domestication, dual meanings of, 109
domestication of microfinance, 109–110, 136–138
domestic/public dichotomy, 113–114, 125
domestic violence, 107–108, 114–115, 182–184, 218n8
domino effect, 16
Donner, Henrike, 133–134
"doorstep" moneylending, 90–91, 98. *See also* loan officers (DENA)
double bottom line, 208n1
Douglas, Mary, 147, 166, 172
Dowla, Asif, 141
due diligence: in assessing loan risk, 147, 152, 164; in offshore banking, 151; qualitative forms of, 206n17; "reasonable care" in, 151; unintended consequences of, 16, 19. *See also* group meetings; house verifications
Dunn, Elizabeth, 99
Durkheim, Émile, 183, 218n11

East India Company, 19
economy-as-patient, 207n23

EDA Rural Systems, 145–146
Edelman, Marc, 153
education, 130, 204; competitive exams for, 117; of girls, 130; language in, 214n18; private schools, 135, 137, 150, 181, 204; time spent transporting children, 113, 115, 124, 190, 193, 195
elder care, 124
Eleventh Five Year Plan (Planning Commission), 66
Elyachar, Julia, 42–43, 47, 59, 111, 186, 206n17, 210n1
embeddedness of economy, 206nn16–17
"emotional capitalism," 102
emotional labor of debt recovery, 97–102
employment insecurity under neo-liberalism, 52
entrepreneurs: and appropriate risk, 50; definition of, 49–50; entrepreneurial personhood, 36, 54
ethics, 219n20; ethical capitalism, 41–42, 54; "ethical imagination," 204; "ethicalization of market rule," 41, 82
ethnography, 92, 202–204
Ewald, François, 18, 172–173, 179–180, 217n2
exchange versus use value, 193

Faier, Lieba, 24
fair-trade movements, 41
Farah (borrower), 196–197
farmer suicides, 187–189
fast-track courts for MFIs, 73
female-run businesses, 45. *See also* women
Fernandes, Leela, 202
"fictitious" financial capital, 13
fieldwork, author's, 24–27
finance: "financescape," 59; as "natural reality," 12; performative nature of, 12
financial flows in Indian microfinance, 10–11 (*11*)

financial inclusion goals, 2, 7, 58–59, 65–66, 74, 113, 204
financialization: abstraction of, 14; of everyday life, 17; as global phenomenon, 12–13; and labor, 88; as peopled, 202; of poverty, 200; social study of, 12
financial system, defined, 205n7
Fistful of Rice, A (Akula), 34
"flexibilisation of production," 47, 88
food self-sufficiency issues, 62
food stalls, 45, 124
Fordism, 52–53
forms, aesthetic criteria of, 149–150
Fortune at the Bottom of the Pyramid, The (Prahalad), 40
foundational narratives of microfinance, 32–35
Fraser, Nancy, 114, 214n9
friendship and emotional labor, 98
"frontiers of capitalism," 13
Fruzzetti, Lina, 129
future loans as incentive, 177–178

GAD (gender and development) paradigm, 112
Gandhi, Indira, 57–58, 62–63
Gandhi, Mohandes K., 37–38, 93–94, 208n8
Garcia, Angela, 184
garib/poor, 131
gender: DENA personnel and, 98; "domestic" and "public" spheres, 213–214n8; "failed patriarchy," 136; flouting norms, 108; GAD (gender and development) paradigm, 112; gendered codes of shame, 8, 114; hidden labor of women, 122, 124; and microfinance, 113–114, 124, 127, 137, 166; redistributive policies, 112; role of working/middle-class women, 132–135, 137; upholding norms, 99. *See also* women

Ghate, Prabhu, 69
Ghertner, Asher, 208n29
ghetto economy, US, 209n18
Ghosh, Parimal, 131
Giddens, Anthony, 178, 181
gifts, 88, 102, 213n9
"good death," 174
Gooptu, Nandini, 20
"Governance and Systems against Reputation Risk" workshop (Sa-Dahn), 26, 77, 100, 145
Grameen Bank model, 7–8, 31, 34, 110, 112, 212n3
Grameen Capital, 145
Grameen Foundation, 145, 215nn7–8
group meetings of borrowers: finding locations for, 113–119 (*116*); homeowner charging rent for, 117; interfering with domestic tasks, 121–122; lack of space for, 115; learning of suicide in, 196–197; open discussions of life, marital issues, 1, 51, 108, 118, 121, 136–137; peer pressure in, 97–98, 110, 189–190; prejudice against Muslims in, 155–156; time pressure of, 84–85, 120–124; tracking down absentees, 1–3, 189–190. *See also* borrowers/borrowers' groups; house verifications
"growth guarantee," 215n8
Guha, Mr. (DENA deputy general manager), 70, 96
Gupta, Vaibhav, 48
Gurumani, Suresh, 71–72

Habermas, Jürgen, 214n9
Halliburton, Murphy, 218n9, 219n18
Han, Clara, 192, 194
"Hard-Core Poor" program, 24, 208n32
Harris, Laurence, 212n5
Harriss, John, 21
Hart, Keith, 209n15
Harvey, David, 13, 84, 87

healthcare sector of economy, 195–196, 204

hedges as "mastering" risk, 172

Henaff, Marcel, 14

hero, entrepreneur as, 36

hierarchical dominance through debt, 88

High Mark Credit Information Services Ltd., 164

Ho, Karen, 172, 209n9

Hochschild, Arlie, 98, 101

Hoogvelt, Ankie, 206n12

horror, Asad on, 219n16

"hostess clubs" (Japan), 98

household decision making, 113–114

house verifications: applicant using neighbor's house for, 149; difficulties for renters, 163–164; documents needed for, 126–130 (*127*); embarrassment, shame over, 163; evaluating guarantors during, 46–47, 127, 140, 147–148; intrusiveness of home visits, 90–91; by loan officers, 84–85; rationale for, 15, 142, 149; space for meetings a plus, 115–117 (*116*); two-step process for, 26; underreporting of income during, 151; untidy house impacting loan, 139–140, 154

ICICI Prudential Bank, 101, 170, 171, 211n12

IDBI bank, commercial for, 101

idealism versus profitability, 39

IDFC Limited, 10, 58

IFMR, 103–104, 145, 215N7

I Have a Dream (Bansal), 36

illness/injury of borrowers, 194–195, 201

Illouz, Eva, 102

ILM (individual liability method), 177–178

IMF (International Monetary Fund), 64

"impact investing," 43

inalienability in exchange relationships, 102

"income smoothing" mechanisms, 173

India: financial inclusion policy, 2; Imperial Bank of India Act (1920), 60; Indian Life Assurance Companies Act, 175; indigenous banking system, 59–61; Insurance Regulatory Act (1999), 176; liberalization of economy (1991), 21; as social laboratory, 60. *See also* Calcutta; Kolkata; West Bengal

indigenous economies and capitalism, 38–39

industrialization: capital investment required for, 61; decline of in West Bengal, 47; postindependence, 52

infectious diseases, 189

informal economy, work in the, 47

inhabiting of norms, 137, 214n20

insurance. *See* life insurance/*bima*

Insurance Regulatory Act (1999), 176

International Monetary Fund (IMF), 64

investment not charity narrative, 35, 41

Ito, Sanae, 112

James, Deborah, 214n17

Jameson, Frederic, 205n8

Jaya, 181

Jeffrey, Craig, 51

JLGs (joint-liability groups), 69, 110, 112, 177

JNNURM (Jawaharlal Nehru National Urban Renewal Mission), 23

joint-stock banks, 60–61

Joshi, Deepali Pant, 63, 67

Joy (loan officer), 127–129, 150, 196–197

Jugaad/"making do," 48

jute mills, 20

Kabeer, Naila, 213n7

Kalpana (borrower), 51–52

Kapoor, Rakesh (in *Peepli Live*), 188
karma and social entrepreneurship, 37
Karnani, Aneel, 50
Kaviraj, Sudipta, 219n17
Keynesian model, 62
Khan, Aamir, 188
Khan, Mehboob, 89
Khan Committee, 66
khomota/"capacity," 153–154
Khurana, Rakesh, 211n11
kinship ties guaranteeing loans, 128–130
"kin work," 123
Kiva peer-to-peer lending site, 34,
    208n5
Knorr Cetina, Karin, 205n7, 212n2,
    215n1
Kohli, Atul, 210n21, 214n14
Kolkata, 19–23 (*22*); goal of "world-
    class" city, 21; micro-entrepreneurs
    of, 44–48 (*46*); slums of, 163; struc-
    tural inequality in, 16. *See also* Cal-
    cutta; West Bengal
Krishna (borrower), 117
Kristof, Nicholas, 8
KYC (know your customer) norms, 164,
    205n3

labor: of debt, 6, 13–15; emotional, 97–
    101; ideologies of motherhood and,
    99; by women, 45, 122–124
Lambek, Michael, 194, 219n20
land as collateral for debt, 61
landless farmers, 188–189
language in Kolkata, 159–160
Laxmi (DENA borrower), 118
Lee, Benjamin, 142
legal fiction, defined, 152
Leyshon, Andrew, 12, 84, 98
liberalization of financial sector, 58–59,
    64–67, 80, 132, 209n21
liberalization of health care, 195
LIC (Life Insurance Corporation of In-
    dia), 170

life insurance/*bima*: claims filed on, 167–
    168; as collateral, 180, 201; collateral-
    izing life itself, 16; historically, 171–
    172, 175–176; managing capital risk,
    179; mandatory for borrowers, 4,
    15, 168, 169; mediating and valuing
    death, 173; methods of, 170; need for
    death certificate to claim, 197; offset-
    ting risk during debt crisis, 178; pop-
    ularity of, 171; premiums for, 4, 76;
    recent government action on, 204; as
    "two-way protection," 169–170
Life Insurance Corporation Act, 175
LiPuma, Edward, 142
liquidity crunch and recovery, 9–10
Livingston, Julie, 186
loan application forms and documents,
    126–130 (*127*), 149–152
loan officers (DENA): alienation of, 88;
    application process, 146–153; avoid-
    ing "excess" of sociality, 102; avoid-
    ing patron-client relationship, 96;
    calling on personal loyalty from bor-
    rowers, 98; code of conduct for, 76,
    100–101; credit risk analysis by, 146–
    147; daily duties of, 84–86, 90; deny-
    ing loans if disrespected, 100; due
    diligence in assessing risk, 147, 152,
    164; forms of address with borrow-
    ers, 85; as mediators, 90; must use bi-
    cycles only, 85; performing financial
    labor, 15, 83–84; personally respon-
    sible for groups' debt, 4, 98; physi-
    cal/emotional labor of, 82–83, 88, 91,
    95, 97–101; as "proxy-creditors," 87;
    reducing loan for dirty house, 139;
    risk assessment by, 16, 90; robberies
    of, 85; stigmatized as debt collectors,
    5. *See also* debt relationships within
    MFIs; house verifications
loan products as commodities, 88
"long-term waiting" for jobs, 51–52
L&T Finance, 17

"lump sum" loans, 6
Lutz, Catherine, 13, 202
Lyons, Laura, 35

M2i Consulting, 145
MacKenzie, Donald, 206n9
macroeconomic risk, managing of, 142
madhyabitta/middle class, 131
Madras Equitable Life Insurance Society, 175
Mahajan, Vijay, 77
Mahila Sewa Cooperative Bank, 67
Mahmood, Saba, 137, 214–215n20
Maira, Arun, 37–38
Maity, Mr., 49–50
Majumdar, Diptos, 132
Malegam, Y. H., 75–77, 211n18
Malegam Committee, 75–78, 165, 211n20, 217n20
male guarantors for loans, 126–129
Mani, Lata, 131
Manjula (borrower), 184
"Maoists," protesting workers labeled, 210n22
market: abstractions in, 14, 205n8; efficiency of, 112; moral limits of, 203
Martin, Randy, 205–206n8
Marwari community, 22
Marx, Karl, 13, 87, 142, 193, 206n13, 212n5
mass migrations, 21
mathematical modeling on Wall Street, 143
Maurer, Bill, 15, 151, 164, 174
Mauss, Marcel, 88
McLean, Bethany, 143
mega city, defined, 207n28
men: domestic violence by, 107–108, 114–115, 182–184, 218n8; stereotypes of working-class, 135–136; wives procuring loans for, 53, 129, 137
mercantile ethnic groups and castes, 36

metaphors, financial, 18
MFIN (Microfinance Institutions Network), 77, 100, 164–165
MFIs (microfinance institutions):
Andhra Pradesh Micro Finance Institutions Ordinance (2010), 72–73; associated with moneylending, 89–90, 92; BC model of, 69–70; as ethical enterprise, 31–32; as financial services not NGO, 32; as for-profit investment, 34–43, 69, 71, 82, 193, 199, 209n10; high risk of default of, 67; high transaction costs of, 67; individual loans from, 69; interest rates of, 6, 72, 76, 201–202; liquidity crunch (2010), 75; loan recovery rates, 4; maintaining own lines of credit, 7; as means of diversifying risk, 68, 144–145; patron-client relationships within, 109; preventing delinquencies, 1–2; required loan recovery rates, 4; risks of, 15, 141–147; self-sufficiency goal of, 39; staff's desire for respect (*samman*), 99–100; state-level regulations of, 72; systemic importance of, 79; as "too big too fail," 144; in United States, 205n4. *See also* DENA
microcredit versus microfinance, 7–8
micro-entrepreneurship, 32–33, 39; encompassing whole person, 54; goal of millions, 39; in Kolkata, 44–48
microfinance: in Andhra Pradesh, 74; defined, 2; domestication of, 137–138; global expansion of, 7–8, 16; government conflicts of interest, 73; loan officer/borrower relationship in, 81, 84–86; as moneylending, 89; regulation of, 74–78, 141; risks of, 17, 141, 145–147 (*146*); self-help groups (SHGs) as, 26, 74; social capital within, 109; systemic importance of, 79. *See also* MFIs

microfinance crisis (2010), 17, 58, 163, 202

Micro Finance Institutions Bill 2012 (proposed), 78, 207n21

Microfinance Institutions Network (MFIN), 77, 100, 164–165

Micro Finance Institutions Ordinance (Andhra Pradesh 2010), 72–75

Micro Financial Sector (Development and Regulation) Bill, proposed, 75

microinsurance providers, 170

middle class: definition of, 130–132; expectations of women in, 133–134, 137; "new" Indian middle class, 132

Millar, Kathleen, 54

Miller, Carol, 112, 213n5

Miller, Daniel, 206n10

Miller, Margaret, 165

Mintu (borrower), 137–138

Mithun (loan officer), 94–95, 100–101, 105–106, 107, 195

modeling of risk, 143

modernization theory, 111, 213n4

Modi, Narendra, 204, 205n3, 210n7

Mondal, Akash, 48

money: to be invested, not "used," 193; as free from quality, 213n9; "poor people's money," 105, 204

moneylending, 49, 61–62, 73, 89, 91–92

Moodie, Megan, 115

Moonmoon (DENA loan applicant), 127–129

Moore, Henrietta, 204

moral economies, 82, 148, 153–154

morality of debt, 184–187

moral limits of the market, 203

Morduch, Jonathan, 177

motherhood, ideologies of, 99. *See also* women

Mother India (Khan), 89

Mukherjee, Pranab, 58

Mukherjee, Sucharita, 103

Mukul (branch manager): disbelieving borrowers' income numbers, 151–152; at group meetings, 51, 119–121, 190; on Muslims, 154–155; and overdue borrowers, 97–98; performing house verification, 147–148; on sari businesses, 45; use of gender norms, 98

multipolar world, 13

Muslim borrowers: deemed high risk, 156; Hindu disgust over beef, 154–155; language issues, 159–160

NABARD (National Bank for Agriculture and Development), 23, 68–69, 75

Nair, Tara, 23

Nandigram, 21, 207n27

Nandy, Ashis, 157, 162

Narasimham Committees, 65

Narayan, Deepa, 111

narratives of microfinance, 34–37

Natha (in *Peepli Live*), 188–189

nationalization of banks, 57–59, 62–64, 175–176

nationalization of insurance sector, 175–176

NBFCs (nonbanking financial companies), 65; NBFC-MFIs, 69, 76–77, 164, 211n18, 215n5

Nehru, Jawaharlal, 23, 52, 62, 209n8

neoliberalism, 10, 42, 52, 64, 109, 186, 192

networks of obligation, 88

"New Communism," 21

"new" Indian middle class, 132

Nilima (DENA worker), 134

Nocera, Joe, 143

Nonini, Donald, 13

nostalgia, 209n20

Obligation of Insurers to Rural or Social Sectors (2005), 176

Occupy movement, 13

OD (overdue) loans, 95, 98, 196–197

Omidyar, Pierre, 8
operational risks, 141
"ordinary ethics," 194
organized labor, weakening of, 52
Oriental Life Insurance Company, 175
"own-account workers," 50–51

Pakistan, war with, 62
PAN (permanent account number)
    cards, 126
Panchali (loan officer), 189–190
Pandian, Anand, 15
Parry, Jonathan, 14, 102
Partho (husband of borrower), 200–202
partition, 21, 157
Parul (borrower), 193–194
Patel, Geeta, 179–180
"paternalism toward the poor," 40
"patients-in-waiting," 215n2
Payal (borrower), 191–193
payment protection insurance (PPI),
    217n5
Peepli Live (Rizvi), 188–189
peer-to-peer lending, 34
People's Wealth Scheme, 204
performativity, 10, 206nn9
permanent account number (PAN)
    cards, 126
PET bottle processing, 154
philanthropic paternalism, 174
Pietz, William, 173
Planet of Slums (Davis), 162
plastic bottle processing, 154
Polish baby food factory workers, 99
"poor always pay back," 141
poor borrowers: alleged harassment
    of, 72, 182; as "bankable" popula-
    tion, 141; capitalizing on, 18; com-
    munity pressure against default, 94;
    connection of to global finance, 80;
    credit-worthiness of, 65; difficulties
    in accumulating capital, 48, 50; as
    "emerging asset class," 43; as entre-

preneurs and consumers, 40; ethics
of loans to, 81; fees attached to loans,
167; financial inclusion goals for, 74;
high death rate among, 169–170; ill-
ness/injury of, 194–195, 201; less dependent on husbands, 137; less integrated into formal economy, 145;
loans used for nonstated purposes,
152; mitigating risks of loans to, 15,
18; money going to social obligations, 201; mortality rates among,
168; multiple loans, continual debt,
49; need for development policy to
address, 203; as "own-account workers," 50; paternalism toward, 40;
paying old debts with new loans,
189–191; pregnant women denied
new loans, 178; pre-independence,
62; producing demand for credit, 17;
seen as homogenous group, 140; status of wives, 107–109; traveling to
pick up loans, 167; urban/rural differences, 160–162; widowed or unmarried women, 129. *See also* group
meetings; SHGs; suicide
Poornima (borrower, group leader),
    1–3, 6
Poovey, Mary, 12
popular life insurance, 174
Portes, Alejandro, 111
postindustrial city concept, 21
PPI (payment protection insurance),
    217n5
Pradhan Mantri Jan Dhan Yojana (Prime
    Minister's People's Wealth Scheme),
    204
Prahalad, C. K., 40
precaution, age of, 172
Preda, Alex, 205n7
predatory lending, 19
"Presidency Banks," 60
PricewaterhouseCoopers report, 195–
    196

priority-sector loans, 64, 65, 79
privatization, 10, 43, 47, 64–65
production versus consumption loans, 193
profit-making institutions, MFIs as, 34–43, 69, 71, 82, 193, 199, 209n10
proxy-creditors, 87, 92
Puhazhendi, V., 68
Purnima (borrower), 48–50, 54
Putul (DENA staff/branch manager): disbursing loans, 167; disrespected by urban borrowers, 100; on gossip among borrower groups, 118; on insurance and suicides, 168, 182–184; performing house verifications, 46–47, 149, 163; tracking down delinquent payments, 1–6; on urban versus rural neighborhoods, 100

Qayum, Seemin, 21, 135–136

Radha (in *Mother India*), 212–213n7
Radha (loan officer), 119–120
Radhakrishnan, Smitha, 133
Rahman, Aminur, 212n3
Rajagopal, Arvind, 208n29
Rajak, Dinah, 41–42
Rajasthan, 22, 115
Rangarajan, C., 23, 66
Rankin, Katherine, 113, 137
Rao, M. R., 71
ratings agencies, 101
ration cards, 126
Ray, Mr. (MFI COO), 31–33, 169–170, 208n2
Ray, Raka, 21, 135–136
Raychaudhuri, Ajitava, 47
Razavi, Shahrashoub, 112, 213n5
RBI (Reserve Bank of India), 10, 60; approving new banks, 10, 58, 70; banks following lead of, 74–75; goal of inclusive growth, 39; on Indian economy, 12; introducing BC model,

69–70; loan officers passing blame to, 91–92; Malegam Committee, 75–78, 165, 211n20, 217n20; overseeing MFIs, 78–79, 91–92, 104, 144, 164; setting cutoff for poverty, 77; setting KYC norms, 164, 217n19; smaller organizations not under, 165; statements on MFIs, 89; survey of rural indebtedness by, 210n5
reappropriation of debt relationship, 95–96
"reasonable care," 151, 164
reciprocity, 14, 42, 68
Reddy, Y. V., 89
Rekha (borrower), 51, 147–148, 150–151
relationality of debt, 14, 141
religion, 156–157
"reputation collateral" from credit bureau, 165
Reserve Bank of India. *See* RBI
"respectable femininity," 133
respect and sense of self, 100
restructuring powers of courts, 62
rethinking risk management, 18
riba/interest, 61. *See also* usury
right to income before work, 55
Riles, Annelise, 83, 149, 152, 180
Rima (borrower), 121
Rimi (child of loan recipient), 136–137
Rio de Janeiro, Brazil, 55
risk, 217n2; diversification of, 143–145; encouragement of, 172; loan officers' assessment of, 166; risk society, 142, 147
risk analysis, 18, 28, 81, 140, 142, 146–147, 164; and insurance, 174, 178; in "zero-risk" military strategy, 217n2
risk management, 5, 16–19, 28–29, 141–147, 151, 164, 168–169; within MFIs, 16–18, 145–147 (*146*), 178, 200; "money management" preferred to, 176

Rizvi, Anusha, 188
Rock, Paul, 91
Roitman, Janet, 18, 207n22
Rosaldo, Michelle, 213n8
Roy, Ananya, 21, 41, 82
Roy, Anup, 187
Roy, Tirthankar, 210n4
Rudner, David, 89
Ruma (borrower), 97–98, 190–191
RuPay debit card, 204
rupee versus dollar, 79
rural versus urban poor, 23–24, 115–118 (*116*)

Saavala, Minna, 133
Sa-Dhan organized workshop, 26, 77, 100, 145
Samit (DENA member), 86, 91
samman/respect, 99–100
Sandeep, 155–156
Sandel, Michael, 203
Sanyal, Paromita, 114
sari businesses, 44–45, 128, 130, 147
Saswati (loan officer), 134
Saurav (branch manager), 48
scholarship on finance, 14, 83
schools. *See* education
Schrader, Heiko, 92
Schwarcz, Steven, 16
Second Narasimham Committee, 65
second-wave feminism, 111
securitization of debt, 12, 77, 82, 103–104, 200
seeds, privatization of production of, 218n15
"self-employed," 50–51
self-help groups. *See* SHGs
self-reliance over welfare, 10
self-sufficiency goal, 35
Sen, Amartya, 111, 209n13
sentimental narratives, 34–35
SERP (Society for the Elimination of Poverty), 72, 182

SEWA (Self-Employed Women's Association), 210–211n8
Shah, Alpa, 140
Shanti (borrower), 120–121
shareholder/stakeholder versus citizen roles, 38
shareholder value, 209n9
Sheuli, (borrower), 130–132
SHGs (self-help groups), 68; Andhra Pradesh Ordinance and, 73–74; and life insurance, 171; as microfinance model, 26, 67–70, 73–74; one-per-person limit on, 73; problems with, 68–69; women's groups as central units, 113
Shilpa (borrower), 168, 182–184, 218n12
Shipra (borrower), 1–6
Shipton, Parker, 104
Shirreff, David, 143
Simon, Jonathan, 172
Singh, Manmohan, 64–65, 188
Singh, Ramendra, 48
Singur, 21
Sinha, Janmejaya, 87, 144
Siraj ud-Daulah, 182
Sitala temples, 189
"site of encounter," credit as, 24
SKS Microfinance/Bharat Financial Inclusion, 208n4, 211n9; and Andhra Pradesh Ordinance, 74–75; effects of microfinance crisis on, 9–10, 72; founding of, 34; internal tensions, firing of CEO, 71–72; public listing of, 9, 71; securitization and, 103; share price volatility of, 71–72, 74, 80; suicides related to, 72, 217n7. *See also* Akula, Vikram
social banking, 63, 66
social capital, 8; building of within groups, 7–8, 24, 28; as collateral for poor women, 28, 109, 121, 141, 178, 197; and empowerment, 110–113; as idealistic and profitable, 39; intel-

social capital (*continued*)
lectual history of, 213n2; in place of
material capital, 177; production and
maintenance of, 123; social networks,
111, 118, 123; theory of, 110–112
social entrepreneurs, 36–37, 42, 202
social evaluations of creditworthiness,
16
social exclusion by loan officers, 140, 166
sociality, 14–15, 102, 150, 152
social networks, 111, 123, 215n1
social productivity of debt, 88
social scientific knowledge as performative, 206n9
Society for the Elimination of Poverty
(SERP), 72, 182
Spandana Sphoorty, 74, 211n9
"special monies," 152
speculative capital finance, 142–143
"speculative raiding," 84
spirit of capitalism defined, 38
Spivak, Gayatri Chakravarty, 218
Standard & Poor, 80
Staples, James, 184, 186
Stark, David, 212n2
state must take on risk, 19
Steingass, Francis, 176
structural inequality, 16–18, 202, 207n19
Subbarao, Duvvuri, 58
subprime crisis in United States (2008),
8, 13, 16, 78–79, 88, 143, 202
subprime microfinance crisis in India (2010): causes of, 78–79, 141; effects of on DENA, 96, 105–106, 163–
165; intensifying discrimination, 155;
MFIs seeking foreign investments
following, 144; microfinance credit
bureau, 163–165; recovery from, 58;
and release of Malegam Committee
report, 217n20; and securitization of
loans, 103–104; and SKS, 71–72; and
"systemic enfolding," 17, 155; "upstream" consequences of, 202; workshop in response to, 26, 77, 100, 145

Subramanian, Ajantha, 208n6
Subramanian, Arvind, 87, 144
subsidized commodities, 126
sūdhe taka newa/"money on interest," 90
suicide: abetment of, 186; of borrowers,
72, 168–170, 182–186, 217–218nn7–
8; by country, region, 14, 182, 186,
218nn9; as criminal offense, 186;
death certificate for insurance, 197;
Durkheim on, 183, 218n11; of farmers, 187–189, 218n14; lack of sympathy, 185–186; of women, 187, 218n10.
See also death
Sukhilala (in *Mother India*), 89
Sunder Rajan, Kausik, 142, 215n2
"symbolic elaboration," 102
syndicate loans, 184–185, 216n17
systemically important MFIs, 79
systemic enfolding, 15–19, 155
systemic risk, 16–18

Tania (loan officer), 51, 98, 150–151, 154,
156, 189
taste, 216n11
Taussig, Michael, 83, 212n6
taxi leases, 51, 147–148
temporality, 192
temporary/contractual labor, 52
"tension," 192
Tett, Gillian, 88
thinking-feeling social entrepreneurs,
36–37
Thompson, E. P., 153, 192, 212n1
Thrift, Nigel, 12, 84
total indebtedness information, 165
trade unions and political parties, 20
trading in risk, 143
"transfer jobs," 96–97
transformative moment, 34
Trinamool Congress Party, 21
triple bottom line, 208n1
Tsing, Anna, 13

Udgirkar, Trushna, 71

unbanked, the, 59, 67–68, 144
United Nations World Conference on
    Women, 112
unmarked citizens, Hindus as, 157
unpaid labor of women, 122–123
urban agglomeration, 21, 207n28
urbanization in India, 23
urban microfinance, 23–24
urban poor: as borrowers, 160–162; de-
    mographics of, 23–24; husband/fa-
    ther as wage earner, 174; paying for
    private-sector services, 200; precari-
    ousness of life for, 200–201
use value, 88, 193
usury, 14, 61, 87

vegetable, fruit stalls, 45
visible hand, 42

Wall Street, 143, 172
Waquant, Loïc, 209n18
"warm" and "cold" money, 68
Warner, Michael, 114
water collection, 122
water delivery business, 46–47
Weeks, Kathi, 53–54
Weingarten, Richard, 211n15
welfare, 10, 19, 35, 42, 64, 174, 204
West Bengal: caste relations in, 158;
    class politics in, 131; DENA in, 71;
    farmer suicides in, 218n25; industrial
    sector, 20–21, 47; microfinance in ru-
    ral areas, 114; problems with photo
    ID in, 126–127; refugees in, 21
Western corporate models, 37–38
Weston, Kath, 18, 207n23, 209n20
White, Hylton, 52
WID (women in development) para-
    digm, 111–112
Williams, Brett, 166
women: age limits for loans, 179; as cen-
    tral focus for development, 111–112;
    considered more responsible, 166;
    credit as part of domestic work, 6,
14–15; effect of loans on status of,
    107–109; empowerment of, 213n6;
    ethnography of, 98–99, 133, 214n16;
    female-run businesses, 45; finding
    child care, 124; home as sphere of,
    113, 135; housewife suicide rate, 187;
    impact of microfinance on, 8–9, 107–
    109, 113–114; labor of, 122–123; preg-
    nancy disqualifies for DENA loans,
    178–179; procuring loans for hus-
    bands, 53, 129, 137; role of in mid-
    dle class, 133–134; social capital as
    collateral for, 28, 109, 121, 141, 178,
    197; teasing of girls, 136–137; time
    demands on, 109, 122; time spent
    transporting children, 113, 115, 124,
    190, 193, 195; unpaid labor of, 122–
    123; waged labor of, 124; water col-
    lection by, 122; widows as borrow-
    ers, 129; working-class stereotypes,
    134–135
Women, Culture and Society (Rosaldo),
    213n8
Woolcock, Michael, 111
working class: gender roles within, 133–
    135; microfinance as credit for, 9;
    shrinking of, 22
World Bank, 64, 100
"world class," 21, 208n29

Yanagisako, Sylvia, 214n8
"Year of Microcredit," 8
Yunus, Muhammad: biography of,
    208n3; on for-profit models, 209n10;
    Grameen Bank model, 7–8; as inspi-
    ration for Amit, 199; moment of rev-
    elation for, 34–35; Mr. Bose meet-
    ing with, 31; "non-loss, non-dividend
    business," 40; problem of collateral,
    110; and problem of collateral, 110

Zaloom, Caitlin, 215n1
Zelizer, Viviana, 152, 174, 213n9
zero-balance accounts, 205n3

ALSO PUBLISHED IN THE SOUTH ASIA IN MOTION SERIES

Jinnealogy: Time, Islam, and Ecological Thought in the Medieval Ruins of Delhi
Anand Vivek Taneja (2017)

Uprising of the Fools: Pilgrimage as Moral Protest in Contemporary India
Vikash Singh (2017)

The Slow Boil: Street Food, Rights, and Public Space in Mumbai
Jonathan Shapiro Anjaria (2016)

The Demands of Recognition: State Anthropology and Ethnopolitics in Darjeeling
Townsend Middleton (2015)

The South African Gandhi: Stretcher-Bearer of Empire
Ashwin Desai and Goolam Vahed (2015)

X 20-99

INTER-BD
APP
28/2/19

65691

Lightning Source UK Ltd.
Milton Keynes UK
UKHW01f0031130618
323925UK00002B/117/P